'a book that has never finished saying what it has to say'... intriguing... essential reflections... emerging theme

By the end of this century, most of us will be living in cities of one size or another but they are forever changing in their composition and shape. Their form is never final, Luca D'Acci's review of multiple forces that coalesce in the places we inhabit which he entitles Anthropological-Evolutionary Urbanism, reflects Italo Calvino's classic dictum of ' … a book that has never finished saying what it has to say'. What is intriguing in his treatise is the echo that haunts us down the ages, of phenomenon that is always contingent, hence unpredictable and temporal, which is a theme that we are only slowly beginning to recognise in our search for stable patterns of urban life. This book provides essential reflections on this emerging theme.

Michael Batty (Urban Analyst)
CBE FRS FBA, Emeritus Bartlett Professor of Planning at University College London where he is Chair of the Centre for Advanced Spatial Analysis (CASA). Four honorary doctorates and a Vautrin Lud Prize winner (known as the Nobel Prize of Geography).

well-informed and provocative... These ideas can stimulate progress

Luca D'Acci's latest book, well-informed and provocative, poses important questions about the impact of urban living on mental health, happiness, and the meaning that we create in our lives by making choices and investing in them. It draws on insights from multiple disciplines to make the argument that many of us are happier living in the country, small towns, or small cities than in large ones, and it raises the possibility that we may not, in the future, have to trade those environments for successful careers as technology continues to free us from prior constraints. It is well worth the read. These ideas can stimulate progress.

Stephen C. Stearns (Evolutionary Biologist)
Professor Emeritus of Ecology and Evolutionary Biology, Yale University, former President of the European Society for Evolutionary Biology, and ex vice-President of the Society for the Study of Evolution, founding editor of *the Journal of Evolutionary Biology* and of *Evolution, Medicine, and Public Health*, and author of *Life History Evolution and of Evolutionary Medicine*. Honorary doctorate from the University of Zurich.

novelty, breadth and depth of thinking

This book reflects on a personal journey that the author has taken over the last 10 years. It emphasises the importance of scale and diversity in urban form, suggesting that there is no ideal but only differences. A strong case is made for taking a holistic approach that integrates perspectives from a range of social, medical and natural sciences. The book is well worth reading for its novelty, breadth and depth of thinking.

David Banister (Geographer)
Professor Emeritus at School of Geography and the Environment, University of Oxford, former Director of the Environmental Change Institute, and of the Transport Studies Unit.

Thought-provoking and inspirational, D'Acci is like a 'Renaissance man' painting on a big urban canvas with an eye for the human-scale detail

Urban Living distils thousands of years of history and millions of years of human evolution into a compelling perspective for the creation of the urban habitat. The book provides a welcome excursion away from the quotidian utilitarianism of much urban research, to step back to ask big philosophical questions, of how to live a good life, urbanistically – or how can we make cities better fitted to us? D'Acci invites us to imagine what scale or kind of settlement we would like to live in – from villages to megacities – drawing from a remarkable breadth of disciplines, from philosophy to neuroscience and evolutionary history. Thought-provoking and inspirational, D'Acci is like a 'Renaissance man' painting on a big urban canvas, but with an eye for the personal human-scale detail.

Stephen Marshall (Urbanist)
Professor of Urban Morphology and Urban Design at Bartlett School of Planning, University College London. Author of *Cities, Design and Evolution*.

could not be more timely... compelling

This book could not be more timely. As cities expand worldwide, understanding how they shape our minds and well-being has become a central challenge. Drawing on the latest findings from neuroscience, psychology, anthropology, and urban studies, Luca D'Acci offers a compelling synthesis of how modern urban life interacts with brains that evolved for very different environments. Rather than idealizing or condemning urbanization, Urban Living integrates diverse evidence into a thoughtful assessment of the opportunities and risks of city life, and how these might be managed through better design and policy. The result is a helpful guide to how humans can thrive in habitats that are, in evolutionary terms, still very new to us.

Andreas Meyer-Lindenberg (Psychiatrist, Neuroscientist)
Director of the Central Institute of Mental Health in Mannheim and Professor at Heidelberg University; Editor-in-Chief of *Neuroscience Applied* and laureate of awards including the ECNP Neuropsychopharmacology Award, Prix Roger de Spoelberch, and Robert Sommer Medal.

... pathbreaking... much-needed assessment

Darwin's study of moths in 19th century Birmingham, England proved that evolution did not cease with urbanization. The epigenetic revolution reveals that genes are not simply inherited and expressed but expressed and even changed (via methylation) through interactions with the environment. With global urbanization currently at 58% and rising, the environment for humans is increasingly urban. D'Acci's pathbreaking book Urban Living offers a much-needed assessment of what scientist have learned about human adaptation, development, and evolution in urban settings.

Douglas S. Massey (Sociologist)
Henry G. Bryant Professor at Princeton University, former President of the American Sociological Association, and 2025 Princess of Asturias Laureate for Social Sciences. Author of *Strangers in a Strange Land: Humans in an Urbanizing World.*

... fascinating... great reading

What is it like for a great ape – furless, but not fearless – to find itself in a novel environment that in many ways deviates from the environment in which it evolved? Does the new environment impact its well-being or its physical and mental health? "Urban living", as we learn from the book by Luca S. D'Acci, is indeed challenging for a creature with our behavioural and genetic make-up. But it is also full of opportunities – otherwise it would not have happened that the majority of members of our species nowadays seem to "prefer" urban life over rural. Luca S. D'Acci has reviewed a huge amount of information and digested it for us readers in the form of a fascinating book on urban living from an anthropological and evolutionary perspective. This is great reading that I highly recommend.

Martin Brüne (Psychiatrist, Psychotherapist, and Neurologist) Professor of Psychiatry and Head of the Division of Social Neuropsychiatry and Evolutionary Medicine at the LWL University-Hospital, Ruhr University Bochum. Author of *Evolutionary Psychiatry and Psychosomatic Medicine*, and co-editor of *The Oxford Handbook of Evolutionary Medicine*, and of *The Evolutionary Roots of Human Brain Diseases*.

... ambitious... enduring value

Luca D'Acci's *Urban Living* is an ambitious interdisciplinary inquiry into how cities shape human life, spanning evolutionary anthropology, psychology, neuroscience, primatology, and sociology. For me, its enduring value is the truth it names: survival is not the same as flourishing. True flourishing calls for cities that join their Neolithic gift—the vibrant intermixing of peoples and ideas—with our older Paleolithic inheritance: nature still visible, tangible, and wild.

Peter H. Kahn, Jr. (Psychologist)
Professor of Psychology and Environmental and Forest Sciences, and Director of the Human Interaction with Nature and Technological Systems (HINTS) Lab at the University of Washington. Author of *Technological Nature: Adaptation and the Future of Human Life*.

Urban Living

This interdisciplinary book lays the foundations for a new critique of human societies examining how humans, as a species, are suited to live across the rural–urban spectrum. It proposes a new perspective for urban studies, ultimately centred on human nature. Evolutionary perspectives are at the core of the book and are linked to other disciplines such as economic geography, sociology, anthropology, geographical psychology, environmental psychology, genetics, and ontogenetics.

The book summarises the academic state of the art of the various fields under discussion, each expressing its own angle which, when holistically presented in the same volume, enriches the integrated understanding of such a multilayered theme. The timing of this book is critical: today, more than ever, we live in urban environments of some description or other and, within the coming decades, large numbers of new dwellers will "choose" cities as their permanent place of residence. For this reason, the author argues that urban planning and design must embrace this unique opportunity to build ex-novo urban and non-urban settlements for billions of people in liveable ways. The interdisciplinary approach brings together the study and understanding of cities from diverse disciplines.

This topical work therefore offers the reader a new understanding of how – and tentatively, why – living in cities affects humans for better or worse. It indirectly underlines the importance of smaller settlements based on empirical evidence, without necessarily having to escape from the big city, which instead could become more attractive if wisely planned and integrated in the larger multivariate territory. The author provides educated insights for policy and planning, inducing habitats which could be optimal for our well-being and progress.

Luca S. D'Acci is Associate Professor at the Polytechnic of Turin (DIST), Honorary Fellow at the University of Birmingham (EPS), and Partner (Visiting Professor) at the Erasmus University Rotterdam (EHERO).

Routledge Advances in Regional Economics, Science and Policy

Cross Border Mobility in Eastern European Union Countries
External Shocks and Regional Resilience
Tomasz Komornicki, Rafał Wiśniewski, Andrzej Jakubowski, Barbara Szejgiec-Kolenda and Eugenia Maruniak

The Urban University and the Knowledge Economy
New Spaces of Interaction
Edited by Patrizia Ingallina

Sustainable Finance and Smart Cities
Izabela Jonek-Kowalska and Aneta Michalak

Inclusive, Smart and Sustainable Cities
Elwira Gross-Gniot, Zbigniew Makieła, Magdalena M. Stuss, Jacek Szołtysek and Grażyna Trzpiot

Evolving Intelligent Environments
Smart Ecosystems and Transformative Innovations in the 21st Century
Nicos Komninos

Urban Living
Anthropological-Evolutionary Urbanism
Luca S. D'Acci

For more information about this series, please visit: www.routledge.com/series/RAIRESP

Urban Living

Anthropological-Evolutionary Urbanism

Luca S. D'Acci

Routledge
Taylor & Francis Group
LONDON AND NEW YORK

First published 2026
by Routledge
4 Park Square, Milton Park, Abingdon, Oxon OX14 4RN

and by Routledge
605 Third Avenue, New York, NY 10158

Routledge is an imprint of the Taylor & Francis Group, an informa business

British Library Cataloguing-in-Publication Data
A catalogue record for this book is available from the British Library

ISBN: 978-1-032-40860-6 (hbk)
ISBN: 978-1-032-40861-3 (pbk)
ISBN: 978-1-003-35501-4 (ebk)

DOI: 10.4324/9781003355014

The Open Access version of this book was funded by POLITECNICO DI TORINO.

Contents

Preface

In the process of developing a different critique of human societies and human habitats, I wrote this book with the aim to collect, sometimes interpret, and disseminate knowledge from different disciplines – typically not considered in urban planning and (e)valuations – reorganising them into a least common denominator helping educated thoughts towards making better human habitats.

Endemic to social sciences and urban studies for over a century, the rural–urban debate lacks an evolutionary perspective.

The growing academic and popular attention to quality of life, happiness, life satisfaction, mental health, and well-being, is gradually shifting the emphasis of the debate, which can now make use of evolutionary and neuro-psychological advances.

We should advance a new analysis of urban–rural living, based on the ultimate perspective – human evolution – more final and appropriate to the current knowledge and social-individual ambitions to have better, healthier, and happier lives in our human habitats. The latter should be wherever one would truly prefer to live: a hamlet, village, town, city, or megacity.

The main question addressed by this book increasingly appears to me as the most fundamental anyone of the contemporary urban era could ask: how can we make cities – and the full spectrum of settlement sizes – better fitted to us?

This book summarises research about diverse types of settlements – mostly in terms of size – to acquire unbiased empirical information regardless of preferences and stereotypes; this can be achieved by studying the academic literature from various disciplines to have a full picture and build knowledge bridges. Then we could apply such knowledge in planning and decision processes regarding the transformation and construction of our built environments to favour better lives and societies.

The introduction of the book, Chapter 1, warms the reader up to one of its main questions: is the human psyche well suited to contemporary urban life?

It then starts its journey by the very beginning of our species and our closest primates' habitat in the second chapter about primatological and prehistorical perspectives.

Chapter 3 circuitously carries on guiding the reader towards the main query of this book by providing evidence of humans' preference for a certain landscape which seems to be innate and plausibly linked to our hominid origins.

Chapter 4 – mostly theoretical and hypothetical – condenses the predominant sociologists' discourses about urban life, while Chapter 5 presents neurological empirical facts about urbanicity. The latter intended as the level of settlements' size, in terms of population, is usually associated with typical densities too.

A psychological and utilitarian perspective is taken in Chapter 6 which reviews stated preferences towards different urbanicity levels, life satisfaction, happiness, and loneliness.

Finally, Chapter 7 faces the ultimate issue: genetics and behaviour eventually modified, modifiable, and adaptable in such terrifically different habitats we can live in, spanning from rural to megaurban areas. These human habitats are actually created, and, sometimes, chosen by us. This is the subject of Chapter 8, which uses concepts and terms from ontogenetic inheritance, economic geography, and geographical psychology.

The book concludes by proposing thoughts about future human habitats, whether rural or megaurban habitats, or a promiscuous stimulating mix of them, in light of the evolutionary and psychological perspective discussed, which urbanism and planning should consider to ensure healthier and happier rural–urban dwellers, namely healthier and happier societies that favour our individual and societal flourishing.

This book, then, reports findings from an extensive academic literature across disciplines not usually talking among each other, consolidating a new perspective for urban planning, centred on human nature, ultimately intended. While picturing an idea of most current big cities being not ideal for our well-being, it also prizes them as a great human achievement which could, and should, get better and better. It underlines the importance of smaller settlements on the basis of the empirical evidence, without necessarily having to escape from the big city, which instead could become more attractive if wisely planned and integrated in the larger multivariate territory.

We live in under-optimal versions of our settlements; the attempt in the end is to bring what could be called the *Anthropological-Evolutionary Urbanism* introduced in this book, to bear on the traditional urban and social studies for the betterment of our settlement living. Anthropological-Evolutionary Urbanism can be defined as an interdisciplinary framework that repositions urban theory and planning around the evolved biological, psychological, and socio-cultural characteristics of humans today, guiding the development of habitats that better support human wellbeing and societal flourishing.

Cities exist *per natura*, they are not artificial objects, but parts of our cultural predisposition built on our biological one. However, when they overgrow – more for economic functionalities than for our own preferences – and they get too big and, sometimes, unpleasant, they need to find ways to keep more in line with our biological nature to have healthier, happier citizens and societies. The same is true for smaller settlements, not to become far too disconnected and under-stimulating for those permanently there.

This book is about settlement *sizes* and their suitability for us, but it takes for granted that *beauty* – however ephemeral and subjective – and life stages play a role too.

Luca S. D'Acci
Hampshire, England, August 2025
Piedmont, Italy, March 2026

No AI-based tools and technologies were used for this book

Behind the book

It is early June, the end of school. My older brother and I start our fantastic train-ferry journey to spend two months in our Mediterranean island aunt's countryside farm. My brother happily carrying me inside the wheelbarrow between chickens, rabbits, fields of basil, parsley, tomatoes, and aubergines; picking peaches and figs, playing with butterflies and ants, eating and napping under a fresh ivy gazebo and the perfume of glycine; falling asleep with the sounds of crickets and waking with those of goldfinches. All around just few cottages, fields and little lanes for walks and bike rides. The mountain far away, the sparkling stars, the moon, and a low adjacent hill from where she was setting, the only things interrupting the limpid sky view. Unforgettable evenings watching stars from the red recliners with my brother and cousins delighted by the jasmine fragrance, enhanced by the silence of the countryside, interrupted only by the sounds of the sea waves on the occasional windy nights.

After these two colourful months, our parents re-join us to all travel back home up to our pre-Alpine 1-million city, but with a special stop around the middle. An enchanted historical village of a few thousand inhabitants, where individual houses are compacted into a picturesque careless hamlet where time seems to have stopped centuries, if not millennia, ago. You can just hear the sound of your feet walking, the bells, birds, people peacefully talking together sitting in front of their houses and children playing everywhere in the streets, courts and little squares of this wholly pedestrian hamlet. Walking all day, hand in hand with my brother, through the village's cozy, meandering little stepped streets, sometimes all the way to the wooded hill in front of us, where we would sit at the top, waiting to watch the occasional car pass along the only road, far below, following it until disappearing into the countryside. There we will spend almost another charming month.

This would happen each year from my 3rd to my 13th. Undoubtedly one of the most enriching and beautiful times of my life.

All this was so drastically different from the scenario we were used to during the year in our 1-million-inhabitant city.

I grew up, from when I was 3 years old to when I was 13, experiencing every year, ¼ of the time in countryside and village life, the rest of the year a 1-million city lifestyle, feeling and reflecting the positive and negative aspects that the size and the entirely different essence of each settlement involved. Thoughts which got more persistent when, since my late twenties, I experienced the incredible life of even bigger cities[1] and of smaller settlements.[2]

The above enriched my surprise and thinking about the following: how built (or unbuilt) places can offer you such terrifically different types of living according to how they are built, how big they are, and many other factors characterising them; and how we end up choosing (or not choosing) our own settlement type in which to live our lives.

Despite the individualities of each settlement, due to unique genius loci, climate, geography, socio-economic context, historical paths and randomness, in my life experiences, I felt some commonalities underlining somehow settlements' life according to their size. It seems that urbanicity, intended as how "urbanized" an environment is (size and density), acts a bit like altitude for the mountains: it makes mountain environments at the same altitudes rather similar to each other regardless of where they are. Even though, cities and villages of similar size/density can be so different to each other to give you dramatically diverse experiences and feelings.

1 São Paulo, Sydney, Rio de Janeiro, New York, Boston, London, Paris, Kuala Lumpur…

2 One year at Barão Geraldo in Brazil; 1 year in cottages of ancient hamlets of a few dozen actual inhabitants within the French forests and in Camargue (Verfeil-sur-Seye, Lavaurette, Saint-Projet, Petit Boisviel); a few months in a little wood house in the Uruguayan "desert" near a small fishing village (Punta del Diablo, Cabo Polonio); regular visits at my brother's cottage in the Piedmont-French mountains, as well as most weekends and holidays in countryside hill (Valle San Bartolomeo), small sea (San Bartolomeo al Mare, Monterosso al Mare, Riva Ligure, Laigueglia) and mountain (Chezal, Gressoney Saint-Jean, Bardonecchia) Italian villages/towns for years. This, plus 3 years in futuristic Rotterdam, parts within 10 years in a traditional English village (Milford-on-Sea), half a year in Glasgow, a few months in Dublin and Barcelona, and half a year in Sydney and São Paulo, were places I actually lived in, alongside, the visiting of around 400 other places across five continents.

Something else amplified my curiosity about how different types of settlements affect people's lives: my mother – born and raised in a 200-thousand-inhabitants' city – loves city life, and the bigger the city the better. My father – born and raised in a few-thousand-inhabitants' medieval village surrounded by a hilly countryside – hates cities. And my older brother in his twenties moved to a mountain- isolated dwelling[3] almost escaping from the big city[4] as soon as he could, despite loving aspects of it.

It is difficult to separate the influence of their judgements and feelings coming from the settlement size they were raised in when young, but, regardless of the reasons, this sharp contrast stayed in my mind.

Now that I can more formally study these experiences, I educated my knowledge and discovered fascinating disciplines such as urban scaling, neuro-urbanism, niche construction, environmental psychology, geographical psychology, urban economy, evolutionary psychology, and neuroanthropology. Such academic study started many years ago during my time as Asst. Professor at the Erasmus School of Social and Behavioural Sciences, when I proposed and taught a PhD course titled "Nature and Nurture. *Homo sapiens* in cities", and studied behavioural aspects of humans: both genetically and environmentally speaking. Something I later revisited in some Anthropology courses at the University of Oxford.

Having recently finished editing a book titled *Urban Scaling*, empirically facing how quantifiable factors[5] change with city size, I now wanted to write this book still dealing with diverse sizes of settlements but from the less standard angle of human evolution and psycho-anthropological perspectives.

Luca S. D'Acci
Hampshire, England, August 2025

3 At 1,400 m, 20 km from a village, 30 km from a town, 50 km from a city, and 120 km from a big city. He later moved slightly closer to towns and cities, but still well away from them: to a pre-mountain traditional Piedmont farmhouse at 6 km from a village, 15 km from a city, and 70 km from a big city.

4 120 km away.

5 GDP, incomes, density, crime, emissions, inequalities, education, infrastructures, diversities, interactions, services … .

1 Introduction

Abstract

Notorious anthropologists, psychologists, biologists, ecologists, geneticists, palaeontologists, behaviourists and neuroscientists are studying how far the brain plasticity engraved in the Homo sapiens' genotype enables behavioural phenotypes suited to current urban life; while sociologists, economists and urban planners are beginning to treat urban phenomena and spatial decisions under an evolutionary lens. Urban scholars would benefit the most from such multidisciplinary perspectives, having as a final goal the facilitation, if not creation, of human habitats enhancing our well-being and progress. Megacities, cities, towns, and villages are a form of ontogenetic inheritance (Niche Construction) which, when free, we can choose (Niche Picking) and, most importantly, alter (Planning). Geographical Psychology and Economic Geography deal with active gene–environment correlations and spatial decision-making processes where utility functions attempt to optimise trade-offs.

Massey (2002), in his American Sociological Association presidential address, states outright:

> sociologists must work to understand more fully our evolutionary history [...] the anthropological literature on hunter-gatherer societies [...] primatologists [...] cognitive neuroscience; [...] we must end our hostility to the biological sciences and work to incorporate the increasingly well-understood biological foundations of human behavior.

DOI: 10.4324/9781003355014-1

In fact, evolutionary explanations are not an *alternative* to other social sciences but operate at different levels: the *ultimate* level for the former and the *proximate* level for the latter.

Among the social sciences themes susceptible to a profitable convergence of disciplines, we discuss urban life.

According to Wilson E.O,[1] "human nature – the epigenetic rules – did not originate in cities and croplands, which are too recent in human history to have driven significant amounts of genetic evolution" (2000, p. viii).

They were probably the earlier books by the Nobel Prize winner Lorenz K. (1963), the zoologist Morris D. (1967), and the anthropologists Tiger L. and Fox R. (1971) whose phylogenetic approach via comparative ethology called attention to academics and the public to see humans as a biological species evolved to adapt to specific environments, although within a certain plasticity.

The attention they received worldwide, positive and critical, was punctual in time to break the extreme behaviourists in vogue who were pushing towards a view of the human mind as a tabula rasa "equipotent response machine", concept which is "neither correct nor heuristic" (Wilson 2000, p. 551).

For generations, the social scientists' conviction that humans escaped its own genes and became exclusively culture-bound was dominating, but today scientific and technical progress tell us a different story.

Is the human psyche suited to contemporary urban life? Starting from the last chapter of Wilson's *Sociobiology* (Wilson 1975), famous for the reactions it generated, an emerging academic literature is facing this question by reasoning on its fundamentals: DNA and environment.

Notorious anthropologists, psychologists, biologists, ecologists, geneticists, palaeontologists, behaviourists, sociologists, architects and urban planners, mathematicians, neuroscientists, environmental economists, philosophers, and archaeologists[2] are getting interested in how and if, as a species, we fit the urban physical-cultural environments of modern societies.

1 The father of Sociobiology (Workman and Reader 2021; Shackelford and Welling 2019; Wilson 1975) – later also called Evolutionary Psychology – whose 1975's book was ranked by the International Animal Behavior Society as the most important book on animal behaviour of all time, surpassing even Darwin's monument *The Evolution of Emotions in Man and Animals*.

2 **Anthropologists** (e.g. Shaw C.N., Longman D.P., Downey G., Odling-Smee J., Kendal J.R., Tehrani J.J., Hare B., Lewis E.D., Churchill S.E., Franciscus R.G., Tan

Massey (2002) is one of them seeking "to illuminate what sort of beings we really are, and to project how we might be expected to function in the dense, urban environments of the future". About 300˙000 generations of humans lived as hunter-gatherers,500 generations as agrarians, 9 generations in the industrial era, and 1 generation in the post-industrial era. Therefore – Massey concludes – "as organisms, we cannot possibly have adapted to the environment in which we now find ourselves".

While urban life insulates us from some selective pressures our ancestors adapted for, it also poses new types of challenges on their own (Downey 2016).

One of the questions is if our notorious phenotype plasticity copes with these new challenges which we are suddenly facing in our recent urban era, or, if not, whether the latter create a sufficient selective pressure to induce the related genetic adaptations and, if so, how fast to avoid prolonged evolutionary mismatch.

Downey reflects upon the evidence – and possibility – that "cities shape their inhabitants, biasing the human phenotype, perhaps even in ways that can inflect the gene pool of our species"; he believes that "urbanization does not produce a niche so well-tailored to our use" (Downey 2016).

As environments often change and organisms can be genetically adapted only to the environments encountered by the previous generation at most, a "certain deviation" from the optimal potential adaptation level is ordinary (Crespi 2000). However, our current societies are transforming dramatically in a within-generation time, which leaves little biological response margin to the evolutionary time necessary for adaptation, and at magnitudes surpassing "little deviations".

To use the words of Buss – one of the fathers of evolutionary psychology – we live "in the modern environment, [but] we have a

J., Shea J.J.), psychologists (e.g. King P.A., Barret J.L., Greenway T.S., Schnitker S.A., Furrow J.L., Brown G.R., Kanheman D., Twersky A., Van Wingerden M., Kalenscher T., Chen C., Kaplan S., Duque J.F.D., Fitzgerald C.J., Danner K.M., Ittelson W.H., Hinds J., and Sparks P.), **biologists** (e.g. Feldman M.W., Gilbert S.F., Creanza N., Kolodny O., Wang E.T., Kodama G., Heinrich B., and Cieri R.L.), ecologists (e.g. Matthews B.), **geneticists** (e.g. Myles S., Moyzis R.K., and Pritchard J.K.), **palaeontologists** (e.g. Ward P.), behaviouralists (e.g. Laland K.N.) sociologists (e.g. Törnberg A. and Andersson C.), **architects and urban planners** (e.g. Downton P., Jones D., Zeunert J., and Deuskar C.), **mathematicians** (e.g. Baldi P.), **neuroscientists** (e.g. Turner R. and Egan G.), **environmental economists** (e.g. MacKerron G. and Mourato S.), **philosophers** (e.g. Buller D.J.), and **archeologists** (e.g. Durrani N.).

Stone Age brain" (Morton 2000); or to use the words of Miller (2016), "we navigate our increasingly urban modern world with Paleolithic brains".

Our urban habitats are "strikingly different from those which came before than that created by the city" (Bloom 2001).

"We are genetically pre-programmed to live outdoors", states Koen Steemers (2015) – a condition that contrasts with the daily life of a typical person of a typical contemporary city, living most of her time enclosed in a cement box and travelling inside a metal one. In the US, people spent on average 93% of their time inside a building (87%) and a vehicle (6%) (Klepeis et al. 2001). The same expression is used by Pinker disapproving urban lives in which planners condemn most urban dwellers by ignoring our genetically encoded nature: "the belief that human tastes are reversible cultural preferences has led social planners to write off people's enjoyment of ornament, natural light, and human scale and force millions of people to live in drab cement boxes" (Pinker 2002).

Noisy urban environments with their asphalted spread surfaces, crowded, polluted streets, and frenetic lives, are a "divergence from [our] ancestral habitats [hence] the neurobiological impact of the transition to city living should be carefully examined" (Lambert et al. 2015).

Assuming that we have retained our ancestral brains, perhaps undergoing slow adaptation processes, and within a non-infinite plasticity, we should study the effect of habitats transitions – as urban dwellings – occurring over just a few generations (Lambert et al. 2015, Maller et al., 2005, Fawcett and Gullone 2001).

2 Primatological and prehistorical perspectives

Abstract

A brief excursus on Homo sapiens' way of life in the earliest times and a few comparisons to our closest primate species' social and physical habitats.

While the ancestor of all primates was solitary or pair-living (Olivier et al. 2024), primate groups vary in size from 1 up to more than 800 (Chapman and Teichroeb 2012), even if most of them vary from 2 to 200 members (Lewin 2005, p. 80) influenced by social and ecological factors, within which among the latter we can mention the kind of food they eat and its spatial abundance and distribution, and the type of predator's defence strategy. According to Wrangham, the ecological pressure is the "principal responsibility in social behavior" (Wrangham 1987).

Gorillas' groups vary from 2 to 20 members, chimpanzees from 15 to 80[1] (Lewin 2005, p. 81), and, a most extreme variation, *Procolobus rufomitratus* (red colobus) from 12 to 150 individuals (Chapman and Chapman 2000), while an across-species comparison reports a variation from 1 individual in the *Pongo* species (orangutans) to more than 800 in the *Mandrillus sphinx* (mandrills) (Abernethy, White and Wickings 2002).

Ecological factors inducing the formation of group life rather than solitary life are possibly many, such as a reduced risk of predation (Dunbar, MacCarron, Robertson 2018, Shultz and Finlayson

1 The average numbers are 10 for gorillas and 30–50 for chimpanzees (van Vugt 2018, p. 10).

DOI: 10.4324/9781003355014-2

2010, Lehmann and Dunbar 2009, Willems and Hill 2009, Shultz et al. 2004, Cowlishaw 1994), more efficiency in discovering and defending patches of food (Cody 1971, Wrangham 1980), in raising offspring, and in defending against predators (Lewin 2005, pp. 80, 81), tracking the positions of conspecifics within a shared home range for foraging efficiency (Isbell 2024); while factors discouraging big group formations are related to competition for food access (Dunbar, Korstjens, Lehmann 2009, Janson and Goldsmith 1995), social stress (Borries et al. 2008, Hill, Lycett, and Dunbar 2000, Srivastava and Dunbar 1996, van Schaik 1983, Dunbar 1988), female fertility (Dunbar 2018), higher disease risk, and higher visibility to predators (Lewin 2005, p. 80), even if the larger the group the more eyes checking for predators, and also the lower the probability of being the one who is eaten (dilution effect, see, e.g., Alcock 1989, Krebs and Davies 1991).

As individuals within the same group have the same dietary range and as food resources are not usually infinitively continuously available in the same location, it means that the speed of eating food and the speed of "regenerating" it are not identical. It follows that individuals within the group must compete for it, which typically happens in two ways: contest competition and scramble competition; the former involves direct fighting, the latter arriving first and eating the food before other individuals of the group (Chapman and Teichroeb 2012). In both cases it means that as food is not enough for the entire group, it is necessary to travel farther to find it, which is a cost. A point will be reached after which the costs of traveling are more energetically expensive than the advantage of keeping that particular group size; then it will split. This model is called Ecological Constraints Model (concept origins: Milton 1984, Janson 1988. Explicitly formalised and named: Wrangham, Gittleman and Chapman 1993. See also Chapman and Teichroeb 2012). The higher the food spatial frequency, the lower the travel distances, the bigger the group can be.

It is a balanced trade-off between costs and benefits that ultimately determines the optimal (rather than the maximum) group size (Krebs and Davies 1991, Boesch 2012, p. 488).

An interesting dynamic, more temporally flexible social organization called fission-fusion, takes advantage of both large and small group sizes, following ecological constraints contingencies.

Among primates adopting this type of social organization are the *Ateles* species (spider monkeys), and the *Pan troglodytes* (chimpanzees); as well as the multi-level (also called modular or nested) organisation in the *Theropithecus gelada* (gelada), the *Papio hamadryas* (Hamadryas baboons) (Chapman and Teichroeb 2012, Aureli et al. 2008), the *Rhinopithecus* species (snub-nosed monkeys), and the *Nasalis larvatus* (proboscis monkeys). See Grueter et al. (2017, 2012) for, respectively, a multi-level versus fission-fusion society definition and a larger list of primate species adopting such social organizations. This flexible modular social organisation allows for regular, or even continuous, proximity among these subgroups which generally also macro-coordinate themselves.

Reasons behind cyclically grouping in different sizes are both ecological (e.g. improving foraging efficiency, Aguilar-Melo et al. 2019, according to fluctuations of the availability of food or oscillations in predators) and social (e.g. sex). A recent alternative view (Isbell 2024) suggests that group formation results from individuals visually tracking others in the same home range to avoid foraging in the same locations.

We now shift to our primate species, *Homo sapiens*.

Referring to multilevel societies, Murdoch (1981) observed, "nowhere on Earth do people live regularly in isolated families. The habitual formation of superfamily level groupings is one of the unmistakable universals of human sociality" (Grueter et al. 2012); or, talking about primate groups in general, Stringer and Andrews (2014, p. 200) remark that "civilized societies have not changed that much from our primate ancestors".

For over five million pre-civilization years we lived in sparse, relatively immobile populations of hunter-gatherers (Wilson 2004a, p. 34) whose economies of subsistence production were gathering wild plants and hunting wild animals. Hunter-gatherer existence covers more than 99% of our time (Wilson 2004a, p. 84, Miller 2016, p. 908).

The basic subsistence unit of those human foragers was the family, composed by 5–8 persons. To make optimal use of dispersed resources, we lived in dispersed families. When food is uniformly distributed – and territorial populations are small enough – the costs of exploiting it are uniform. Dispersing populations in scattered families, minimizing individual competition maximizing efficiency, was the natural tendency to avoid interference. Competitive food procurement favours dispersion – as long as populations in the territory are small enough to allow such dispersion and avoid overlaps. However, when food procurement requires cooperative forms, aggregation is favoured. According to these cost–benefit cycles of scale over time, families seasonally aggregate in a camp of 4–6 families, 25–50 persons,[2] and disperse according to where food is available and how to procure it (Johnson and Earle 2001, pp. 32–33, 41, 50–51, 54–57).

Parallel to cooperative food procurement reasons, families occasionally gathered also to share food in case of lack (risk management) or of abundance (fandango festival, ceremonies, and trade). A subsequent networking level occurred for security and food territorial defence, when regional networks of 10–20 camps provided an extra alliance system (Johnson and Earle 2001, pp. 56–57, 63, 88).

Even with plentiful vacant land suitable for horticulture, early hominids preferred to disperse in family units as procuring and processing food required only 2–5 hours per day (Hayden 1981), allowing easy and non-competitive access to wild foods (avoiding interferences and conflicts). Small scattered group settlements were a cost-efficient solution to respond to basic economic necessities for which the economies of scale required cooperation among only 1–6 persons (Johnson and Earle 2001, pp. 61–62, 77, 91). To keep subsistence costs down and constant access to foods and resources, we scattered in small family units and moved frequently. Under these circumstances we were then able to avoid the diseconomies of agglomeration of larger groups such as less efficient food procurement and mobility, social tensions, and lack of freedom and of independent decision-making.

During this first hominids era, the family-level forager was the self-sufficient unit of social and economic organisation (avoiding diseconomies of agglomeration); however, when opportunities or problems occurred, it cyclically moved in and out of superfamily camps for the benefit of all (thereby enjoying economies of agglomeration).

Having lived more than 99% of our history like that, it might call into question our current megaurban lives' natural predisposition, even considering a certain malleability inbuilt in our own nature.

However, a particular view is presented by Turner and Machalek (2018): they emphasise that such small groups in which our ancestors lived – as well as some of our current closest primates – often were not permanent. They make the point that we generally take for granted

2 Each camp was composed of several extended families, where a family of a man, a woman, and few children was augmented by grandparents, cousins, aunts, and uncles. These extended families moved across camps around eight times a year. Until around 12,000 years ago, humans' bigger social network was a tribe of around 150 individuals spread over camps within a large territory, getting together once a year or so, for gossip, parties, partner searches … (van Vugt 2018, p. 10).

that humans are naturally social and group-forming animals, while they are not. Our human's primate ancestors were genetically oriented to be weak-tie, low-sociality animals forming non-permanent groups. Then natural selection had to work (enhancing humans' emotions) to overcome such genetic propensity and make us more social and group oriented. This Darwinian cognitive, emotional, and behavioural selection took millions of years, but, according to them, it might not have cleared out the original more individualistic nature towards large communities, which, [if true], could be an advantage because it provides us with the genetic behavioural "preparation" to handle the large population of urban life too.

In their book they summarise how both cladistic[3] and comparative analyses show the individualistic side of our ancestral nature, more community (large) oriented than group (small) oriented.

Turner and Machalek list the following cladistic results:

All great apes share common traits in their social structure:

1 Male-female promiscuity
2 At puberty, all females (and males in gorilla and orangutan, but not in chimpanzee) abandon their natal community to migrate to other communities and never return
3 Not permanent group structures

The only strong tie is the mother-young offspring (point 1 implies that fathers are never known, which undermines ties with "fathers"), which is in any case broken for point 2. Then the intergenerational continuity is not fully possible.

Among great apes the ***group*** is not a natural formation: it is temporary and following a fusion-fission pattern. Groups are fluid. Even the most permanent group of the lead silverback male gorilla is not permanent.

The only truly permanent social structure is the ***community***, which is much larger.

Indeed, great apes are very individualistic, mobile, sometimes autonomous, don't make permanent groups, but consider themselves part of the larger community.

3 In language, cladistic analysis aims to find common roots: what all languages have in common. In biology, the common features of species which evolved from a common origin. In our case, it focuses on the behavioural phenotypes of the last common ancestors.

It seems that 30 million years ago (Mya) apes and Old-World monkeys were similar but 20 Mya monkeys, being smaller, took control of the treetop habitat where the abundance of food and room supported larger and more permanent groups. The opposite happened for the apes, who were larger and then confined in the lower part of the trees. In Maryanski's analysis, monkeys are group oriented, while great apes are community oriented.

Then, when 10 Mya African forests began to recede in favour of savannas, there were no room/resources for all arboreal primates, and many were forced to come to the ground. Monkeys were able to defend themselves from predators even in the savanna due to their large, organized groups, while apes declined because they didn't form such groups. Eventually, the latter too started to form a more stable subgroup within the larger community: between 1.8 and 3.5 Mya, under natural selection, our subcortical brain developed probably reinforcing emotions allowing social ties to be sufficiently strong to form groups, essential for the survival in the savanna.[4]

Then, up to 6 Mya, most great apes were weak-tie, non-group species – something that might still have left a mark in our human nature,[5] given that we are evolved great apes.

"A monkey could never create a macrosociety because they are programmed to form local troops. The community is the natural unit of orientation for great apes rather than the local groups, which are always temporary"[6] (Turner and Machalek 2018, p. 320).

Turner and Machalek's argument is that our pre-adaptation to form macrosocieties, to live in large population, in frequent changes

4 Around 6 Mya, an ape species in African forests bordering open fields was divided into two subspecies: one remained in the forests and became the current chimpanzees and bonobos and the other moved to the savannah and became humans (van Vugt 2018, p. 8).

5 Turner and Machalek attribute the human conflict between individualism and collectivism to the above reasoning. Each of us is neurologically wired to lean either towards individualism or collectivism, but this conflict cannot be resolved by choosing one over the other: embracing individualism may lead to loneliness, while embracing collectivism can feel emotionally overwhelming.

6 Attention is needed in the reasoning because we might still talk about permanent ***groups*** of non-permanent ***members***. If so, it would mean that they were still used and designed to (***daily***) live in groups (even if smaller) regardless of the regular change of its members, and their capacity to see the larger community behind the group, in which however they didn't live ***daily***.

and among strangers,[7] could in fact stem from this great ape ancestral capacity to see beyond the group. They argue that although natural selection made hominins more social and group oriented, it did not eliminate their cognitive ability to comprehend broader social structures beyond their immediate group. The latter, despite all, made macrosocieties socio-psychologically possible.

Great apes perceive a larger macro-level social structure, while monkeys and most mammals are kin and group oriented without the capacity to see larger social structures.

We started indeed forming such megasocieties[8] 5˙000 years ago, after 200˙000 years of small foraging societies, and most of our previous times in kin units, small societies of various nuclear kinship units in a gathering/hunting band within a delimited area. Starting with horticultural and agrarian societies, we had to deal with strangers and be organized in much larger social structures beyond kinship. In a way, what was maladaptive[9] 10 Mya, it could be seen as a pre-adaptation for the later macrosocieties: great apes are neither confined to tightly bonded kin groups nor do they automatically form strong social ties, and they often live alongside others who remain social strangers; therefore, descendants of great apes, as us, are better positioned to deal with strangers[10] (Turner and Machalek 2018).

As – Turner and Machalek continue – natural selection, while enhancing apes emotions to form groups, did not select out their weak ties and larger community orientations (interaction with strangers), humans today have two minds: feeling lonely in the absence of strong ties, yet overwhelmed when too many; "this duality can make for personal problems for individuals if out of balance" (Turner and Machalek 2018, pp. 417–18).

This "out of balance", makes me think of the two extremes of the continuous spectrum of human settlements (in terms of sizes – and often subsequent densities): village (too overwhelmed *if* suffocated by the lack of freedom and privacy when literally everyone knows and daily sees/checks everyone), and big city (too lonely *if*[11] it's difficult to

7 Despite all the negative socio-psychological aspects listed in this book.

8 Agrarian, industrial, post-industrial.

9 The ape incapacity to form large and stable groups.

10 At least up to a point, as evidence collected in this book reports. See also the previous footnote about *daily* group life versus *non-daily* community life.

11 See next chapters of the book for more discussions empirically based.

have a few strong ties). Even though, social space[12] is not necessarily overlapping with geographical space: you can have intimate friends in the other side of a megacity with whom you regularly engage, while having no real intimate friends even if living in front of you in your small village.

Van Vugt (2018) believes that a hunter-gatherer life was profoundly anti-depressant due to exercise, omega-3, social network, and enough sleep, while modern environments generate stress and loneliness.[13] The latter was [probably] not present within the strong social structures of our ancestors.

Even though, we have evolved to be *supercooperators* (Fuentes 2017) able to live in large-scale societies (Gross 2019). Contrary to chimps, we are capable of creating ordered patterns even when living with thousands and thousands of others.[14] Such larger "groups" are possible by emotional threads of co-operation (Winston 2002).

However, upon reaching the modern era, scholars such as Henricks (2022), question whether the new style of life "developed in ways that no longer respond to fundamental human needs".

12 For example, the description of the anthropologist Donald Brown in Green (2013, p. 49).

13 However, as mentioned earlier, living in a big city might lead to less loneliness and deeper friendships than in a village – provided one is good at making friends and has the opportunities to do so (due to lifestyle, activities, personality, etc.). In that case, the city could even be better, offering a much larger pool from which to find well-matched friends.

14 "The real difference between us and chimpanzees is the glue that binds together larger numbers of individuals, families and groups" (Harari 2015, p. 25).

3 Landscape preferences

Abstract

Why do we tend to prefer a certain type of landscape rather than another?

We face this question from two angles: socio-anthropologically and evolutionarily.

3.1 Socio-anthropological perspective

The same place can assume different meanings for different people or for the same person across time (D'Acci 2015). Each of us has a personal-unique vision of the world, a distinctive life path which builds up in a stratified accumulation of events, emotions, feelings, and relationships, which time slowly sculpts – and sometimes re-sculpts – in our mind in the form of memories, worldviews, and personalities. The latter, summed with innate tempers-inclinations, shape our world's idea and our meaning we attach to spaces which are privately translated into places, with personalized flavours which, like voices and fingerprints, can never be the same as another person.

This subjective experience transforming objective spaces into personalised-symbolic places has been studied in geography during the 1960s–1980s (Lynch 1960, Tuan 1977, Buttimer and Cosgrove 1980, Cosgrove 1985, Daniels and Cosgrove 1988).

As Bender (1993) pointed out, groups of different people assign different values to the same place. Interpreting the concept of culture in Geertz's meaning, groups sharing the same culture also share a similar world view (Geertz 1973).

DOI: 10.4324/9781003355014-3

An anthropological investigation on how landscape, space, and place are conceptualised as a cultural dimension appeared in the middle of the 1990s in Feld and Basso (1996), Hirsch and O'Hanlon (1995), and Low and Lawrence-Zuniga (2003). Hirsch (1995) proposed an ego-centred idea of landscape as a relationship between two personal "poles of experiences": background and foreground(s). The "ongoing cultural process" concept of landscape according to Hirsch is a dynamic interplay between the "here" (background) and the "there" (foreground), where the latter is our own horizon of experience which can be objectified as space, or can be imaginative horizons mentally constructed upon stories/movies/novels.

Talking about humans and nature, we briefly explore how the idea of nature itself, and related "natural" places, changed over time in some European societies (Ducarme and Couvet 2020).

The Ancient Greek term used for nature was *phusis,* which means "growing, producing", whose Indo-European root *bheu* is the precursor of the verb *be* in English.

Some pre-Socratic uses such as those of Heraclitus added a metaphysical religious meaning to the phusis' concept of "general property of being", somehow similar to some modern use of nature with the capital N.

Aristotle, in one of his opus, *Physics* (which was so titled after his death, based on the term *phusis*) defined nature as the essence of things, and in his *Metaphysics* he gave four meanings of nature: what grows (a process), the primordial element (a principle), spontaneous movement (a spontaneous cause), and the matter of things (substance). Most importantly, most definitions of *phusis* include humankind. Even when Aristotle uses *tecnè* as differing from *phusis*, he still collocates humans as part of nature, though with the ability to make artifices. In this regard civilised humans are natural as they follow the natural process of their development (humanity progress, technology, science …). Therefore, nature is not a synonym of wild because it is a spontaneous process rather than a fixed state. This meaning of nature as a process was shared by the ancient Romans in their *natura*, meaning "birth, initial character", etymologically deriving from the verb *nascor* (in modern Italian *nascere* means to get born). They also associated it with a bucolic meaning of the countryside where, for the Romans as for the modern Americans, it was the place of the good life rather than in cities. Meaning that fortified with the advent of the Christian who view cities (e.g. the "perverted"

Babylon) as evil, while nature as a delightful wilderness where you encounter God. This Christian meaning culminated at the end of the Middle Ages when Nature lost the meaning of process and became a static vision created by God, who, together with humans, transcends nature itself. This Neo-Platonism (spirit greater than matter), coupled with the Cartesian-Baconian dualistic-mechanistic interpretation of nature, radicalised this static and "raw material for humans" vision. Progressively, the idea of nature lost its moral meaning, opening the door to the exploitation of the subsequent industrial-capitalistic times of the 18th–19th centuries. Nowadays, not surprisingly, a neo-romantic vision of nature is reaffirming itself, re-adding its lost moral value – closer to the picturesque vision of the term "landscape", coming from the Dutch *landschap* (a painted rural view) and of the Italian, French idea of *paesaggio*, *paysage* as the proper space for nature.

3.2 Evolutionary perspectives

Basically, all cultures studied by anthropologists share some common aesthetic behaviours (Benton and DiYanni 2012), suggesting that it might be "rooted in innate tendencies" (Grinde and Husselmann 2023).

In terms of landscape aesthetic, it seems that humans tend to prefer a view of nature, compared to a view of a cityscape or an artificial environment (Grinde and Patil 2009).

Despite subjective differences in personalities and the related selective migration rich variety, there might exist a kind of universal tendency towards preferring certain ranges of landscapes.

According to evolutionary aesthetics, the landscapes we incline to prefer could be an atavistic reminiscence of those in which survival and reproduction were higher (Kaplan and Kaplan 1989, Kaplan 1987, Lothian 1999, Mealey and Theis 1995, Škorić and Kišjuhas 2020, Smith 2005, Xenakis et al. 2012, Orians and Heerwagen 1992, Dutton 2003, Thornhill 1998, Hartmann and Apaolaza-Ibáñez 2010).

Four decades ago, Wilson (1984, 2004b) coined the term "biophilia" for this hypothesis which current research in neurourbanism, life satisfaction, preferences, and housing values appears to indirectly confirm.

We lived in forests from around 85 million years ago till at least 4.4 million years ago when earliest hominids (e.g. *Ardipithecus ramidus*) were still preferring woodland habitats; subsequently (e.g.

Australopithecus) we adapted also to open landscapes with scattered trees (Lewin 2005, White 2018).

Intriguingly, children manifest stronger preferences than adults (Balling and Falk 1982), suggesting a largely innate aesthetic sense toward an appreciation for some range of habitats (Heinrich 2013).

A reason behind our attraction for park-like views might reside in our latest evolution time on open land with spread trees; our sympathy for animals might be unconsciously due to linking them with signs of environments suitable for our life; as well as the presence of flowers which usually associates with the presence of animals and fruits (Heinrich 2013). It is also not random that our feeling of refuge is a covered space as a cave-like (Appleton 1996).

Research has shown that we tend to prefer natural overbuilt environment (Liu and Green 2026, Mascherek et al. 2025), savannah-type view (Orians and Heerwagen 1992, Balling and Falk 1982, Falk and Balling 2010, Klasios 2016, Townsend and Barton 2018) or rainforest (Moura et al. 2018, Hartmann and Apaolaza-Ibáñez 2010, 2013), indicating as a potential cause our Pleistocene time spent in such environments shaping "innate" silent preferences (Roberts et al. 2016).

It also appears that most of us prefer curvy rather than straight streets (D'Acci 2019), and find depressing the areas with identical house or street types repeated; in line with the finding that most prefer intriguing complex (although no too much) visual scenes over too simple ones (Grinde and Husselman 2023, Papadimitriou 2020, Landwehr et al. 2011, Taylor et al. 2011, Hagerhall et al. 2004) and with authors stressing people's preferences towards curved streets as stimulating mystery and curiosity (Kaplan 1987, 1988, Kent 1989, Matsumoto et al. 1997, Herzog and Miller 1998, Bell et al. 2001, Ewing and Handy 2009).

Evolutionarily thinking, it is possible that the above is partially influenced by the fact that "*Humans* are pushed toward exploratory behaviour, as are many other animals, because that way we may discover novel opportunities (Xu et al. 2021)" (Grinde and Husselman 2023).

Zeller et al. (2023) recently found that "hominins lived in areas with multiple biome types [forest, savannah, grassland …] in close proximity, suggesting that hominins preferred landscape mosaics rather than uniform environments" probably for maximizing food in terms of both abundance and variety (Figure 3.1). *Homo* species, particularly *H. sapiens*, were well equipped to heterogeneous habitats: "behavioral

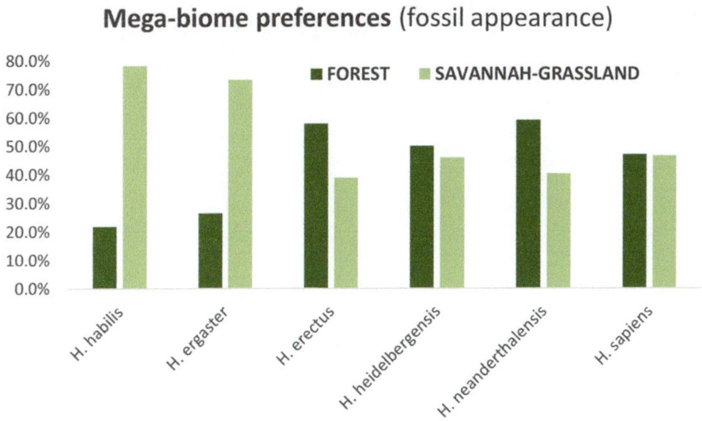

Figure 3.1 Mega-biome preferences in terms of time of fossil appearance. Forest: tropical forest, warm-temperate forest, temperate forest, boreal forest. Savannah-grassland: savannah and dry woodland, grassland and dry scrubland, dry tundra, tundra, barren.

Source: Adapted from Zeller et al. (2023).

and cultural plasticity may have allowed humans to exploit habitat diversity"; over the Pleistocene we adapted and migrated to areas very diverse in their landscapes, while "modern humans have clearly taken an unprecedented path away from our ancestors' resilience and diversity-based strategies" (Zeller et al. 2023).

4 Sociological perspectives[1]

Abstract

The thoughts on urban life of Tönnies, Durkheim, Simmel, Park, Weber, Wirth, Fisher, Ullman, Stokols, Lowry, Gieryn, Gans, Marx, are introduced.

The sociologists Tönnies (1887) and Durkheim (1893) followed by Simmel (1903), Park (1915), Weber et al. (1921), Wirth (1938), and Fisher (1972, 1973, 1975) studied the effects of urban life on us.

The Tönnies's shift from *Gemeinschaft* (Social solidity built on family/kin group of instinctive habitual relations) to *Gesellschaft* (Weak family-friendship cohesion, social relations based on contractual commitments among professional peers) communities is interpreted by Durkheim from a labour division point of view: from primitive societies with minimal division of labour, if any, to modern complex societies with extreme division of labour creating higher efficiency at the cost of too many interactions which for Simmel lead to a "mental change" and for Weber to a money-oriented, self-seeking society with larger and larger frenetic cities and consequentially lower moral unity and happiness.

In the Wirthian model – based on the sociological foundation of Tönnies and Durkheim, and the socio-psychological model of Simmel – impersonality, superficial-transitory relationships, formal organisation, unhappiness, isolation, and deviance are grouped under the label of *social malaise*, correlated with city size, density, and heterogeneity.

1 Some parts from D'Acci (2021).

DOI: 10.4324/9781003355014-4

Fisher poses the following question: are the cities themselves (size, density, and heterogeneity) leading to unhappiness, or other associated factors (e.g. crime, poverty, absence of support …)?

In this regard, for Michael Foucault – despite "urban space has its own dangers" (Foucault 1984, p. 243) – the fragmented realm of cities is an opportunity of freedom as the place to experiencing "otherness", a pluriformity heterotopia in which a spatialized otherness can flourish (Sudradjat 2012).

Also Herbert Gans points to some positive aspects of urban life laying in the density itself which for someone is a desirable factor (Gans 2002, p. 332) and whose public places and compactness may explain the creativity and cultural effervescence of cities (Gieryn 2000, Hannerz 1992).

We can adapt to the strangers' close presence of modern city life but at a psychological cost although high density usually provides a variety of stimulation and learning opportunities (Sommer 2002, p. 650).

Thomas F. Gieryn (2000, p. 476) epitomises this urban life dichotomy: "Places bring people together in bodily co-presence – but then what? (Boden and Molotch 1994, Sennett 1994). Put crudely, the possibilities are two – engagement or estrangement (Sennett 1990)". The debate about these two pendulum swings was already considerable in the second half of the 1970s, and reviewed in Fischer (1975) and Choldin (1978).

Gieryn (2000, p. 476) reminds us how in one extreme of this pendulum, cities are the locus of freedom, creativity, interactions (Young 1990), diversity, tolerance, sociation, integration, participation (Fischer 1977, 1982); in the other extreme are the locus of anonymity, mental illness, loneliness, egoism, detachment, isolation (Halpern 1995).

Torsten Hägerstrand talks about "the fate of the individual being in an increasingly complicated environment or, if one prefers, questions as to the quality of life" and likes to see people, not locations, as the core of regional sciences (Hägerstrand 1970).

The search for quality of life seems to be an omnipresent compromise between the positive aspects linked with urban life and those linked with village-country life. This difficulty of maintaining the economies of agglomeration and scale without paying their diseconomies is expressed in the presidential address of Ullman: "problem remains to design cities to take advantage of scale economies and the other advantages of concentration, and at the same time to provide optimum livability" (Ullman 1962). Around two decades earlier, Stokols used the term "optimal environments" as those maximising the fulfilment of people needs in a "human–environment optimisation" cyclical feedback coupling "human transactions with the sociophysical environment", even if "in actuality, people are often forced by situational constraints to accept undesirable environmental conditions" (Stokols 1978, p. 258).

As Lowry exemplified, "people seem able to extract apparently equivalent values from diverse environments […] when cities become too dismal for comfort, we retire to the suburbs and substitute the amenities of gardening for those of museums and bright lights" (Lowry 1967).

Indeed, we cannot choose "our moment in life […] but we do have a range of choices as to location" (Harvey 1993).

This bicentennial academic discussion culminated in the Neurourbanism: "a new interdisciplinary field of research […] on the interdependencies between urbanisation and mental wellbeing" (Adli et al. 2017, p. 183).

This attempt to measure the link between cities and, in this case, mental well-being is mostly a quantitative approach as the very beginning of "sociology" itself with August Comte's description of sociology as the new science of societies, seeing it as a positivistic science, a kind of social physics such as the abstract laws of Newton's equation of gravity.

Does urban life make our brains more inclined to mental-health problems? Early studies (Malzberg 1930, Schroeder 1942, Park and Burgess 1967 [1925], Milgram 1970, Glass and Singer 1972) are in line with contemporary neuroscientists' analysis associating urban life with mental issues and stress (Fitzgerald et al. 2016), suggesting that the "*intensification of nervous stimulation*" of urban life (Simmel 1903) would leave a mark on our psyche (White 1903).

Since then, the work on urban stress has evolved rapidly (Lipowski 1971, Calhoun 1973, Craik 1973, Altman 1975, Seeman 1975, Schopler and Stockdale 1977, Cohen and Lezak 1977, Ramsden 2012, Collins et al. 2024) also including comparative studies to speculate analogies with other animal behaviours under stress due to over density.

We saw how various earliest sociologists were worried about the pathologies of "modernity" due to social conditions violating human nature. A worry also investigated by contemporary sociologists today is called "critical sociology" (Turner and Machalek 2018).

Awaiting the advent of the more recent sociobiology, such "human nature" investigated by early sociologists during the 19th–20th century, was rather speculative. Examples are the following.

Marx wrote that human pathologies (e.g. alienation) arise when *fundamental needs of human nature* are not enabled to be satisfied. For Durkheim, a fundamental need of human nature is being part of collective organisations, while for Herbert and Codey the development of self.

Pareto instead used the terms *fundamental sentiments* to indicate the driving behavioural forces behind social organisation patterns.

This wide critique of the modern society and its pathologies – raised as a consequences of violating human's basic nature (the fundamental needs of human nature) – started during the 18th and 19th centuries in a rather speculative manner. However, from the 20th century, the social sciences "adopted the tenets of science" (Turner and Machalek 2018), as biology, and became less speculative, until Sociobiology (Wilson 1975) saw them even as subfields within biology.

Before the advent of Sociobiology, there was a resurgence in human nature interest by anthropologists (Ardrey, Morris, Tiger, and Fox), sociologists (van den Berghe), and ethologists (Lorenz), but typically speculative, while sociobiology forced scholars to be less so and more precise (Turner and Machalek 2018).

Let's now shift the discussion to another level: how societies themselves evolve/change. Our built environment is a mirror of our society types, which could either enhance or obstacle our flourishment.

Being cities – particularly megacities, suburbs, conurbations, and urban agglomerations – and urban living a relatively recent product of societies; and being our lives in current cities not always the best that they could be for our well-being (which ultimately also means humanity progress in any terms), understanding how societies change adds useful knowledge for our reasoning.

Social organisations have been seen as a larger "body social" in Comte's (1830) and Spencer's (1851) words: "social organism", and "superorganism" respectively.

Spencer was the first to elaborate the idea of an evolution at the superorganic level in addition to the organic one. He was also the one who first coined the expression "survival of the fittest", after reading Darwin's natural selection.

Durkheim reminded us that differently than the biological one, sociocultural evolution is highly Lamarckian, evolving by acquired characteristics. He (1893) developed a theory of societal evolution which goes like this: as population grows, we have two types of increases: material density (physical concentration) and moral density (rates of interactions) which create an increase in competition among actors, which creates selection, which creates differentiation.

The latter is a similar concept of the "social speciation" of Comte described in his theory of social evolution: as societies get larger they differentiate (or "speciate") into greater levels of complexity of their sociocultural components. This would increase problems of the social world, as a kind of selection pressure, using the modern terminology.

Similarly, Spencer's theory of societal evolution initiates with population growth which begins differentiating social structures.

Durkheim, Comte and Spencer were all implicitly referring to selection pressures in societies.

Following Turner and Machalek (2018), we can list the following non-Darwinian selections, where selection operates by the human social universe rather than the natural:

1 Spencerian selection
2 Durkheimian selection
3 Marxian selection

Spencerian selection can be of two types:

Type 1 when the population must adapt to face issues in one or more crucial lines: production, distribution, reproduction, and regulation.[2]

Type 2 when different societies fight (war) among each other over limited resources.

The Spencerian selection Type 1 reminds us an important aspect which we sometimes forget thinking that things[3] are as they are

2 Or, in nowadays projection, fault lines in our human habitats: cities generating unlivable environments and unhealthy direct and indirect effects on our lives.

3 Traffics, urban dispersions, pollution, commuting times, poor quality and poor connections of urban peripheries, and so on, seen as "inevitable" results of (again "inevitable") forces guiding various urban processes.

and cannot be changed. But humans are teleological animals with a strong capacity to reorganize themselves. They can either plan or "let" emerge new variants of "social morphologies" via invention, diffusion, or simply luck. More generally, any species, as us, with the capacity of agency, transmit new sociocultural form in a Lamarckian-type evolution.

Durkheimian selection coined the two terms previously anticipated in this chapter: material density and moral density. The first related to population density, and the second related to the number of interactions. They both cause competition among individuals where the less fit would migrate to new niches or, thanks to their capacity of agency, would create new (better) niches.[4]

Finally, the Marxian selection is based on the conflicts for class inequalities.

Let's now see social evolution from a chronological point of view described by Marx, Weber, Simmel, and Lenski.
Marx's stage model of societal evolution has the following five stages, chronologically:

1 Primitive communism (nomadic hunting and gathering)
2 Slavery (horticulture early agrarianism)
3 Feudalism (advanced agrarianism)
4 Capitalism (our current industrialisation and market-driven economies)
5 Socialism and Communism

Weber's stage model theorised an epoch driven by "rationalism" where money and calculations are the dominant approaches to treat gods and means to gods – a kind of "steel enclosure" constraining feasible options among available ones.

In contradiction to this negative view of market-driven economies and societies of Marx and Weber, Simmel's stage model of evolution sees the open market as a good option for expressing preferences.

Early stage models of societal evolution suggest that societies evolved towards more and more complexity via a differentiation of their cultures and structures. Their evolutions show the following specific temporal pattern:

4 As nowadays we are trying to design better cities after suffering for decades their negative degenerated aspects.

1 Nomadic nuclear families in bands
2 Settled hunter-gatherer's communities
3 Horticultural communities
4 Fishing and pastoral, herding variants of 3)
5 Advanced 3), larger and urban formations
6 Agrarian societies
7 Advanced 6)
8 Industrial societies

Lenski's theory on social evolution is based on empirical research and highlights *technology* as the driving force of societal evolution. In his *Ecology-Evolution Theory* (2005), human needs and desires – enabled/limited by their own capacities – push new sociocultural forms which, contrarily to genetic forms, can be transmitted by other societies in a Lamarckian fashion and they can do even within 1 generation.

However, such push for new (often better) sociocultural forms (or codes) is typically constrained by conservative forces labelled as follows:

1 Socialisation: resist changes if deviate too much from crucial believes
2 Ideology: moralize current cultural forms which in turn mean biases in perceptions and propensities
3 Interdependence: the interconnectedness of social factors can make change more difficult
4 Vested interests: people in position of power can control changes
5 Sociocultural inertia: when current forms are perceived satisfactory

Despite the above, technological innovation induces change and related societal evolution developing new sociocultural forms, usually overall better, somehow similar to Parsons' concept of "adaptive upgrading": *technology* plus *capital* gives *societal evolution*.

Stage models indicate a type of directionality in the evolution of societies toward getting larger and more complex. At least so far.

5 Neurological perspectives

Abstract

Empirical research indicates a link – often proven to be causal by longitudinal and dose–response analyses – between mental health and urbanicity, particularly for those genetically predisposed and those who lived in cities during their youth.

We need quantifiable evidence based on scientific methods to develop audacious well-being policies. Cities have profusely positive influences on our psychological well-being and brain development in terms of stimulus (if without degenerating into *over*-enriched environments), variety (ethnicities, life styles, and life philosophies), possibilities to find individuals matching/stimulating/enriching/complementing our personalities, creativity and wealth (both superlinearly increasing with urban size, although selective migration might influence), and services and opportunities to culturally and educationally grow as individuals and as a species. Cities usually offer richer opportunities in terms of social mobility, wealth, education, career, services, cultural and recreational activities, and social interaction and related creativity stimulation, but there is a cost for it, at least for someone: they are associated with worse mental health compared with town-village-rural areas. Decades of empirical evidence confirm a statistically significant association between urbanicity and mental health issues, often proven to be causal by longitudinal and dose–response studies. Urban rates of such mental disorders are – although relatively low – roughly double compared to the rural rates.

DOI: 10.4324/9781003355014-5

5.1 Cities and mental health

The World Health Organization (WHO) defines mental health as "a state of well-being in which every individual realizes his or her own potential, can cope with the normal stresses of life, can work productively and fruitfully, and is able to make a contribution to her or his community" (WHO 2014) – a condition affected during the lifetime of at least one-third of the global population (Ginn and Horder 2012, Steel et al. 2014). To what extent do cities and urban lifestyles influence it? One of the classics in the study about mental disorder and cities, Faris and Dunham (1939) paved the way to a multitude of similar research in America and Europe during the following decades, mostly confirming the link between urban life and psychiatric disorders. We can go back until the very beginning of the 20th century to see the first most comprehensive American analysis associating insanity prevalence with geographical area differences (White 1903), even though earlier attempts in the United States track back to the sixth decennial Census in 1840 (Cohen 1982).

Since then, a consistent body of empirical research indicates urban dwellers being healthier overall than their rural counterparts, even though this benefit is greater for the rich than the poor (Dye 2008), but according to abundant studies this is not often valid for mental health (Wiers et al 2025, Freeman et al. 2015, Krabbendam et al. 2014).

In natural scenarios the physiological stress response helps mammals to survive threats (predators, aggressive enemies …), and activates hormone release (e.g. cortisol and adrenaline) which increases the blood sugar levels and blood flow to make muscles and lungs ready to respond to the danger (running, hunting, or fighting); the issue is when the stress response remains continuously on, raising psychiatric problem risks particularly in those genetically inclined and in the young when the brain is developing (Abbott 2012).

Psychosocial challenges in modern cities are a substantial portion of these threats (D'Acci 2021), which robustly activate the hypothalamic–pituitary–adrenal axis which, by feedback loops, controls the neuroendocrine system that in turn regulates the secretion of cortisol and physiological responses to stress in mammals such as humans (Hermann and Cullinan 1997) throughout the interaction between adrenal glucocorticoids and glucocorticoid receptors (highly expressed in limbic regions), modulating the structural and functional organisation of the neural circuitry responsible for behavioural response under stress (Tost et al. 2015).

Research literature shows the physical and mental damage of prolonged social adversities and related hypothalamic–pituitary–adrenal axis activation, especially during the brain development years (McEwen 2013); in fact, enduring stress exposure during neurodevelopmental times reprograms the limbic and prefrontal systems with consequential lasting modifications in the neural plasticity potential, the region-specific gene expression, the neuroendocrine function, and the behavioural response to stress (Champagne 2013, Tost et al. 2015).

For humans, urban upbringing has been significantly and repetitively associated with lasting modifications in the reactivity of the hypothalamic–pituitary–adrenal axis (Steinheuser et al. 2014), as modern and big cities are notoriously stressful for most people, even if most likely the nature of this urban link is synergistic with genetic susceptibility (Lecic-Tosevski 2019, Meyer-Lindenberg 2010).

Numerous scholars indicate the fast pace of urban environments as the hostile psychosocial stimuli providing the "toxic social circumstances" (Bentall et al. 2008) that induce chronic stress and related anomalous neural development in susceptible persons (Christmas 1973).

In addition to the over-speed of city life, possible types of *psychosocial* factors of urban stress might include (Tost et al. 2015) the following: ephemeral social relationships, break-up of the traditional family composition and closeness, lack of supportive social linkages, remote interactions due to new telecommunication technologies and consequent real-life social isolation, greater socio-economic inequalities, higher crime per capita, continuous and greater social competition at the expense of a reduced feeling of social cooperation, and daily personal space intrusions. The latter point, as all the others in different ways, might be an evolutionary reminiscence of the neural threat system originally programmed to promptly respond to forthcoming physical attack: recurring crowds – forcing daily close contact with thousands of strangers – might trigger the continuous involvement of the amygdala (Kennedy et al. 2009) and consequentially the sympathetic and hypothalamic–pituitary–adrenal stress systems, which in turn elicit defensive and emotional behaviours (Graziano and Cooke 2006).

Adding to psychosocial factors, the lack of natural daily experience typically suffered by urban dwellers has been extensively proven to be associated with mood and physical and mental health (among many: Haluza et al. 2014, Park et al. 2010, Bowler et al. 2010, Maas et al. 2006, Fuller et al. 2007, Frumkin 2001).

Urban planning and design should induce daily green contact, pleasant public and private spaces, views, walking, and cycling (D'Acci 2019) to offer opportunities for daily psychological relief from urban stressors to quickly restore the homeostatic state where our body-mind functions in a normal way. Or, using the General Adaptation Syndrome terminologies (Selye 1951, 1950, 1946), to allow a proper and rapid *Resistance* stage after the initial *Alarming reaction* stage avoiding reaching the *Exhaustion* stage. Urban planning, by implementing policies and urban forms-structures enabling to reduce over-isolation, crowds, pollution, and congestion, can also diminish the urban stressors, which consequently means mitigating the initial *Alarm reaction* stage itself.

5.2 Urbanicity and mental health: empirical evidence

As for life satisfaction and urbanicity (Hoogerbrugge and Burger 2022), self-selection migration might play a role for the higher mental health rates observed as cities get larger.

A meta-analysis of urban–rural differences in psychiatric disorders conducted by Peen, Schoevers, Beekman, and Dekker shows a significant association with urbanisation and higher prevalence of psychiatric disorders, specifically for mood disorders and anxiety (Peen et al. 2010). However, it might not be universal across countries[1] (Mascayano et al. 2025. Finnemann et al 2025, Xu et al. 2023), as for subjective wellbeing (Jurčišinová et al. 2026).

Vassos, Agerbo, Mors, and Pedersen confirmed in a study on almost three million people born in Denmark between 1955 and 2006 followed from 1995 to 2012 (with an overall cohort followed for more than 45 million person-years) that being born in large cities is associated with higher risk of developing mental illness (Figure 5.1). They found (Vassos et al. 2016) an even marginally higher effect of large cities on the incidence of psychiatric disorder (trend 1.29, 95% confidence interval (CI) 1.27–1.30) than those of the Peen et al.'s

1 As discussed later in this book, especially between poor and rich countries.

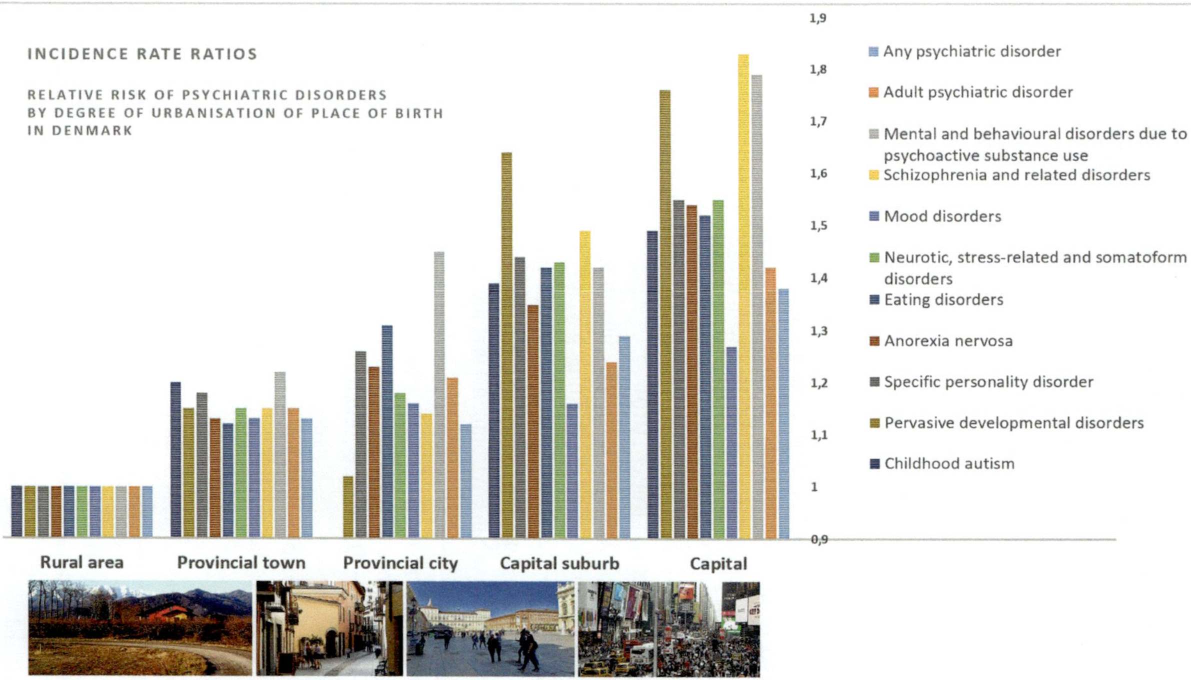

Figure 5.1 Incidence rate ratios for relative risk of psychiatric disorders by degree of urbanisation of place of birth in Denmark. The images on the bottom are symbolic (author's photos in Caraglio, Susa, Torino, and New York).

Source: Author's elaboration from table 2 in Vassos et al. (2016).

meta-analysis (pooled adjusted odds ratio (OR) = 1.21) even though the two approaches are dissimilar.

In a considerable review McGrath et al. (2004) summarise the epidemiological evidence on the influences of (among other environmental factors) urbanicity on schizophrenia from 68 studies, concluding that the schizophrenia rate is almost double in urban than in mixed urban/rural sites (Figure 5.2).

A research on a population-based cohort of almost 2 million people (more than 27 million person-years of follow-up) in Denmark established similar results, confirming the hypothesis of a dose–response connection between urbanicity during upbringing and schizophrenia risk exposure (Pedersen and Mortensen 2001a). By a log-linear Poisson regression and after adjusting for age, age-sex, calendar year, family history of mental illness, and change of municipality, their relative risks related to urbanicity are shown in Figures 5.3, 5.4, and 5.5. The above dose–response association with urbanicity has been repetitively shown in meta-analytical studies using a wide-ranging set of methods, data collection approaches, and definitions of urbanicity (van Os, Kennis and Rutter 2010).

The cautiously selected urbanicity literature review in March et al. (2008) includes 20 studies[2] relating psychosis to urbanicity, where (excluding two[3] resulting in no significant influences on psychosis from urbanicity and one[4] showing a risk increase as high as fourfold associated with urban environment) urbanicity determines an approximately twofold increase in psychosis risk.

These findings suggest an etiologic effect of urbanicity rather than being attributable to reverse causation or service utilisation (March et al. 2008). van Os, Kennis, and Rutter (2010) opine that:

> studies have controlled for a wide range of possible confounders including variables indexing genetic risk in order to exclude

2 Lewis et al. (1992), Eaton (1974), Thornicroft et al. (1993), Marcelis et al. (1998), Marcelis, Takei, and van Os (1999), Mortensen et al. (1999), Eaton, Mortensen, and Frydenberg (2000), Schelin et al. (2000), Allardyce et al. (2001), Pedersen and Mortensen (2001a,b), van Os et al. (2001), Harrison et al. (2003), Sundquist, Frank, and Sundquist (2004), van Os, Pedersen, and Mortensen (2004), Pedersen and Mortensen (2006a,b), Kirkbride et al. (2006), Haukka, Suvisaari, and Lonnqvist (2001), and Torrey et al. (2001).

3 Lewis et al. (1992) and Thornicroft et al. (1993).

4 Eaton, Mortensen, and Frydenberg (2000).

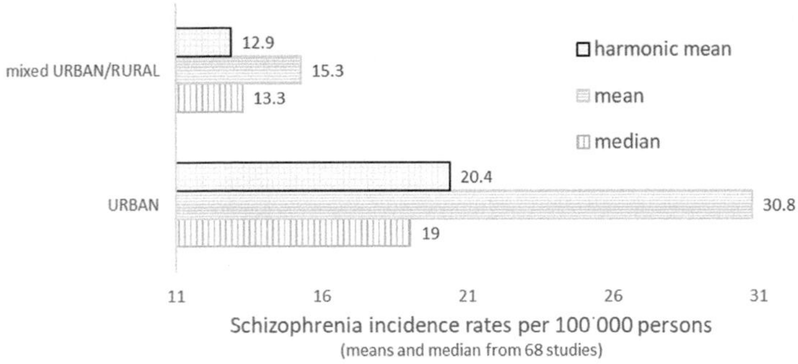

Figure 5.2 Incidence rate ratios of schizophrenia in urban sites and mixed urban/rural sites. Averages from 68 independent studies.

Source: Author's elaboration from table 2 in McGrath et al. (2004).

> genetic confounding [March et al. 2008, Krabbendam, van Os 2005, Kelly et al. 2010, Mortensen, Pedersen, Pedersen 2010]. Longitudinal studies of natural experiments show that changing the environmental exposure, for example moving from an urban to a rural environment in childhood, brings about a corresponding decrease in risk for psychotic outcome [Pedersen, Mortensen 2001] which argues against urbanicity representing a non-causal genetic epiphenomenon.
>
> (p. 204)

Also Lederbogen et al. (2011, p. 498) emphasise this *causal* link: "longitudinal studies [Krabbendam and van Os 2004, van Os, Kenis and Rutten 2010] indicate that urbanicity effects on mental illness are causal and not mediated by other epidemiological variables".

A logistic regression run on a representative sample of more than 7'000 people in the Netherlands computed unadjusted and adjusted (for gender, age, education, income, occupational status, and household composition) odds-ratios showing (Figure 5.6) how urbanisation significantly remains associated with higher mental disorders even when considering confounders (Peen et al. 2007).

In a later meta-analysis review (Peen et al. 2010), adjustment for numerous confounders has been confirmed to have a limited impact on the urban–rural odds-ratio regarding prevalence of psychiatric

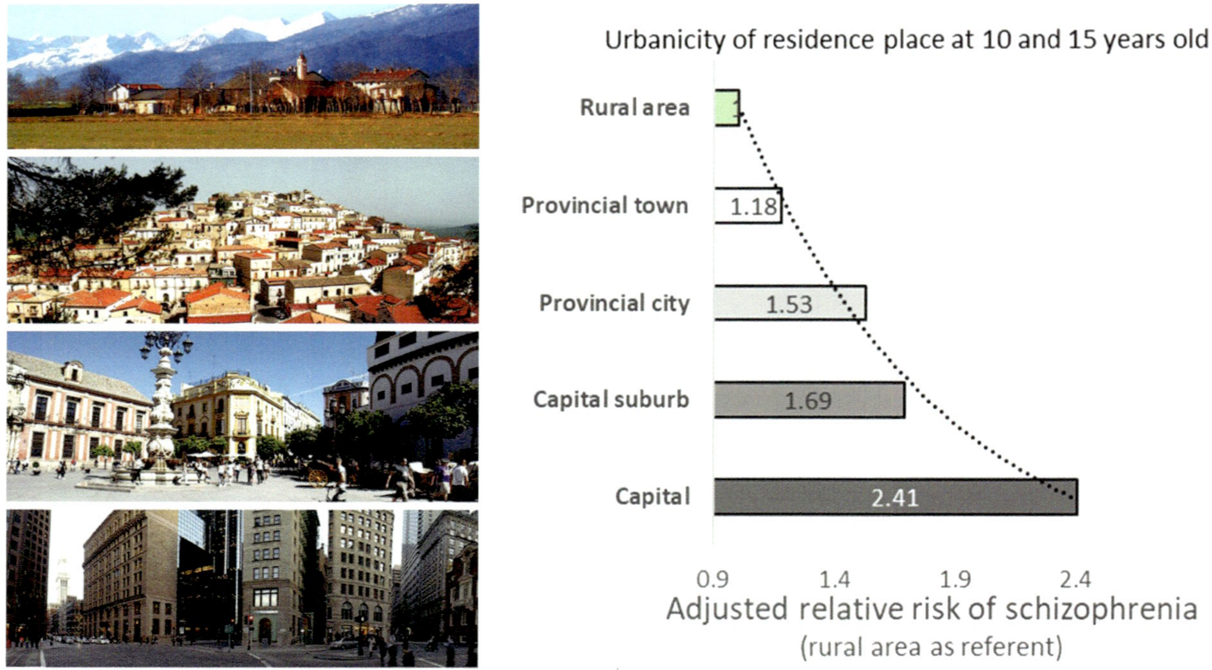

Figure 5.3 Relative risk of schizophrenia and urbanicity.

Source: Author's elaboration from table 3 in Pedersen and Mortensen (2001a). The images on the left are symbolic (author's photos from Caraglio (Italy), Candela (Italy), Seville, Boston).

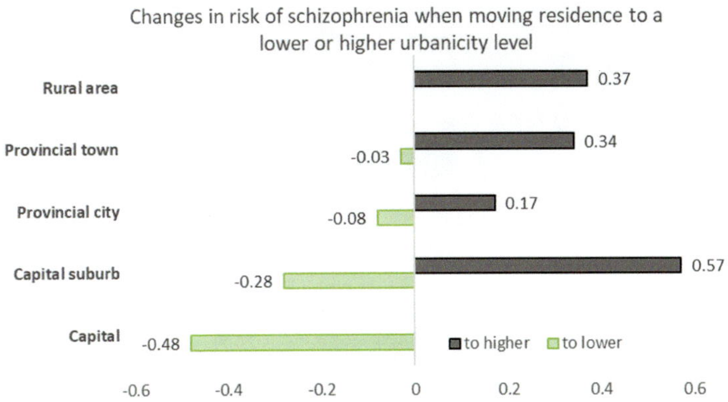

Figure 5.4 Changes in risk of schizophrenia when moving residence from a certain urbanicity degree (Capital, Capital suburb, Provincial city, Provincial town, Rural area) to a lower or higher one. Both adjusted for age, age-sex, calendar year, family history of mental illness, and change of municipality.

Source: Author's elaboration from table 3 in Pedersen and Mortensen (2001a).

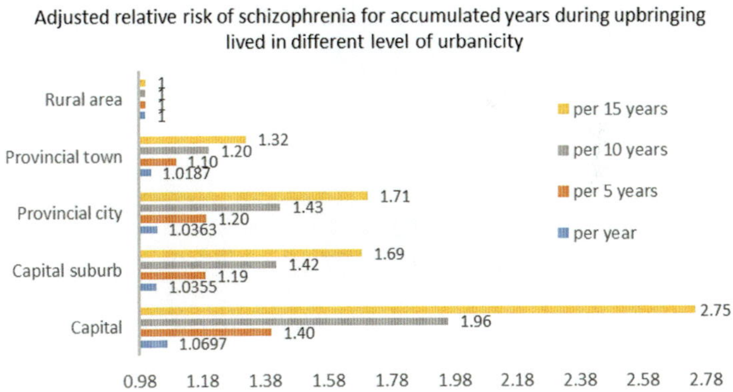

Figure 5.5 Relative risk of schizophrenia for accumulated years during upbringing lived in different levels of urbanicity, adjusted for age, age-sex, calendar year, family history of mental illness, and change of municipality.

Source: Author's elaboration from table 5 in Pedersen and Mortensen (2001a).

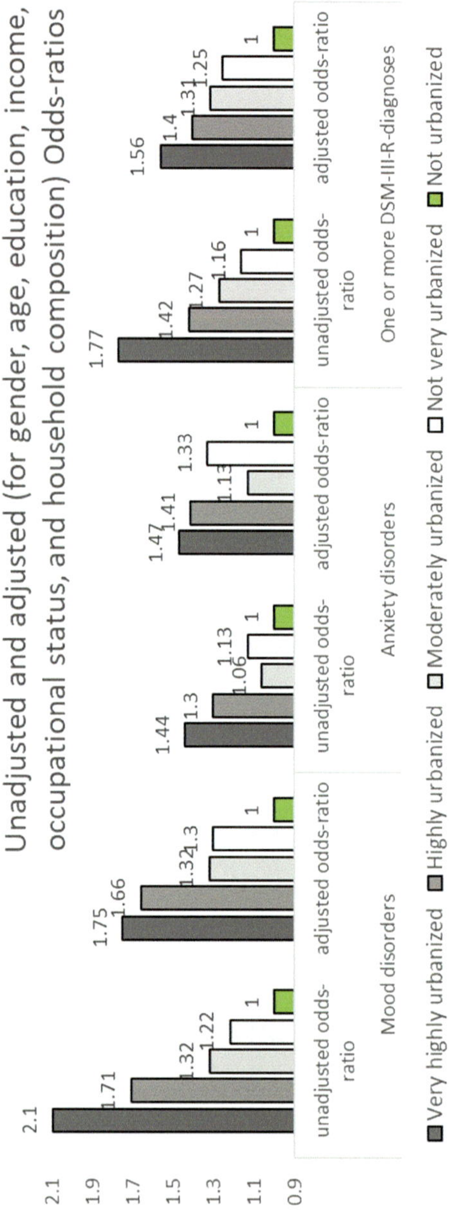

Figure 5.6 Unadjusted and adjusted odds ratios for mental disorders associated with urbanisation level.

Source: Author's elaboration from table 4 in Peen et al. (2007).

disorders, mood disorders, and anxiety disorders, suggesting the relevant direct influence of the urban context on mental health. More precisely their meta-analysis shows city dwellers having a 21% higher risk for anxiety disorders and a 39% higher risk for mood disorders.

Numerous other reviews and studies have reported urbanicity level to be associated with higher mental health issues, such as Lee and Kaufman (2020), Adli and Schöndorf (2020), Abrahamyan Empson et al. (2020), Krabbendam et al. (2021), Reichert et al. (2020), Sampson et al. (2020), Gharib et al. (2020), Pykett et al. (2020), Manning (2019), Costa et al., Lowe (2019), Hoare, Jacka, and Berk (2019), Fett et al. (2019), Okkels et al. (2018), Evans et al. (2018), Kirkbride et al. (2018), Castillejos et al. (2018), Teng et al. (2018), Gruebner et al. (2017), Besteher et al. (2017), Adli et al. (2017, 2016), Newbury et al. (2016), Chen et al. (2016), Heinz et al. (2013), Weich et al. (2006), and Wang (2004), while others did not find such an association, and sometimes the opposite (e.g.. Kovess-Masfety et al. 2005, Probst et al. 2006, Baxter et al. 2013, Wu et al 2026); while some others indicate findings suggesting that as high as 30% of all cases of schizophrenia might be associated with urbanicity (van Os 2004).

Research also suggests linkages between urban density (+ pollution) and poor mental health (Zijlema et al. 2024), natural landscapes and positive mental health effects (Ryan et al. 2024, Williams et al. 2018, Beyer et al. 2014, Maas et al. 2006, Yamaguchi et al. 2006), well-being, mood, cognition (Cassarino and Setti 2015, Tennessen and Cimprich 1995, Hartig et al. 2003, Berto 2005, Berman et al. 2008, 2012, Taylor and Kuo 2009, Kaplan and Berman 2010), longevity (Takano et al. 2002), mortality (Mitchell and Popham 2008), less felt stress and better diurnal cortisol responses (Roe et al. 2013), reduced anger (Cackowski and Nasar 2003, Kweon et al. 2008), enhanced positive emotional states (Berman et al. 2008, 2012, van den Berg and Custers 2011) and reduced stress (Ulrich et al. 1991, Parsons et al. 1998, Wells and Evans 2003, Kweon et al. 2008, van den Berg et al. 2010, van den Berg and Custers 2011, Ward Thompson et al. 2012, Hartig et al. 2014).

Some of the above results have been confirmed to be causal by longitudinal studies (Alcock et al. 2014).

Some also reported reduced daily outdoors play in urban children possibly leading to short- and long-term emotional weaknesses (Joens-Matre et al. 2008, Tandon et al. 2012, Larson et al. 2011).

Other mental effects related to urban life also involve nocturnal artificial light which significantly affects many physiological, social, and behavioural aspects (Bedrosian and Nelson 2013, Stevens et al. 2013), and dramatically alters the endogenous circadian system (McClung, 2007, 2011). The same is true for the urban sounds which are usually perceived as less pleasant-restorative than the natural (Krzywicka and Byrka 2017).

Lastly, also air pollution appears to permanently damage the brain especially when exposure happens during prenatal and infant periods (Brockmeyer and D'Angiulli 2016, Wilker et al. 2015, Peterson et al. 2015, Calderón-Garcidueñas et al. 2013, 2014, Fonken et al. 2011, Levesque et al. 2010).

5.3 Urbanicity and neural replies: empirical evidence

The neuroscientific literature shows that urban upbringing and urban living might negatively affect stress processing in humans (Tost et al. 2015).

A research published in *Nature* in 2011, using a functional magnetic resonance imagining, found an increased stress-related amygdala activity associated with people currently living in cities, and an increased perigenual anterior cingulate cortex associated with urban upbringing (Lederbogen et al. 2011). The latter is a brain region regulating amygdala activity, negative affects and stress; while the amygdala itself is deeply involved in depression, anxiety disorders, and violence. In a first cohort of 32 participants (the discovery study), individuals were asked to solve some tasks (with automatically adapted difficulty to keep between 25% and 40% the success rate) under time pressure and under repeated verbal negative feedback (social evaluative threat) through headphones, during functional magnetic resonance imaging. To make sure that individuals were actually under subjective stress during the test, salivary cortisol, heart rate, and blood pressure were measured repeatedly. Both cardiovascular and cortisol increased during the test, proving that it successfully induced a stressful situation. Stress-related brain activations were quantified in comparison to a control condition in which the social evaluative threat was not used: these activations resulted more conspicuous in the right temporoparietal junction, in the anterior, posterior, and insular cingulate cortex, and in the hypothalamus. The associations between urbanicity and each of the stress-related brain activations areas were determined by a T-test (testing for statistically significant difference between conditions), resulting in an association between current urbanicity and amygdala activations (Figure 5.7), and between urbanicity upbringing and the perigenual anterior cingulate cortex activation (Figure 5.8). The childhood urbanicity was measured as the addition of the multiplications between the number of years spent up to the age of 15 years in an area and the "urban level" of that area, where the latter is quantified as 1 for rural areas, 2 for towns (between 10˙000 and 100˙000 inhabitants), and 3 for cities (more than 100˙000 inhabitants). While the "current urbanicity" simply considers the settlement size (in terms of inhabitants) one is living in. A different second cohort of 23 participants (the replication study) was tested with different tasks to check the results' validity of the first (discovery) study.

Their own study cannot explicitly prove a causal connection, however, "in light of the epidemiological evidence that urbanicity is causal for mental disorders [Peen et al. 2010, Krabbendam and van Os 2005, van Os, Kenis and Rutten 2010]" (Lederbogen et al. 2011, p. 500) they contemplate the parsimonious suggestion to causally link social stress as contributors to urbanicity impacting the neural areas identified in the study.

At the same time studies have repetitively indicated beneficial influences that forest viewing and exploration have in stress pointers such as cortisol level, pulse rate, blood pressure, and sympathetic and parasympathetic nerve action (Craig et al. 2016, Park et al. 2010).

A near-infrared time-resolve spectroscopy (TRS) method was used to measure concentrations of haemoglobin in the left prefrontal area in subjects walking 20 minutes and seated 20 minutes once in a forest scenario and once in an urban scenario: in the forest scenario the haemoglobin level resulted significantly (p-value <0.05 and <0.06, by paired or unpaired one-side t-test) lower, indicating a calmer activity in the left prefrontal cerebral area (Tsunetsugu and Miyazaki 2005). In the same study also salivary cortisol (thought as an indicator of stress level) was sampled and resulted significantly (p-value <0.08) lower after sitting for 20 minutes in the forest area compared with the urban area.

Other studies used functional magnetic resonance imaging (fMRI) – a non-invasive technique measuring the blood-oxygenation-level-dependent (BOLD) signals from the brain – to assess brain activation areas of subjects while viewing natural and urban sceneries.

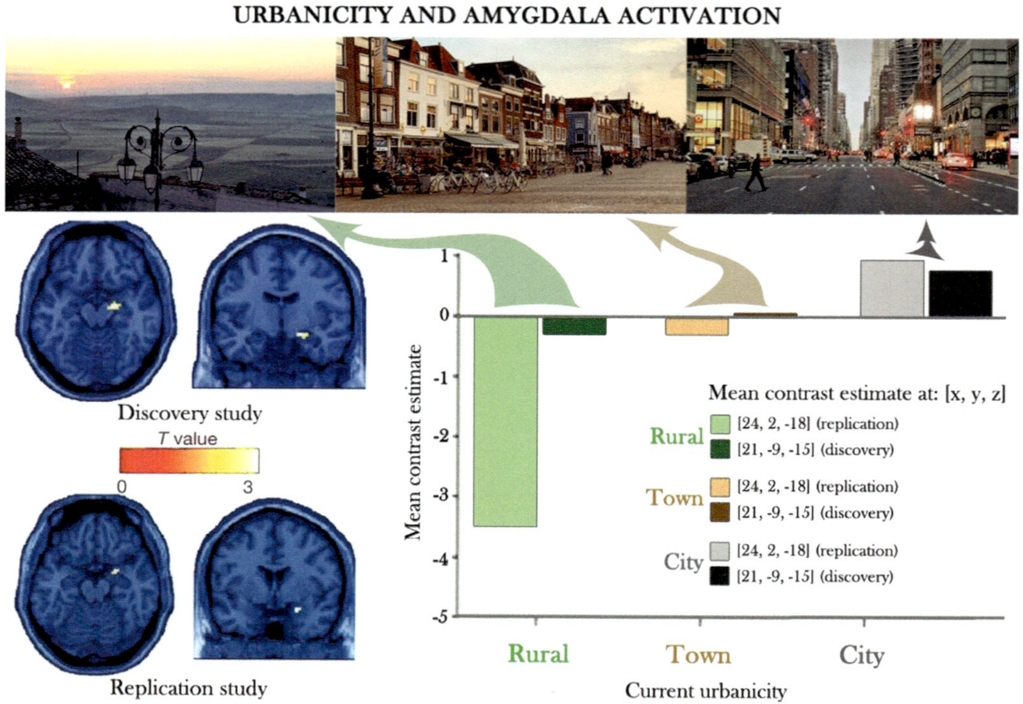

Figure 5.7 Current urbanicity and amygdala activation. The pictures on the top are symbolic (author's photos of Candela (Italy), Delft, and New York).

Source: Graphical variation from Lederbogen et al. (2011, figure 1).

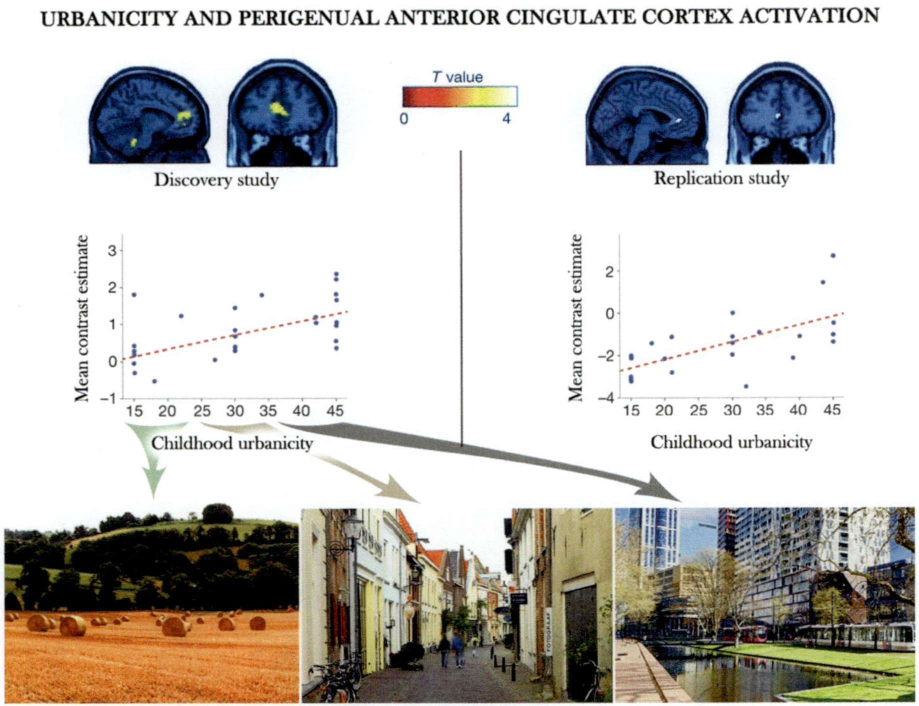

Figure 5.8 Childhood urbanicity and perigenual anterior cingulate cortex activation. The pictures on the bottom are symbolic (author's photos of Southeast France countryside, Deventer, and Rotterdam).

Source: Graphical variation from Lederbogen et al. (2011, figure 2).

When watching natural sceneries, the following brain areas resulted more active than when watching the urban: the superior and middle frontal gyri, superior parietal gyrus, precuneus, basal ganglia, superior occipital gyrus, anterior cingulate gyrus, superior temporal gyrus, and insula; when watching the urban views: the middle and inferior occipital gyri, parahippocampal gyrus, hippocampus, amygdala, anterior temporal pole, and inferior frontal gyrus (Figure 5.9) (Gwang-Won et al. 2010).

Increased activations in the amygdala (Paradiso et al. 1999) occipito-temporal cortex, parahippocampal gyrus and hippocampus are associated with unpleasant emotions (Lane et al. 1997a,b). Amygdala and parahippocampal gyrus activations are also associated with recall/re-experiencing of emotional distress (Sinha et al. 2004). Studies in humans and other animals suggest that the amygdala is involved with negative attainments, anxiety, fear, aversion, and unpleasantness (Lane et al. 1997a,b, Royet et al. 2000, Zald and Pardo 1997). The activation of the anterior temporal pole has been linked with negative emotions, anger (Dougherty et al. 1999), and unpleasantness (Kaplan et al. 2007).

The activation of basal ganglia (including globus pallidus and caudate nucleus) has been measured in response to pleasant pictures (Lane et al. 1999, 1997b, Davidson et al. 1999) and happiness-induced recall (Damasio et al. 2000, George et al. 1996).

In the above Gwang-Won et al. (2010) experiment, the activation of the parahippocampal gyrus, hippocampus, amygdala, and anterior temporal pole happened only when viewing urban scenes, while the activation of the basal ganglia happened only when viewing natural scenes.

In the same year another publication from partially similar researchers described that the "activation of the anterior cingulate gyrus, globus pallidus, putamen and head of the caudate nucleus was dominant during rural scenery viewing, whereas activation of the hippocampus, parahippocamus and amygdala was dominant during urban scenery viewing ($p < 0.01$)" (Tae-Hoon et al. 2010).

Both articles conclude underlining how these types of neural response tests suggest "an inherent preference towards nature-friendly living" (Tae-Hoon et al. 2010), and "can be utilized as a neural index for the assessment of objective preference of the living environments on human habitation" (Gwang-Won et al. 2010).

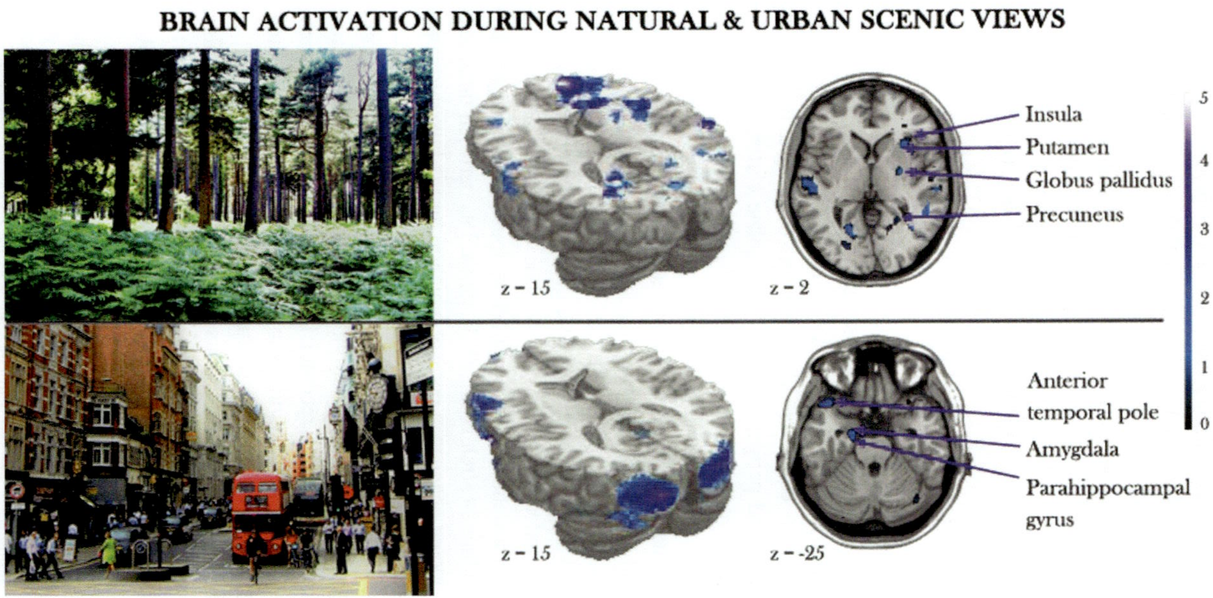

Figure 5.9 Brain activation patterns during natural and urban scenic views. "Z" indicates the coordinate of the z-plane of the brain section. The pictures on the left (author's photo of London and The New Forest in Hampshire) are symbolic, not the ones used for the test.

Source: Graphical variation from Gwang-Won et al. (2010, figures 1 and 2).

A chronic over-involvement of the amygdala may be facilitated by the recurring contact with strangers and intrusion of personal space (both characterising urban life) because of eliciting the brains' threat system (Kennedy et al. 2009).

Amygdala integrity was also found to have a statistically significant positive link with the forest environment around home (Kühn et al. 2017), more generally the positive impact that nature experience has on our cognitive function and mental health has been well documented (Bratman et al. 2012).

Another neurological study (Steinheuser et al. 2014) suggests urban upbringing as a causal factor altering the (re)activity of the hypothalamus–pituitary–adrenal axis (one of the major stress response systems of our body), which in turn is associated with numerous psychiatric disorders, and Haddad et al. (2015) identified a relevant inverse correlation between early-life urbanicity and both right dorsolateral prefrontal cortex and perigenual anterior cingulate cortex grey matter volume, which are linked with the risk of schizophrenia.

An interesting epigenetic link suggesting alterations in DNA methylation as a potential mechanism through which urban location (violence, pollution, social stress, noise, low social cohesion …) contributes to psychopathology is proposed by Galea, Uddin, and Koenen (2011). Other studies reported an interaction between a gene which modulates amygdala responses under stress (the neuropeptide S receptor gene, whose phenotypes manifestation usually involves anxious and stressed profiles) and urban childhood (Strelt et al. 2014), as well as between urbanicity and stress-inducing changes in cortisol which in turn is linked to dopamine (Vaessen et al. 2015), important for optimal prefrontal function.

Gene–environment interactions between urban rearing and three dopamine genes (catechol-O-methyltransferase (COMT), dopamine receptor D1, and dopamine receptor D2) and altered prefrontal activation have recently been found during working memory tests where subjects were asked to memorise sequences of numbers (Reed et al. 2018). More specifically the influence of a functional polymorphism of the gene COMT made by a replacement of methionine (Met) in place of valine (Val) at codon[5] 158 (Figure 5.10) was investigated.

5 A codon is a sequence of three nucleotides which together build a unit of genetic code. A nucleotide is the basic building block of nucleic acids and is formed by a sugar molecule (ribose in RNA, deoxyribose in DNA), a phosphate group, and a nitrogen-containing base. The bases in DNA are adenine (A), cytosine (C), guanine (G), and thymine (T).

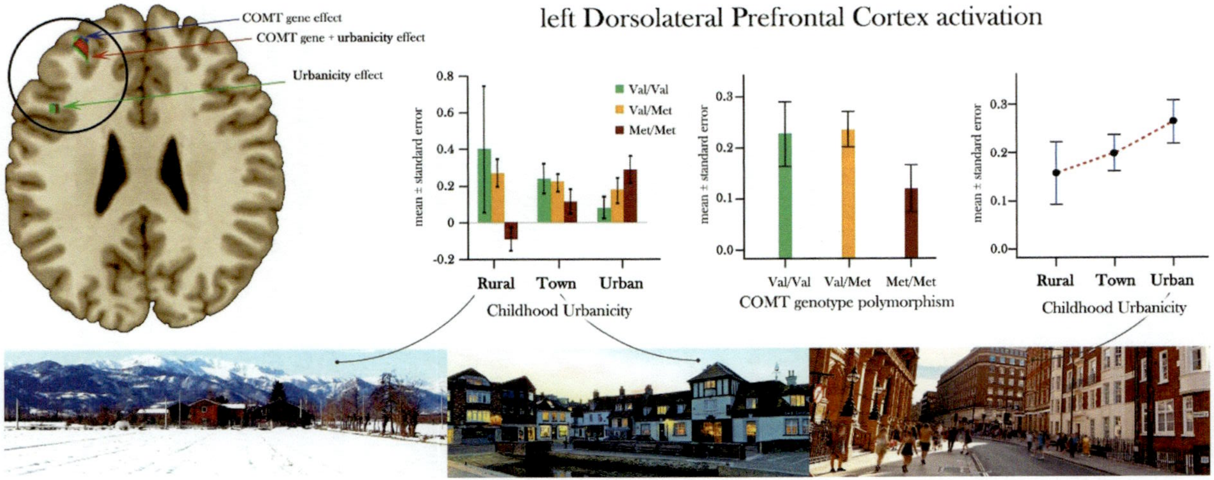

Figure 5.10 Left dorsolateral prefrontal cortex activation measured by blood-oxygen-level-dependent signal acquired with functional magnetic resonance imaging, during working memory tests. From the first graph on the left is evident a reverse effect that urbanicity has for those with the COMT Met/Met gene version related to those with the Val/val and Val/Met genes. The pictures on the bottom are symbolic, not those for the experiment (author's photos of Palazzasso in Italy countryside, Lymington, and London).

Source: Altered visualisation from Reed et al. (2018, figures 1 and 2).

Dopamine is a neurotransmitter involved in the motivational part of reward-motivated behaviour, in movement, attention, learning, emotional responses, and in the feelings of pleasures and satisfaction. Dopamine is affected by stress, both acute and chronic (Pani et al. 2000, Mizrahi 2010, Wand et al. 2007, Booij et al. 2016), and the combination of urbanicity and stress is linked with alterations in cortisol, which is itself connected to dopamine (Vaessen et al. 2015).

A higher depression proneness in adults exposed to stress in their juvenile time has also been linked to an allelic variation in the serotonin transporter gene SLC6A4 (Caspi et al. 2003).

These types of environment and gene–environment interactions altering brain development (neurogenesis, neurotransmission, brain size, and cognition) have been well known since a long time in non-human animals (Hebb 1995, Turner and Burne 2013, Kempermann et al. 1997, Krech et al. 1962, Henderson 1970, Gardener et al. 1975).

Another recent study investigating 85 proteins (125 peptides) abundance ratios at birth between urban–rural environments, linked with psychosis, showed an excellent predictive performance for the prediction model for urbanicity (Cooper et al. 2017).

5.4 Conclusions

Empirical evidence robustly and repetitively has shown negative mental health outcomes[6] associated with urban life, in some cases also proven to be causally linked. However, cities have plenty of precious positive influences on our psychological well-being and brain in terms of more stimulus (as long as we are able to not degenerate in over-enriched environments and their adverse mental effects), more variety (ethnicities, life styles and life philosophies …), more possibilities to find individuals matching/stimulating/enriching/complementing our personalities, more creativity and wealth (both superlinearly increasing with urban size, although the former may be due to selective migration), and more services and opportunities to culturally and educationally grow as individual and as a species.

From a macroeconomic perspective, when individuals make decisions (if they can) about the type of settlement where to live (rural area, village, town, city, megacity, and conurbation), they should also

6 City life notoriously disturbs sleep and our natural circadian rhythms too (Zielinska-Dabkowska et al. 2023, Muzet 2007).

evaluate psychological effects typically associated with different urbanicity levels, even though different personalities, life stories, and genetic predispositions might alter or even reverse these effects.

It might be that people say to prefer – *stated* preferences (we directly ask them about their preferences) – or appear – *revealed* preferences – to prefer a particular environment (we indirectly estimate preferences by regressing the influence that several attributes, including the type of settlement/area, have on their real actions, e.g. how much they actually paid to buy a house in a specific place) even though they *inherently* and *unconsciously* do not, as brain neural activities visualisation, hormones measurements, and gene–environment interactions quantification and their consequent phenotypic manifestations can objectively tell.

From a macroeconomic perspective, if, as I believe, cities will still be there in our future (although conceptually entirely different than the current ones) regardless of the contemporary emergence of artificial intelligence, robots, telework, teleservices, hologram communication, and hyperloops which might challenge their own fundamental necessity to exist as a *physical* socio-economic agglomeration, we should allow their dwellers to not have to pay psychological costs and reduced underground happy mood potentials in order to enjoy their benefits. This cost is not "only" a psychological "internal" cost at the strictly personal expense level of the individual suffering it at various magnitudes of visibility/invisibility; it can be translated in monetary and societal terms as a global roughly 3 trillion US dollars yearly (in 2010), which will probably reach more than 7 trillion yearly in 2030 (Bloom et al. 2011). If we assume to be able to level urban mental illness rate down to the rural rate, more than 1 trillion US dollars can be saved every year (D'Acci 2020).

As Marie Curie says, "science is at the base of all the progress that lightens the burden of life and lessens its suffering"; this implicit common goal (beyond pure curiosity) across scientific fields in our case means to increase our understanding about our environments (e.g. cities) to improve them and their link with our quality of life. As the medical sciences' ultimate implicit aim is to provide better medicines, cures, interventions to live better and longer, the urban and socio-economic-political sciences' ultimate aim is to provide better habitats and societies to live better and longer.

Realising that we could also save trillions of dollars per year by doing so highlights it even more as a clever path to follow, and the sooner the better. Urbanisation is happening with a unique speed in human history (an additional two and a half billion urban dwellers by 2030 only), meaning we need to physically build these new cities within the next few decades, and once a city is built, it is for centuries.

6 Socio-psychological and utilitarian perspectives[1]

Abstract

This chapter reports findings about preferences, preference mishmashes, life satisfaction, loneliness, friendships, and happiness related to urbanicity levels, and utilitarianistically discusses the question "why do people choose cities?"

6.1 Urbanicity preference[2]

"Many surveys about quality of life in cities invariably suggest that it is in smaller cities that the highest quality of life is achieved" (Batty 2018, p. 95).

Attitudinal surveys show that 44% of Americans nominated small towns or rural environments as the best kind of places to live; 30% nominated suburban environments, and only one in five indicated cities (Figure 6.1). European surveys suggested similar results (Knox and Pinch 2006).

When asked about: "If by living in a city (Figure 6.1) or not in a city (Figure 6.2, 6.3, 6.4, and 6.5) you would have the same services, the same job and level of wealth, and the same closeness to your job, family and friends, where would you prefer to live?", an even higher percentage related to the "natural or small town" option was found,[3]

1 Parts from D'Acci 2021.

2 I assume that results might differ if city residents could still live in a "cottage" or villa with a private garden and the usual associated comforts. This could affect both preferences for urbanicity and several psychological well-being outcomes. In short, not only settlement typology, housing typology matters too.

3 More details in D'Acci (2021).

DOI: 10.4324/9781003355014-6

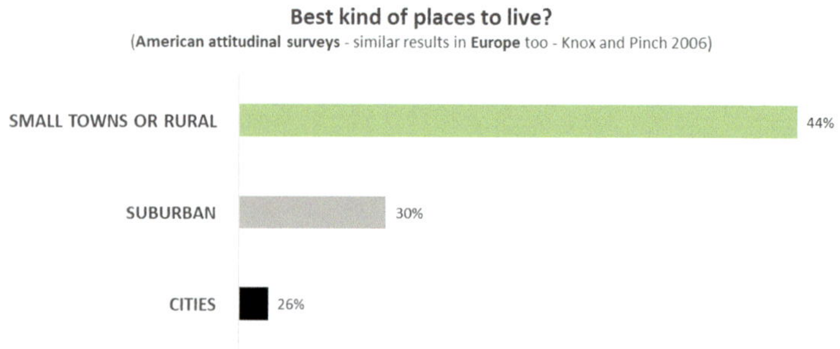

Figure 6.1 American attitudinal surveys. Percentages of replies about the best kind of places to live being small town or rural environment, suburban environment, or cities.

Source: Author's elaboration from Knox and Pinch (2006). (Fig. 1, D'Acci 2021).

followed by a figure (Figure 6.2) as reference for the visual idea of "city" and "not city": by underlying the *ceteris paribus* imaginary condition, a very high percentage of respondents indicated the best place to live as the natural environment (Figure 6.3); however, still around one-third would prefer cities.

Studies consistently indicate rural living as being preferred in the richest countries while urban living is being preferred in the poorest. A first interpretation is related to the difference between *preferring* urban life and *needing* it. Possibly the richest contexts allow opportunities[4] also in/from low urbanicity environments, therefore people are freer to decide the *preferred* place.[5]

4 Job, income, social status, services, education, amenities, cultural inputs, mobility, and access to health systems.

5 This concept is expressed also by Okulicz-Kozaryn in his recent paper: "The fact that people are happy in cities in poor countries [Glaeser 2011] is arguably not due to cities' 'greatness.' It may be simply that life outside of the city in a poor country is unbearable and lacking the necessities, such as food, shelter, sanitation, and transportation. Quality of life or so called 'livability' differs greatly between urban and rural areas in developing countries [...] Simply, the urban happiness in developing countries is rather due to unfavourable conditions outside of cities, not due to virtues of cities" (Okulicz-Kozaryn 2017, p. 145).

He also makes a point in another often-misinterpreted link:

> People are happier in more urbanized countries than in less urbanized countries, but it does not mean that people are happier in cities than in smaller areas [Glaeser

Figure 6.2 "City or not city?".

Source: Author's photos (Sydney, Paris, London, Dronero, Verfeil-sur-Seye, Palma de Maiorca, Alps around Turin, wood house in Uruguay, around Milford-on-Sea). (Fig. 2, D'Acci 2021).

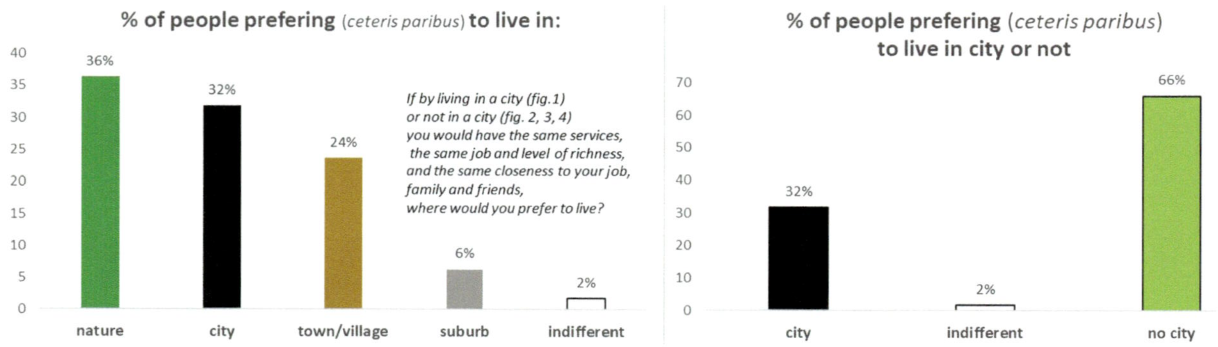

Figure 6.3 Percentage of people preferring, *ceteris paribus*, to live in cities or not. (Fig. 3, D'Acci 2021).

Fuguitt and Zuiches (1975) provide some very insightful empirical information, which, even if very old, still gives elements for thoughts. The following figures are made based on data from their article which I re-elaborated in slightly different forms.

Figure 6.4 shows results from different surveys made in the United States over around two generations ago (Fuguitt and Zuiches 1975). A ***near zero*** percentage of respondents declared having no opinion, while the assumption of ***indifference*** between different locations[6] is at the very basis of spatial equilibrium approaches.

Figure 6.5 groups the same replies into two categories: "city" and "no city". On average, only 14% declared a preference to live in cities, while 86% declared to live in smaller settlements.

Figure 6.6 shows again a ***near zero*** percentage of these "no ascertained" about their preferred residence. This figure is very useful in discerning a possible bias which common sense could suggest: one living in a place might tend, as a reaction,[7] to *think* to prefer a different

> 2011]. More urbanized countries are simply richer, healthier, better governed, etc., than less urbanized countries. This is one of the most agreed upon findings in happiness literature: In a cross-section of countries, people are happier in more developed areas.
>
> (Okulicz-Kozaryn 2017, p. 145)

6 "The spatial equilibrium model requires homeowners (or renters) to be indifferent between different locations" (Glaeser and Gyourko 2008, p. 3). "Individual choice over locations produces the single most important concept in urban or regional economics: the spatial equilibrium. This core insight comes from the idea that if identical people are choosing to live in two different places, then those two different places must be offering an equivalent bundle of advantages, like wages, prices and amenities. Essentially, there must be no potential for arbitrage across space" (Glaeser 2008, p. 4). "When there are some people who are identical and when those people live in more than one area, this means that utility levels must be equal across space" (Glaeser 2008, p. 47). But people are not *indifferent* between different locations because people are *not identical*. Having a similar income, education, etc., does not mean to be identical as they might strongly differ in preferences: one certainly preferring living in a rural village while another in a megacity. When asked about their residential preferences between settlement sizes and typologies, those replying to be "not ascertained" were only between 0% and 2% (Figures 6.3, 6.4, 6.6, 6.7, and 6.11 of this chapter). Apart from some cases of real indifference, when one can choose and chooses, it means that, even necessarily losing something, the overall gain is positive and not zero; the different scenarios are not anymore in equilibrium for her specific own point of view; the equilibrium is broken and therefore he chooses. As long as we can decide, it is doubtful to think that we decide with a coin (because it is indifferent) if spending our life in a rural village or a megacity.

7 The neighbour's grass is always greener.

Preferred residence	(%) Roper 1948	Gallup 1972	NWF 1969	Harris 1970	Population commission 1971	Zuiches-fuguitt 1971
Cities	15	13	6	21	17	10
Suburbs	20	31	18	27	18	11
Small towns	41	32	25	31	30	44
Rural areas	24	23	54	16	34	35
No opinion/other	0	1	1	5	1	0

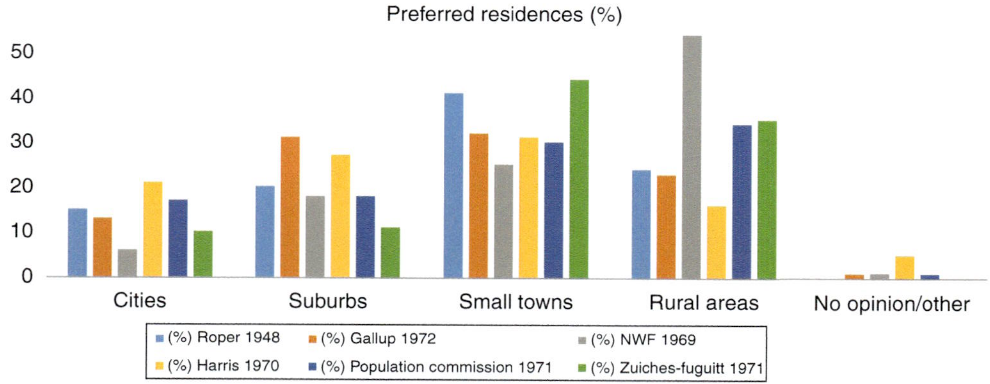

Figure 6.4 Percentage of people preferred residence from various reports.
Source: Author's elaboration from table 1 in Fuguitt and Zuiches (1975).

place instead. Or, the opposite, that one would tend to prefer a type of place because one is already used to it. Figure 6.6 instead indicates a neat and continuously increasing preference towards smaller settlements from those already living there: namely, the smaller the settlement one lives in, the stronger the preference for living there. For example, among those living in bigger cities, only 36% would prefer to live in bigger cities; while among rural dwellers, 82% would prefer to live in rural areas.

Figure 6.7 shows the same but emphasises the preference for smaller or bigger settlements in relation to the current one where one already lives.

Figure 6.8 is another way to see it. It shows the mismatch between the current and the preferred residence in terms of settlement size. Namely the percentage of respondents currently living in a certain settlement size but wishing to live in another settlement size (typically smaller as shown in Figure 7).

Fuguitt and Zuiches (1975) later in their article explore the second of the two possible biases mentioned before: that one could tend to prefer a type of place because one is already used to it.

They found that "people who live in an area [current residence] are more likely to prefer it than people who do not, regardless of

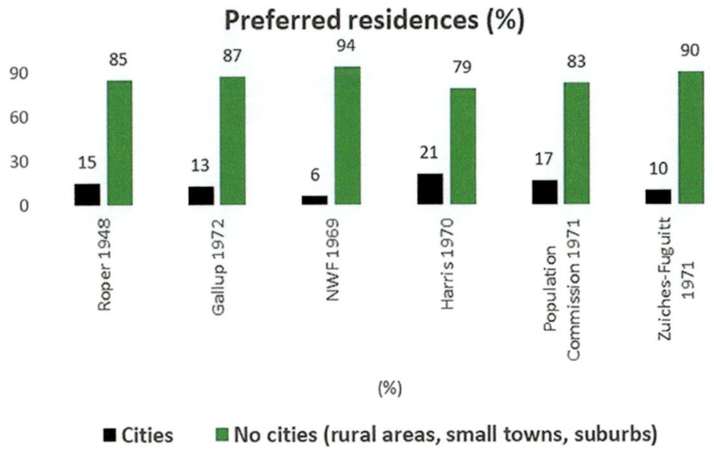

Figure 6.5 Percentage of people preferred residence grouped between "city" and "no city", from various reports.

Source: Author's elaboration from table 1 in Fuguitt and Zuiches (1975).

Current residence	Preferred residence: City > 500k	City 50k - 500k	City 10k - 50k	Town < 10k	Rural area	Not ascertained
City > 500k	36%	15%	17%	16%	16%	0%
City 50k - 500k	4%	41%	23%	10%	22%	0%
City 10k - 50k	4%	10%	50%	14%	21%	1%
Town < 10k	1%	5%	10%	54%	30%	0%
Rural area	1%	2%	5%	8%	82%	2%

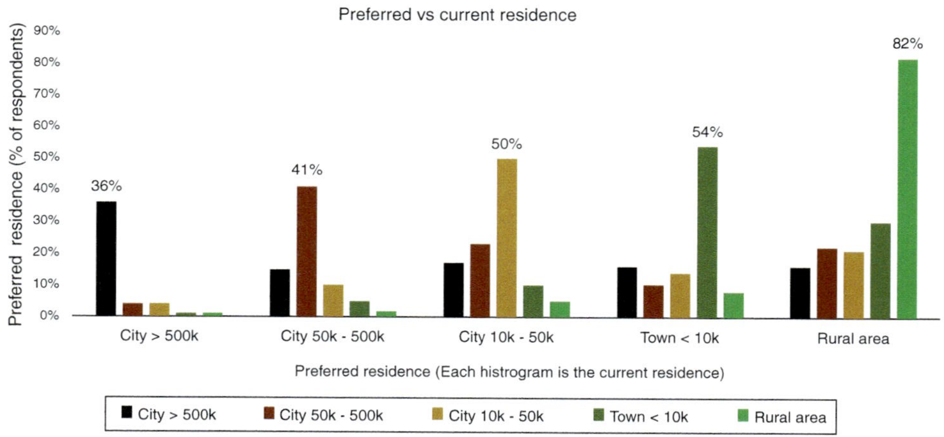

Figure 6.6 Preferred versus current residence. The smaller the settlement one lives in, the stronger the preference for living there. The horizontal axis grouped the preferred residence stated by these currently residents in the settlement size of each histogram (see the legend). Namely it is read like that: 36% of these currently living in a city > 500k stated to prefer living in a city of that size; 41% of these living in a city between 50k and 500k stated to prefer living in a city of that size. And so on.

Source: Author's elaboration from table 3 in Fuguitt and Zuiches (1975).

CURRENT SETTLEMENT SIZE (RESIDENCE)	PREFERRED RESIDENCE Bigger settlement	Current settlment size	Smaller settlement	not ascertained
City > 500k	/	**36%**	64%	0%
City 50k - 500k	4%	**41%**	65%	0%
City 10k - 50k	14%	**50%**	35%	1%
Town < 10k	16%	**54%**	30%	0%
Rural area	16%	**82%**	/	2%

Figure 6.7 Preference towards smaller or bigger settlements in relation to the current one.

Source: Author's elaboration from table 3 in Fuguitt and Zuiches (1975).

origin [residence of birth]. But place of origin, representing an influence which may be more remote in time, also has a smaller but consistent effect on people's preferences" (Fuguitt and Zuiches 1975, p. 499). Despite this current and origin residence bias, Figures 6.6 and 6.7 clearly display that the smaller the settlement one lives in, the greater these preferring it (Figures 6.6 and 6.8) and that the majority of people prefer living in smaller settlements then their current ones (Figure 6.7).

A possible confirmation of the greater urban mishmash compared to the rural comes from a survey of 6˙251 US adults where a higher percentage of urban dwellers than rural "would move if given a chance" (Figure 6.9), (Parker et al. 2018), even though the question didn't ask where. When the latter was asked, the replies were in line with these in Fuguitt and Zuiches (1975): among urban residents, only the 28% would like to move to another urban area, while 71% to a lower urbanicity level (rural, and suburban); the opposite is true for the rural residents: only 20% of them would move to an urban area, while 40% of them would stay in a rural area (Figure 6.7).

The same study indicates that almost half (42%) have always lived in or near the community where they grew up. A direct open-ended question asking them the main reason for never leaving or for coming back to the place where they grew up revealed to being close to their

Mismatch between actual and preferred

Current residence	% mismatched
City > 500k	64%
City 50k - 500k	59%
City 10k - 50k	50%
Town < 10k	46%
Rural area	18%

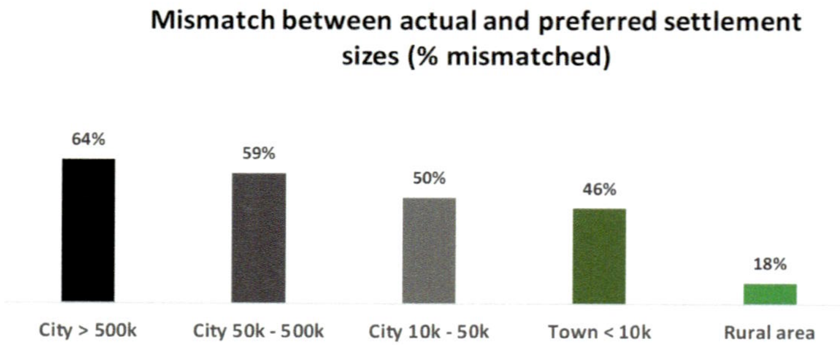

Figure 6.8 Mismatch between actual (current) and preferred residence. The smaller the current settlement of residence, the greater the match of its size and the preferred one. Residents in bigger cities preferring instead another settlement size are 64%, while among rural residents only 18% would prefer to living in other settlements' size.

Source: Author's elaboration from table 3 in Fuguitt and Zuiches (1975).

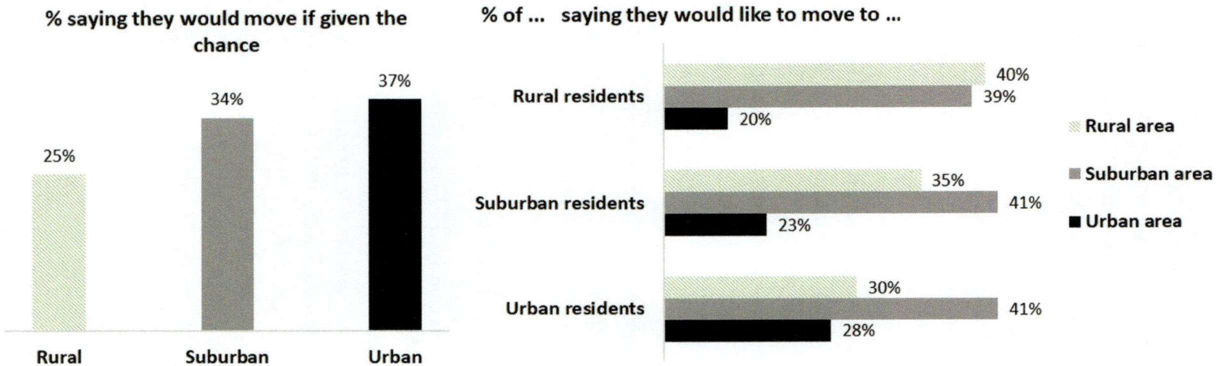

Figure 6.9 Percentage of rural, suburban, and urban people saying they would move if they could. And where they would like to.

Source: Graph elaborated from Parker et al. (2018).

family as the most frequent reason and because they like the place as the least reason.

Considering that most of the world's population is becoming urban, this could mean that a relevant percentage of us would stay in cities across generations not because they like them but because they were born/raised there and therefore having their family there. About 42% never left the place where they grew up, or still leaving nearby it; among them around 74% stay because of family, jobs, friends, inertia or moving costs (Figure 6.10). These numbers, together with the previously shown *settlement mishmash preferences*, provide interesting information regarding the question "Preferring or needing cities?" raised in D'Acci (2021).

Jansen (2020) interviewing a sample of 3˙107 Dutch residents found similar results which are summarised in Figure 6.11. Those indifferent are only 7%. The majority stated to prefer living in a small municipality, while the minority reported to live in the city centre.

Preference towards smaller settlements is again[8] confirmed in Ströbele and Hunziker (2017), as shown in Figure 6.12, from a 1˙208 Swiss sample.

In Scotland, the percentage of people describing their area as a very good place to live was much higher in rural areas than in urban areas (Figure 6.13) (Scottish Government 2020).

6.2 Urbanicity and life satisfaction

A regression analysis on nearly 300˙000 respondents across countries found that life satisfaction is higher in urban areas than in rural areas at low development levels but equalises or reverses in advanced economies, mainly due to similar occupations, income, and education (Easterlin, Angelescu and Zweig 2011). Knox and Pinch (2006) describe this as an "apparent ambiguity", where people prefer rural living but move to cities for better material conditions. The city emerges as neither good nor bad, but as a "necessary evil", or, to use the words of Lynch (1984), "an unfortunate economic necessity."

Studies have shown that life satisfaction is generally higher in smaller towns and rural areas.

8 However, we should also consider that proportion of people who would prefer smaller settlement/countryside mostly because of the pleasure of living in an independent house with private garden rather than for the settlement size itself.

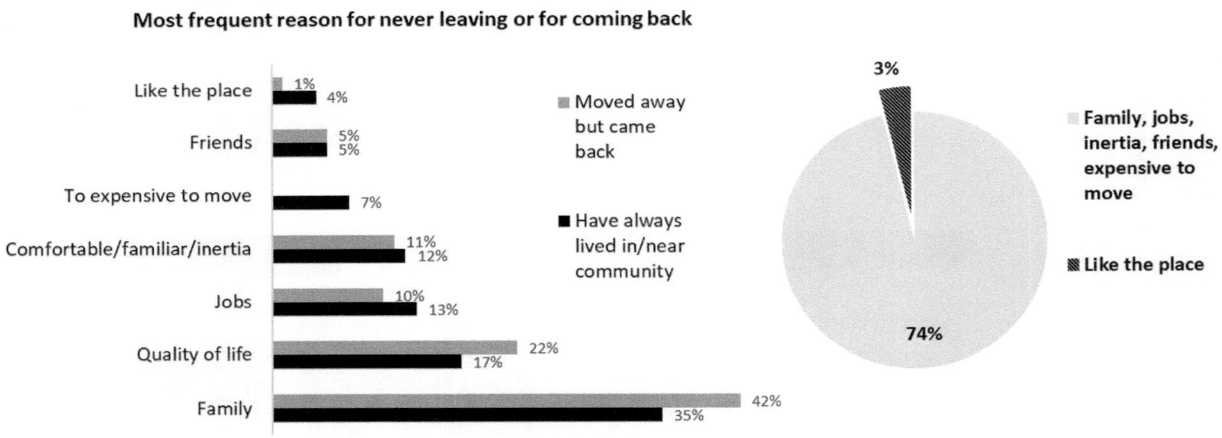

Figure 6.10 *Family* is the most frequent reason given for never leaving or returning to the place where they grew up. The pie chart indicates the mean percentage. Only 3% on average never left or decided to come back to the place where they grew up because they actually *like* the place.

Source: Graph from Parker et al. (2018).

Preferred type of residential environment (% of respondents)

rural	smaller municipality	city edge	city centre	no particular preference
14%	39%	34%	12%	7%

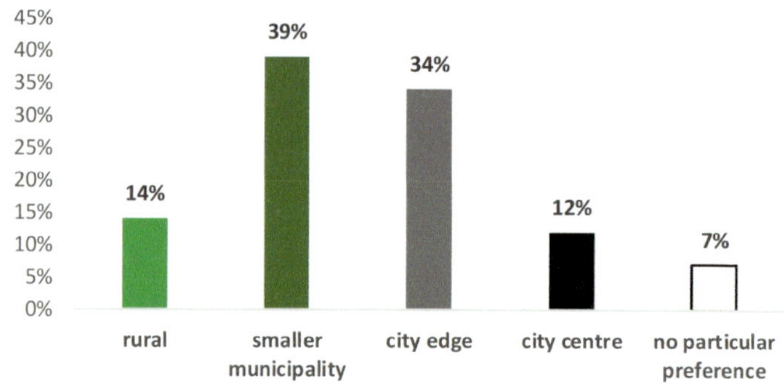

Figure 6.11 Preferred type of residential environment between rural, small municipality, city edge, and city centre.

Source: Author's elaboration from Jansen (2020).

Preferred residence (1–5 scale)

City	Suburb	Small town	Country village	Rural
2.92	3.16	3.84	3.98	3.3

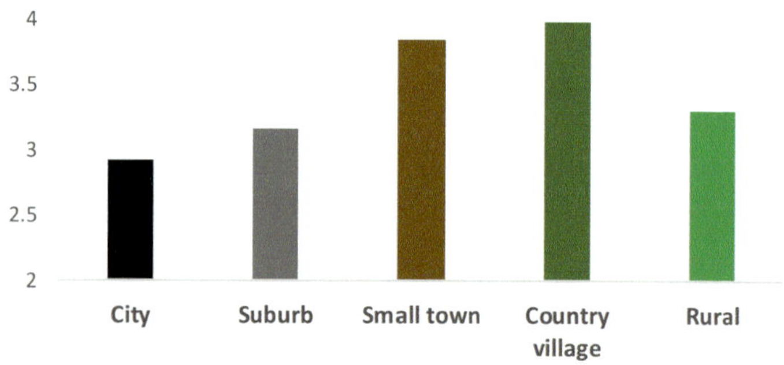

Figure 6.12 Preferred residence (1–5 scale).

Source: Author's elaboration from Ströbele and Hunziker (2017).

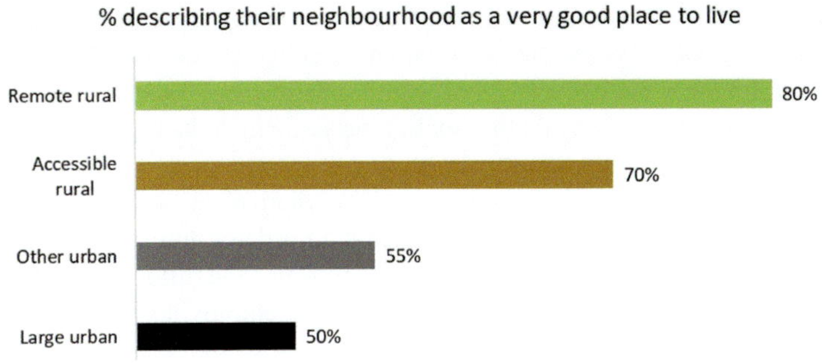

Figure 6.13 Rural dwellers in Scotland are much more likely to describe their area as a very good place to live, rather than the urban.

Source: Graph from Scottish Government (2020).

A study on a sample of more than half a million respondents in Canada indicates that life satisfaction in towns and rural areas is higher than in cities (Helliwell et al. 2018).

Fassio et al. (2013) and Lawless and Lucas (2010) found higher density associated with lower life satisfaction after controlling for key variables. The former controlled for sex, age, marital status, income, and chronic diseases in a northern Italy region (Piedmont) and the latter indicated that Americans are *happier* in smaller areas, rather than "just" *preferring* them (as already resulting from much earlier studies such as Fuguitt and Zuiches 1975 and Fuguitt and Brown 1990).

Other studies empirically associating high density with low life satisfaction, quality of life, or various social-psychological processes are, respectively, Lawless and Lucas (2010), Bell (1992), and Adams (1992).

The fact some people might be unhappy in big cities is not a novelty, but rather a continuous confirmation under different types of variables, methods, and circumstances; since the beginning of the 1970s Fischer (1973) wrote about an "urban malaise" making urban dwellers unhappy, regardless of the specific causal factors.

A regression analysis in Okulicz-Kozaryn and Mazelis (2018) explored the association between nine levels of urbanicity, called "urban-rural continuum", ranging from 1 (>1 million inhabitants) to 9 (<2˙500) and self-reported life satisfaction.[9] When introducing controlled variables (density, crime, housing stress, education, employment, poverty, personal income, percentage of Black people) they found a statistically significant[10] positive coefficient[11] for the "urban-rural continuum": the smaller the settlement the higher the life satisfaction.

Among other studies examining the urban–rural continuum life satisfaction, Sørensen (2014) conducted an ordered logit model on a sample of almost 30˙000 people across Europe, and, after controlling for age, gender, health, family size, education, employment status, and monthly household income, found city areas as statistically significantly unhappier than rural areas and towns (Figures 6.14 and 6.15) (Sørensen 2014, table 4, p. 1457). The result was confirmed also when he tested different criteria to define rural–urban areas. As Figure 6.10 shows, the gradient is monotonic for the richest countries.

Berry and Okulicz-Kozaryn (2013) using a similar sample size (around 30˙000 individuals[12]), classifying urbanicity level into four categories[13], life satisfaction on a Likert scale of three values[14], and controlling for age, income, marital status, employment, family composition, nationality, year and census region, by an ordinal logistic fixed-effect regression, obtained statistically significant odds ratios[15] continuously increasing from large cities to rural areas (Figure 6.16), indicating that the lower the urbanicity degree the higher the life satisfaction.

In another study (Berry and Okulicz-Kozaryn 2009) they also regressed data from the World Value Survey during the period 1995–2004 and found that the higher life *dis*satisfaction in the richest

9 "In general, how satisfied are you with your life?", quantified from 1 (very dissatisfied) to 4 (very satisfied).

10 p-value <0.05 for two models, and <0.001 for one model.

11 0.0094 in the model including all the control variables, and 0.0121 the one most statistically significant with the lowest p-value. Even if apparently small it is rather relevant if we consider that more than 90% of respondents indicated 3 (satisfied) or 4 (very satisfied), with a very small standard variation across counties (only 0.06).

12 Data collected from the General Social Survey from 1972 to 2008 in the USA.

13 Rural-small towns: 2˙500–5˙000 or smaller or open country; suburbs: suburbs of medium-large cities, or in towns between 10˙000 and 50˙000; small cities: 50˙000–250˙000; large cities: >250˙000.

14 1: not too happy, 2: pretty happy, 3: very happy.

15 p-value smaller than 0.001 for "rural-small towns" and "suburbs", and smaller than 0.01 for "large cities", having "small cities" as reference.

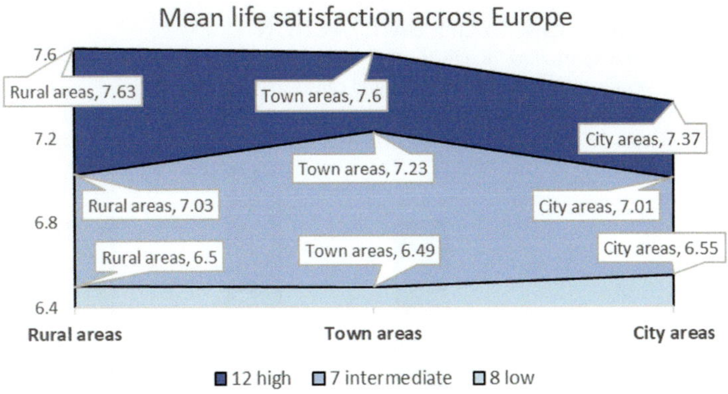

Figure 6.14 Mean life satisfaction across European Union countries (12 richest, 7 intermediate, and 8 poorest). From a sample of almost 30˙000 people across Europe. Life satisfaction measured from 1 (lowest) to 10.

Source: Elaboration from Sørensen (2014, tables 3 and 4, p. 1457). (Fig. 4, D'Acci 2021).

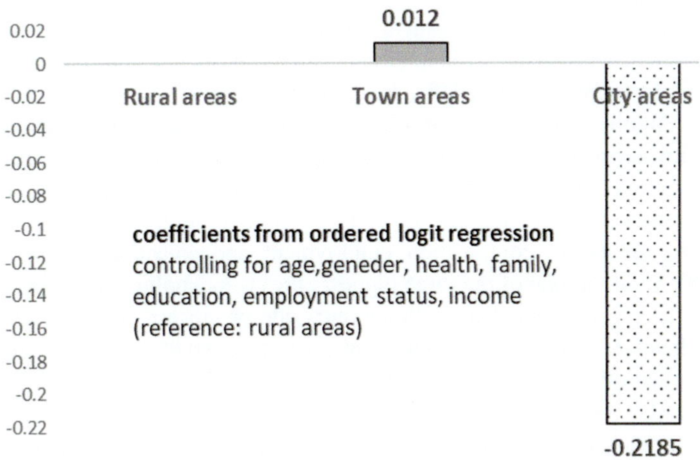

Figure 6.15 Coefficients from an ordered logit regression. From a sample of almost 30˙000 people across Europe. Life satisfaction measured from 1(lowest) to 10.

Source: Author's elaboration from Sørensen (2014, tables 3 and 4, p. 1457). (Fig. 5, D'Acci 2021).

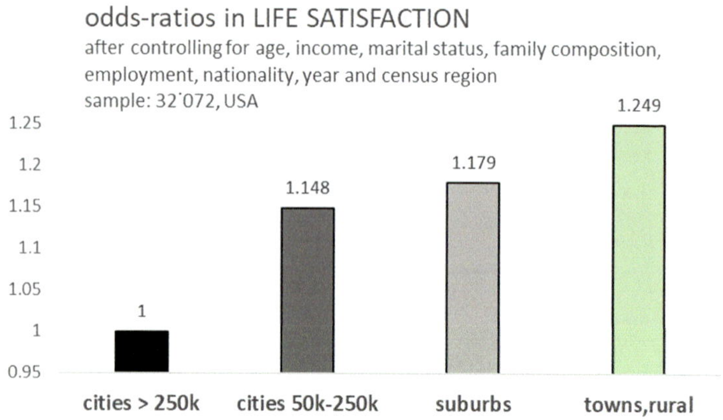

Figure 6.16 Odds ratios, coefficients from an ordinal logistic regression on a sample of more than 30˙000 people from the United States (1972–2008: General Social Survey).

Source: Author's elaboration from Berry and Okulicz-Kozaryn (2013, table 1, p. 879). (Fig. 6, D'Acci 2021).

countries was, again, statistically significant[16] in big cities compared to small settlements, even after controlling for income, marital status, employment, age and GDP per capita (Figure 6.17).

Another confirmation of urban living having negative associations with self-reported life satisfaction was found in Sweden from a study of Gerdtham and Johannesson (2001). The authors regressed (ordered probit model) life satisfaction[17] of 5˙106 Swedish adults controlling for sex, age, family composition, employment, and education and found that living in one of the three biggest cities (Stockholm, Gothenburg, or Malmo), rather than in the countryside or cities < 30˙000 (30k) inhabitants, statistically significantly (p-value <0.05) decreased the probability of feeling "satisfied most of the time".

Also, Glaeser, Gottlie, and Ziv (2014, table 2, p. 45) in a regression analysis controlling for year fixed effects, month fixed effects, age, race, sex, education, marital status, and family size found

16 p<0.001 for the coefficient "settlement<2k", and p<0.05 for "city>500k".

17 Measured in a three-level scale: the daily life is a source of personal satisfaction: "never", "sometimes", and "most of the time".

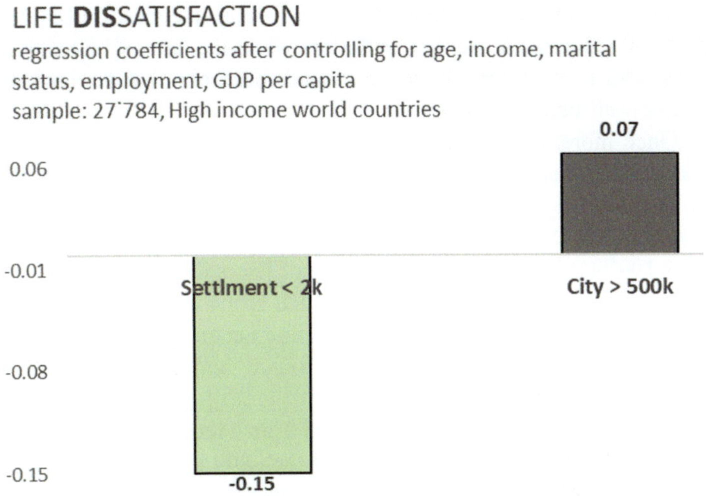

Figure 6.17 Life dissatisfaction regression coefficients after controlling for age, income, marital status, employment, and GDP per capita. Sample: 27˙784, high-income world countries.

Source: Author's elaboration from Berry and Okulicz-Kozaryn (2009, table 3, p. 121). (Fig. 7, D'Acci 2021).

self-reported life satisfaction negatively associated with population size in the United States.

Peiró (2006) made an ordered logit regression on a sample of 20˙440 individuals across 15 countries and also found in most cases greater life satisfactions in settlements with less than 10˙000 inhabitants.

Again, in Italy a regression of over 204˙892 individuals, with 27 control variables (personal-regional characteristics and amenities), reported that urban dwellers are less satisfied than rural dwellers (Biagi and Meleddu 2024). as Also in the United States controlling for personal and geographical factors, population density and size were associated with lower life satisfaction (Winters and Li 2017). Idem in New Zealand (Morrison 2010), while in Australia (Dockery 2003) living in a major city is associated with lower life satisfaction.

Same results appear in Finland where metropolitan dwellers show lower life satisfaction than non-metropolitan dweller (Morrison and Weckroth 2017) and the possible reasons were not merely linked with the place itself, but with the individual values of metropolitan dwellers versus the non-metropolitan; the former was in fact associated with personal values of power and ambition, while the latter with benevolence and conformity which are indeed more correlated with subjective well-being.

Once more, an ordered logit regression controlling for personal and geographical factors in Eastern Europe shows that, in relation to living in a place with less than 5˙000 inhabitants, living in places between 5˙000 and 20˙000 inhabitants, 200˙001 and 100˙000, and over 100˙000, has a higher probability of less satisfied dwellers, and the greater the inhabitants the greater such probability (Hayo 2004).

Again, in a 4˙284 Scottish sample, Gilbert et al. (2016), controlling for personal, socio-economic factors, found "remote rural" dwellers more satisfied than non-rural dwellers.

Similar results are typically obtained from a remarkable number of studies regarding the developed world (actually in *all* the developed world, urban dweller are no happier than the rural ones(Okulicz-Kozaryn and Valente 2021). However, a study about life satisfaction in a developing country, China, on a sample of 1˙288 people, indicated that the new urban dwellers (rural-to-urban migrants, and *in situ* urbanised rural residents) settling in small cities (200˙000–500˙000 inhabitants) rather than larger (or smaller) ones, have higher life satisfaction (Chen et al. 2015).

Literature, in fact, well shows that life satisfaction is higher in bigger settlements in *developing* countries, while the opposite happens in *developed* ones (Tassinari et al. 2023, Deb and Okulicz-Kozaryn 2023, Burger et al. 2020, Morrison 2020, Easterlin et al. 2011).

This could mean that when people are truly free to decide where to live – due to richness, infrastructures, and facility to enjoy services and amenities even if far away from urban areas – they would rather live in smaller settlements.

Finer research found that, in line with common sense, in the richest world people prefer and are more satisfied (the latter is sometimes referred to as "subjective well-being") in smaller settlements but being close to a big city is a plus, as long as not too close, nor too far (Lenzi and Perucca 2021, 2022, Fuguitt and Zuiches 1975).

By making interacting control variables among each other, Lenzi and Perucca (2022) found that being educated and rich mitigates the lower satisfaction typically found in big cities.

Castelli et al. (2022) used a different question ("I am satisfied to live in my city") to test the satisfaction of living in the city where one lives, rather than the satisfaction of their own lives overall as typically asked. They regressed 56˙198 responses across Europe and, controlling for key socio-economic characteristics, found city size to be negatively and highly statistically associated with lower satisfaction with living in that place. See also Finnemann et al. (2026) for the UK.

Besides cross-sectional studies, as the ones so far described, longitudinal studies show analogous results: people moving from bigger to smaller settlements are more satisfied than those moving the other way around (Okulicz-Kozaryn 2023, Hoogerbrugge and Burger 2022, Chen et al. 2015).

6.3 Urbanicity and happiness/subjective well-being

Using a sample of 6˙563 surveys from the General Social Survey for the years between 2000 and 2008 in the United States, Sander (2011) found a continuum monotonic gradient in the percentage of respondents reporting being happy ("very happy" or "pretty happy") across six degrees of urbanicity (Figure 18): rural; other urban; suburbs of 13–100 largest metropolitan areas; suburbs of 1–12 largest metropolitan areas; central city of 13–100 largest metropolitan areas; and central city of 1–12 largest metropolitan areas. He then ran a probit regression considering only two degrees of happiness replies ("very/pretty happy" or "not happy"), and using only the variable "less urban" indicating areas which are outside the 100 largest metropolitan areas. After controlling for health, income, age, Black/Hispanic, nationality, religion, employment, marriage and family status, education, and region, he found a statistically significant (p-value <0.001) positive coefficient for the variable "less urban" (0.14), indicating that people living in a less urban environment are more likely to be happy than those living in one of the 100 largest metropolitan areas.

Similar results appear in Peiró (2006), whose ordered logit regression on a sample of 20˙440 individuals across 15 countries reported that, in most cases (although often not statistically significant) people living in places smaller than 10˙000 inhabitants are a bit happier and more satisfied with life.

An ordered probit regression by Kalyuzhnova and Kambhampati (2008) shows rural inhabitants being happier than citizens in Kazakhstan; as well as a regression in China showing higher subjective well-being in rural households than urban (Knight and Gunatilaka 2010).

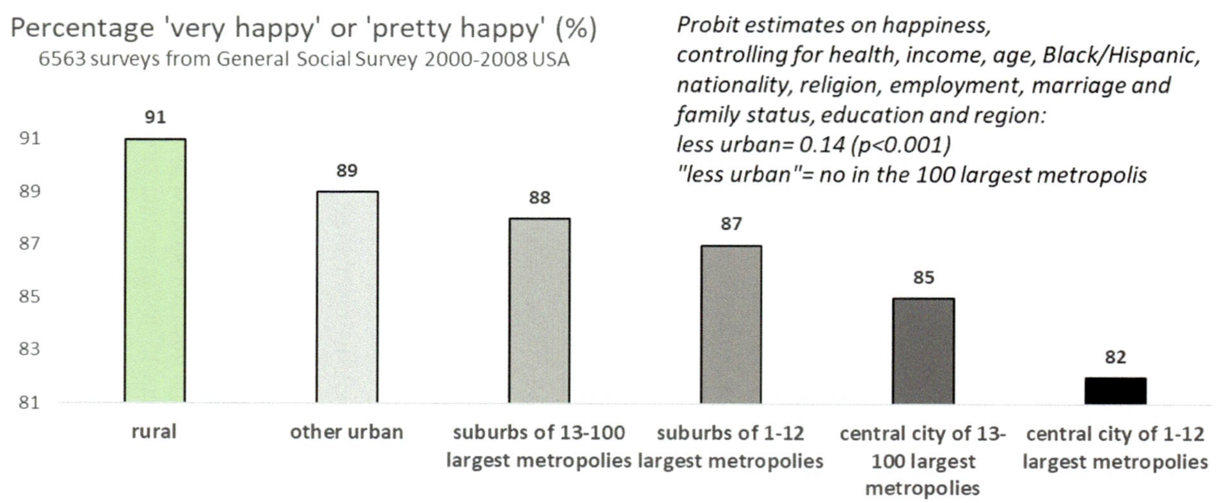

Figure 6.18 Percentage of respondents self-declaring "very happy" or "pretty happy" from 6˙563 individuals (General Social Survey 2000–2008 USA) and Probit regression coefficient for the variable "less urban" (not living in one of the 100 largest metropolis) controlling for relevant key variables.

Source: Author's elaboration from Sander (2011, tables 1 and 2, p. 278). (Fig. 8, D'Acci 2021).

Using data from European Values Study, a multilevel mixed-effects linear regression analysis nesting 507˙452 participants (from 115 countries) within the country, controlling for socio-economic demographic variables, Prati (2024) confirmed (Figure 6.19) that higher urbanicity level (in terms of population size) is associated with lower happiness and life satisfaction, in a continuous way (excluding the category 5k–20k for both happiness and satisfaction, and 20k–100k for happiness as resulting not statistically significant). The direction and the coefficient (-0.05) related to "happiness" for the population category ">500k" are also confirmed by using another data source (World Values Survey), while the other categories were heavily not statistically significant.

Shucksmith et al. (2009) show how, in Europe, the richest the country the smaller the income gap between urban and rural dwellers (Figure 6.20). In the richest countries rural dwellers are also happier, more satisfied, and with greater subjective quality of life, while in the other countries it is the opposite, in line with other research previously mentioned (Tassinari et al. 2023, Burger et al. 2020, Morrison 2020, Easterlin et al. 2011).

This again emphasises the hypothesis that money makes people freer to choose where they actually would prefer to live because richer places

Inhabitants	**Life satisfaction**	*p-value*	**Happiness**	*p-value*
<5k (reference category)				
20k-100k	-0.08	*0.035*	-0.01	*0.634*
100k-500k	-0.13	*< 0.001*	-0.02	*0.019*
>500k	-0.19	*< 0.001*	-0.05	*< 0.001*

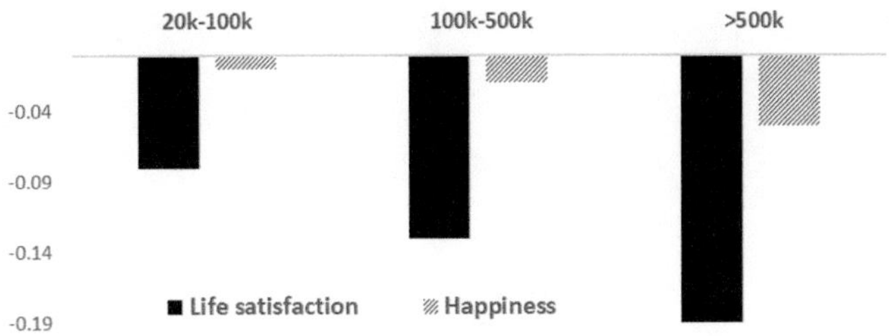

Figure 6.19 Happiness and life satisfaction controlling for socio-economic and demographic variables across 115 countries.

Source: Elaboration from Prati (2024).

European countries	Difference between rural and urban values (%)			
	Income (mean)	Life satisfaction	Happiness	Subjective quality of life
12 richest	-9%	1.4%	1.3%	1.3%
7 intermedie	-18%	-4.0%	-2.6%	-4.0%
6 poorer	-31%	-3.3%	-2.9%	-3.1%
3 (acceding and candidate) poorest	-54%	-1.8%	-6.0%	-3.2%

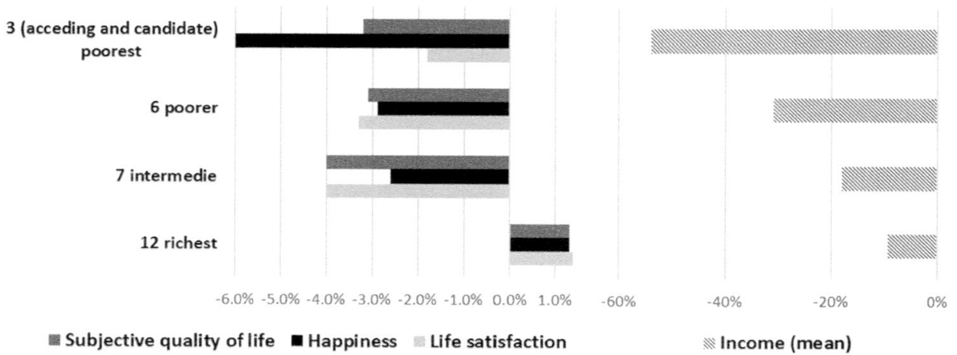

Figure 6.20 Percentage differences between rural and urban values $[(rural - urban) / urban]100$. The richest the country, the monotonically smaller the urban income superiority over the rural. For example, in the richest countries rural dwellers have only 9% less income than the urban dwellers, while in the poorest countries it is 54% (less than half income than the urban dwellers). Similarly, in the richest countries rural dwellers have greater happiness, life satisfaction, and subjective quality of life than the urban dwellers, while the opposite is true for the other countries.

Source: Author's elaboration from Shucksmith et al. (2009).

might have better infrastructures, transports, services, amenities also enjoyable from rural areas and small settlements rather than only in the biggest cities. Money also enables rural residents to afford their higher commuting costs. Richer countries may also have more availability of a variety of jobs also in smaller settlements than the poorer countries.

Another confirmation that the urban–rural differences in life satisfaction and subjective quality of life variables are of opposite signs between richer and poorer places (Figures 6.21 and 6.22) is shown in Counted et al. (2024).

Finally, in line with Lenzi and Perucca (2021) and Fuguitt and Zuiches (1975), Weckroth et al. (2022), controlling for socio-economic and personal variables, found that "Rural areas close to urban areas" have greater perceived quality of life in a 26k Finnish sample.

6.4 Urbanicity and loneliness

In Manitoba, Canada, a sample of 1˙868 senior people aged 72–104 years indicates that the lonelier are more common in rural areas than in urban areas but these more socially isolated are more in urban areas; the ones both lonelier *and* more socially isolated are more in rural areas (Figure 6.23; Havens et al. 2004). For "Social Isolation" they measured interactions (e.g. monthly) with family (living together and not), friends, neighbours, co-workers, and others member of the community. For "Loneliness" they measured feelings of belongingness or sociability (e.g. "there are many people I can count on completely"), and missing relationships (e.g. "I miss having a really close friend").

A sample of 616 random adult respondents from Washington State indicated (Figure 6.24) the greatest mean loneliness in urban areas, while the lowest in small rural and suburban areas (Abshire et al. 2022).

Menec et al. (2019), from a sample of 48˙330 Canadians respondents aged 45–85 years, measured "urban fringes"[18] and "rural areas" as

18 "'Urban core' refers to census metropolitan areas (CMA) with a population of at least 100˙000 (50˙000 or more of whom live in the core) or census agglomerations (CA) with a core population of at least 10˙000. 'Secondary core' refers to a population centre within a CMA with at least 10˙000 residents that was the core of a CA but has now been merged with an adjacent CMA. Urban and secondary cores were combined in the present study. 'Urban fringe' refers to population centres within a CMA or CA that are not contiguous with the core or secondary core with fewer than 10˙000 residents. 'Urban population centres outside CMA and CA' are defined as settlements outside CMA and CA with a population of at least 1,000 and a population density of 400 persons or more per square kilometre. 'Rural' is defined as areas within CMA or CA not classified as core or fringe, or areas not defined as population centres" (Menec et al. 2019).

	Life evaluation today		*Well rested*		*Treated with respect*		*Smile or laugh*	
	(mean)		*(% yes)*		*(% yes)*		*(% yes)*	
	URBAN	*RURAL*	*URBAN*	*RURAL*	*URBAN*	*RURAL*	*URBAN*	*RURAL*
Middle East &	5.84	4.87						
North Africa	7.27	7.32					71.51	76.3
Australia &			83.63	77.95	90.14	83.56		
New Zealand			84.1	88.91				
Southeast Asia					93.38	94.19		
East Asia							59.48	53.34
Europe-Other								
South Asia								
European Union								
Sub-Saharan								
Africa								

Figure 6.21 Differences between urban and rural values (urban – rural) in various quality of life and satisfaction variables in different world regions.

Source: Author's elaboration from Counted et al. (2024).

places with the lowest percentage of socially isolated residents; "rural areas" and "urban centres outside census agglomerations (CA) and outside census metropolitan areas (CMA)" these with lowest lonely residents; while the highest percentage of socially isolated are those in the "urban core", as well as the lonely (Figure 6.25).

In line with the findings in life satisfaction and subjective well-being between the richest and the poorest countries (the former usually reporting greater values in smaller settlements while the latter in the bigger), also for the loneliness a relatively poor European country shows slightly less loneliness among urban rather than rural dwellers: 14.7% (urban) and 15.8% (rural) (Tobiasz-Adamczyk and Zawisza 2017). However, the latter is not in line with the Manitoba (a Canadian place) results previously shown where the lonelier are the rural not the urban dwellers.

In Ireland, Burholt and Scharf (2014) found precisely the same mean loneliness in rural and urban areas.

A sample of 1˙074 Australian adolescents indicated that rural people are *lonelier* than their urban counterparts, and a successive sample of 1˙143 of Australian adolescents (10–16 years old) added

Calmness		*Worry*		*Sadness*		*Stress*		*Contentment*		*People to count on*	
(% yes)		*(% yes)*		*(% yes)*		*(% yes)*		*(% yes)*		*(% yes)*	
URBAN	*RURAL*	*URBAN*	*RURAL*	*URBAN*	*RURAL*	*URBAN*	*RURAL*	*URBAN*	*RURAL*	*URBAN*	*RURAL*
										93.89	94.08
80.67	79.03					22.26	27.11				
		33.52	27.82			20.29	16.43	78.09	88.09		
				21.86	16.43						
		48.25	56.08	39.08	46.46						
66.21	71.36										
								63.43	57.12	69.49	63.3

that the rural people are also more *isolated*[19] and with more *negative attitude to solitude*[20] but with *less friendship loneliness*[21] (Houghton et al. 2014, 2016): Figure 6.26 provides non-parametric correlations.

Indian adolescents were found lonelier in rural areas rather than in urban areas (Shukla et al. 2017), while in Taiwan, a sample of 356 persons aged 19–29 years (Sun and Liang 2022) indicated differences between rural and urban areas (metropolis and suburban) in "unsupportive relationship",[22] "perceived stress",[23] and loneliness[24] (Figure 6.27).

19 Having few friends or feeling that there is no one supportive.
20 Being alone felt as boring, unhappy, isolated time.
21 Reliable, supportive, and trustworthy friends.
22 "'How often do you feel that your family, relatives, and friends are demanding?', 'In the past 4 weeks, how often have you felt nervous because of the important people in your life?', and 'How often do you feel burdened by your interpersonal relationships with your relatives and friends?'. Response categories were 1 = never, 2 = rarely, 3 = sometimes, 4 = often, and 5 = very often" (Sun and Liang 2022).
23 "'How often do you get upset?' and 'How often do you feel anxious and worried?'. Response categories were 1 = never, 2 = rarely, 3 = sometimes, 4 = often, and 5 = very often" (Sun and Liang 2022).
24 "'How often do you feel lonely?', 'How often do you feel that you lack companionship?', and 'How often do you feel isolated from others?'. The items were rated

	Urban minus rural	
	Less developed region	More developed region
Life evaluation today	0.97	-0.05
Well rested	5.68	-4.81
Treated with respect	6.58	-0.81
Smile or laugh	6.14	-4.79
Calmness	1.64	-5.15
Worry	-7.83	5.7
Sadness	-7.38	5.43
Stress	-4.85	3.86
Contentment	6.31	-10
People to count on	6.19	-0.19

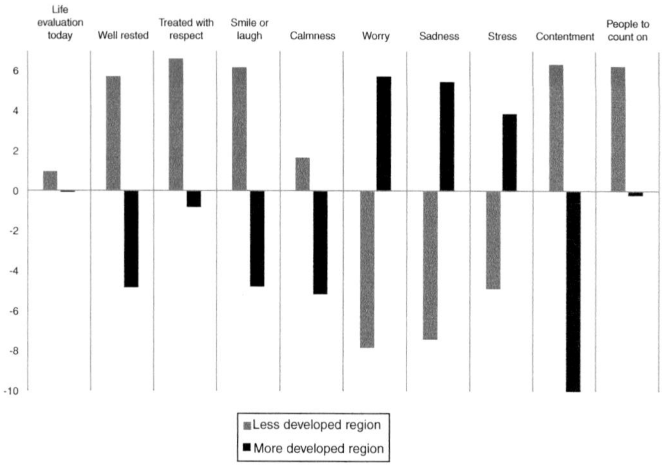

Figure 6.22 Differences between urban and rural values (urban – rural) in various quality of life and satisfaction variables in different world regions, as from Figure 6.21, but regions are separated between less and more developed. Systematically in more developed regions, rural values are better than the urban values. The opposite is true in less developed regions.

Source: Author's elaboration from Counted et al. (2024).

In Scotland, urban dwellers reported (Figure 6.28) higher loneliness (2.05 for urban, 1.60 for rural; range 0–4) and poorer well-being (Long et al. 2025). The latter, called personal well-being, is a composite measure about nowadays life satisfaction, happiness of yesterday, and feeling that life is worthwhile. A multiple regression confirmed that living in urban areas, rather than rural areas, is statistically

	MORE LONELY	MORE SOCIALLY ISOLATED	SOCIALLY ISOLATED *and* LONELY
Rural - Urban	**4%**	**-4%**	**3%**
RURAL	47%	84%	49%
URBAN	43%	88%	46%

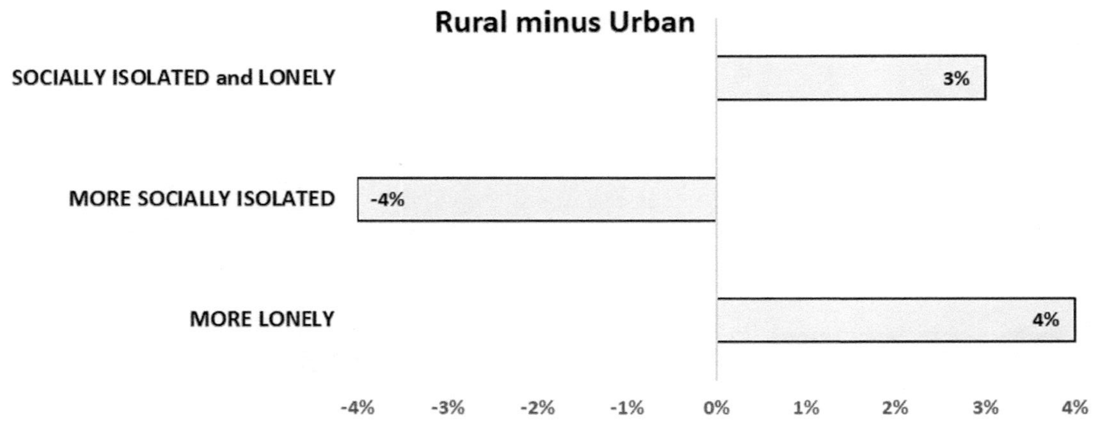

Figure 6.23 Differences between rural and urban values the percentages of Manitoba (Canada) respondents who are lonelier, more socially isolated. And percentage of respondents who are both lonelier and more socially isolated.

Source: Author's elaboration from Havens et al. (2004).

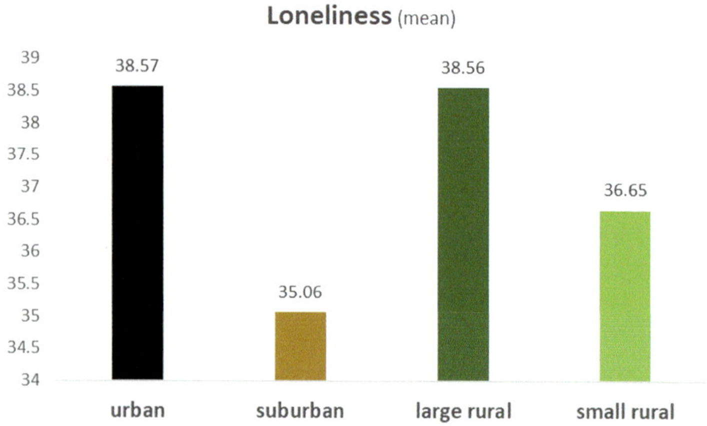

Figure 6.24 Urban, suburban, and large rural and small rural areas mean loneliness in Washington State.

Source: Author's elaboration from Abshire et al. (2022).

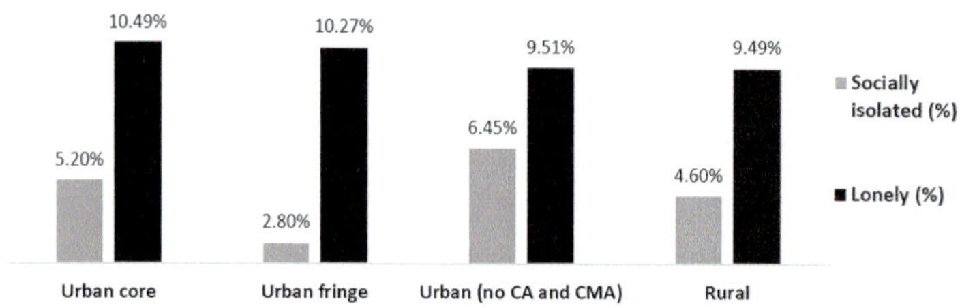

Figure 6.25 "Urban core", "urban fringe", "urban outside agglomeration and metropolitan areas", "rural" loneliness in Canada.

Source: Author's elaboration from Menec et al. (2019).

significantly associated (−1.161***)[25] with lower personal well-being also when controlling for personal factors (Heterosexual, British, Live alone, Finances, General health, and Digital connection), and still (−0.933**) when additionally controlling for personal social network

using a 5-point scale, 1 = never, 2 = rarely, 3 = sometimes, 4 = often, and 5 = very often. The mean scores were calculated; higher scores indicated higher levels of loneliness" (Sun and Liang 2022).

25 −1.161 is the coefficient (the magnitude of the effect: urban dwellers score 1.161 lower than rural; range 0–12); the asterisks are a marker of how strong the evidence

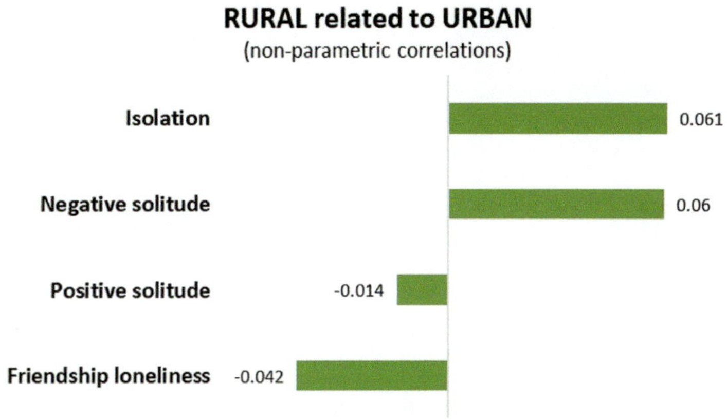

Figure 6.26 Non-parametric correlations between loneliness measures and the categorical variable Australian Rural adolescents (reference category: Urban). Rural dwellers have higher isolation and negative solitude (and lower positive solitude), but less friendship loneliness.

Source: Graph derived from table 2 in Houghton et al. (2016).

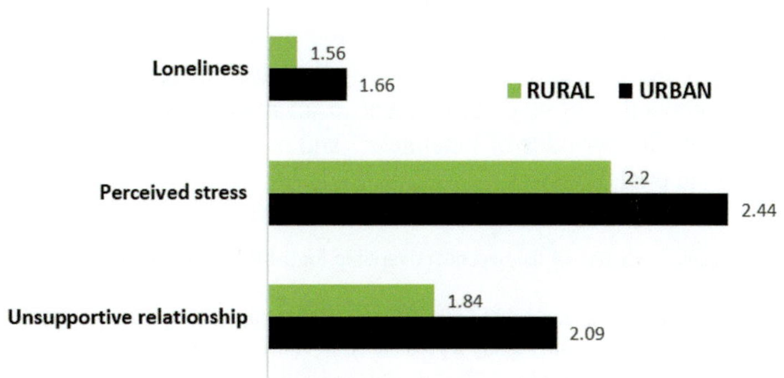

Figure 6.27 Loneliness, perceived stress, and unsupportive relationship between rural and urban dwellers in Taiwan.

Source: Author's elaboration from Sun and Liang (2022).

is for an effect (how likely it is to see a result this big [the coefficient, in this case −1.161] or bigger, just by chance if there were no real effect). More asterisks mean a smaller p-value (stronger evidence): $*p < 0.05$, $**p < 0.01$, $***p < 0.001$.

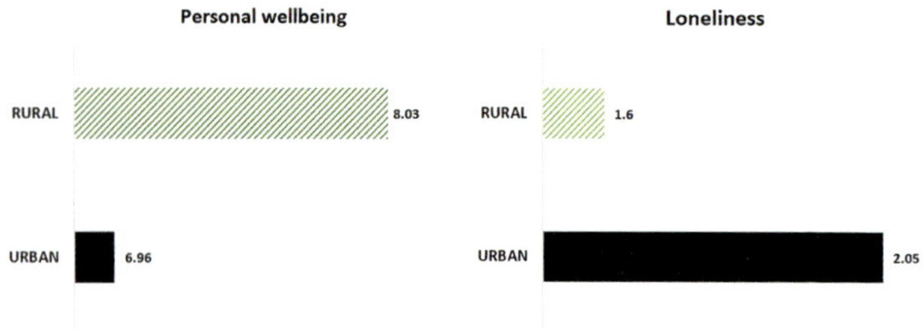

Figure 6.28 Statistically significant means of personal well-being (composite measure about nowadays life satisfaction, happiness of yesterday, and feeling that life is worthwhile), and loneliness in rural and urban dwellers in Scotland.

Source: Graph derived from Long et al. (2024).

factors (Loneliness, Support, Meet up, Network size, Closeness, and Relationship diversity).

Rural dwellers in England and Wales report higher positive views about their neighbourhood than urban dwellers (Figure 6.29; Office for National Statistics 2016).

A multiple regression on a 405˙925 UK Biobank sample aged 37–73 years estimated the density elasticity[26] of loneliness: every 1˙000 units/km^2 increase in residential density,[27] controlling for personal and environmental confounders, resulted in an association with a 2.8% and 11.4% higher odds of loneliness[28] and social isolation,[29] respectively (Lai et al. 2021).

26 Percentage change of the dependent variable for a 1% change of the independent variable.

27 "within a 1-km street catchment"; an even higher elasticity was found within a 2-km spatial scale, suggesting a possible scale effect: the larger the area which is denser, the higher the loneliness and social isolation.

28 "'Do you often feel lonely?" (0 = No, 1 = yes). 'How often are you able to confide in someone close to you?' (0 = almost daily/2–4 times a week/about once a week/about once a month, 1 = once every few months/never or almost never)" (Lai et al. 2021).

29 "'Including yourself, how many people are living together in your household? Include those who usually live in the house such as students living away from home during term, partners in the armed forces or professions such as pilots' (0 = >1, 1 = living alone). 'How often do you visit friends or family or have them visit you?' (0 = almost daily/2–4 times a week/about once a week/about once a month, 1 = once every few months/never or almost never/no friends/family outside household.

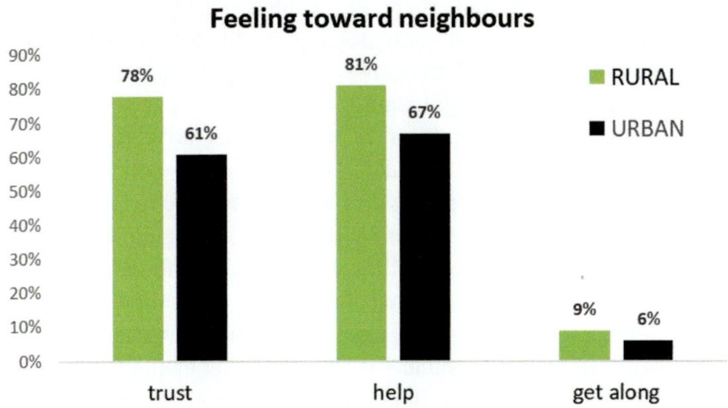

Figure 6.29 Rural dwellers in England and Wales are more likely to trust their neighbours, "feel that others in their local area are willing to help their neighbours", and "less likely to feel that people in their neighbourhood do not get along".

Source: Graph derived from the Office for National Statistics (2016).

Another multiple regression over a 2˙439 US respondents, conducted by Henning-Smith et al. (2019), compared *micropolitan rural* (rural counties centres with < 50k inhabitants and/or substantial commuting to a metropolitan area) and *noncore rural* (rural counties centres <10k inhabitants and/or limited commuting to metropolitan or micropolitan counties) dwellers. Adjusting for sociodemographic and health cofounders, it found lower rates of loneliness[30] in *micropolitan* rural than urban residents ($b = -0.31$, p-value < 0.05).

A binary logistic regression over a 605 elderly people in Uganda found, again, that urban dwellers are more likely to be lonely than their rural counterparts (Nzabona et al. 2016).

'Which of the following do you attend once a week or more often? You can select more than one' (participation in sports club or gym, pub or social pub, religious groups, adult education and other group activities. 0 = engaging in one or more of weekly social activities, 1 = not participating in any weekly social activities)" (Lai et al. 2021).

30 "Loneliness was measured using 3 items: how often the respondent felt "left out", isolated, or lacked companionship. All 3 items had a range of 0 (rarely/none of the time) to 3 (most of the time). We combined these into a 3-item loneliness scale, following prior research using these variables, 28 with a range of 0–9; 9 indicated the highest level of loneliness" (Henning-Smith et al. 2019).

Marquez et al. (2023), using a UK sample of 6˙503 people aged 16–24 years, via a multiple regression controlling for a large number of sociodemographic, environmental, and health confounders, found a very small magnitude effects between rural and urban residents, and this was not statistically significant.

In Germany, on a sample of 17˙602 representative respondents, loneliness[31] was found to be nearly equal in urban and rural areas (means: 0.98 and 1.02, respectively, on a 0–5 measurement scale; and a standardised regression coefficient both zero in magnitude and statistically non-significant, controlling for several confounders); when multiple regression was conducted at a regional level, rural areas were found to be associated to –0.02 loneliness, which however was non-statistically significant (p-value = 0.581) (Buecker et al. 2021).

Beer et al. (2016), again, found a lower, although slightly, urban (metropolitan) dwellers as lonelier and with less friends (when asked about the last month) related to rural (or remote areas) dwellers in Australia, despite both, metropolitan and rural dwellers, feeling equally isolated from other people (Figure 6.30).

Given the differences in urban and rural typologies, specifically among some countries, comparisons and universalisations are problematic.

6.5 Urbanicity, friendship, and social exclusion

Since the post-industrial city with its size and density, urban living has often been described as "to live in a city is […] to live surrounded by large numbers of people one does not know" (Lofland 1973, p. ix). Perhaps the focus of most urban theorists has been too much on contacts with strangers in cities rather than with friends (Wirth 1938, Simmel 1950, Milgram 1970, Lofland 1973), as we saw in a previous chapter on social perspectives. Milgram and Fisher, however, positioned themselves differently than Wirth and Simmel: Milgram thought that this mass of strangers and related non-involvement wouldn't affect personal relationships; Fisher didn't expect differences in both intensity and number of personal relationships across urbanicity levels, instead cities offer the necessary "critical mass" allowing the selection

31 "On a 5-point scale ranging from 0 ¼ never to 4 ¼ very often, participants indicated how often they miss the company of other people, feel left out, and feel socially isolated" (Buecker et al. 2021).

During the past four weeks I felt isolated from other people

	Almost always (4)	Most of the time (3)	About half the time (2)	Occasionally (1)	Not at all (0)	Mean
metropolitan	2.4	4.1	7.9	32.5	53.1	0.702
rural or remote	2	5.3	7.8	30.7	54.3	0.702

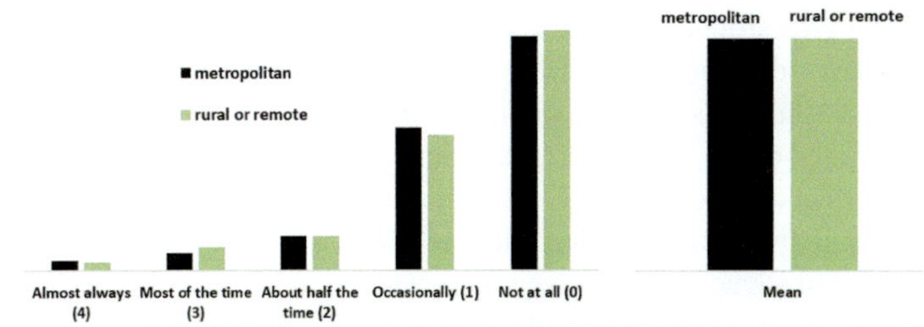

During the past four weeks I felt alone and friendless

	Almost always (4)	Most of the time (3)	About half the time (2)	Occasionally (1)	Not at all (0)	Mean
metropolitan	1.8	4.4	6	26	61.9	0.584
rural or remote	1.4	3.6	6.4	22.6	66.1	0.518

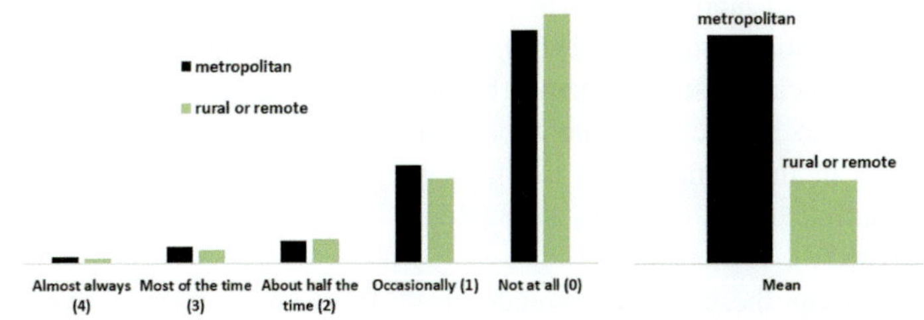

Figure 6.30 Metropolitan versus non-metropolitan (i.e. rural and remote areas) residents in Australia. Despite metropolitan and rural dwellers felt equally isolated from other people, the former felt more alone and friendless than the latter.

Source: Author's elaboration from Beer et al. (2016).

of friends ("personal social worlds") based on common interests rather than simply proximity (Fisher 1976, 1978), while Simmel and Wirth assumed that the larger the city the more socially isolated its dwellers (Franck 1980). Although, "in positive terms, the move to the metropolis entails, Simmel argues, an escape from the coercively oppressive bonds of the little community" (Werbner 2018).

Fisher (1976, 1978), therefore, preferred to see urban dwellers not as isolated individuals living an anonymous life, but as members of "personal social worlds" selected[32] based on common interests.

These theoretical assumptions were empirically tested in a comparative, longitudinal study on two groups of newcomer university students: one moved to New York, one to a town of 31k inhabitants in a rural area around New York. They were interviewed after 2 months they arrived in their new place, and again after 7–8 months. Variance analysis showed statistical significance of the effect of place (p-value <0.05) and of the interaction place-time (p-value <0.01) but no significant effect of time alone. Despite initially being easier to get friends in the small town, after a reasonable time, there were no differences in the number of friends between New York and the rural town (Figure 6.31). However, this sample was not representative. For example, university students might make friends within their own courses, regardless of the place they live.

Nevertheless, earlier empirical research found no link between settlement sizes and number of friends (Sutcliffe and Crabbe 1963, Kasarda and Janowitz 1974).

A previous study (Key 1968), which suggested non-urban residents as less socially isolated than urban residents, only reported less frequency in contact with neighbours (Franck 1980), but other three works at that time found the frequency of contact with friends to be unlinked to settlement size (Reiss 1959, Key 1968, Glenn and Hill 1977).

Among these earlier studies from the last century, Guterman (1969) observed a more "intimacy" of friendships in the smaller settlements, however this was measured by including the duration of the friendships, and the fact of knowing the family's and friends' friends. All these three factors are much more likely to happen in smaller settlements. The results of Guterman's study were opposite

32 However, I guess that this capacity to select friends within a big city depends on personal characters and life styles: one can be a more social type, easily going out or frequent various environments allowing meeting many people and selecting them; while another one could be shyer, or introvert, or too poor to attend events and purchase memberships, all factors which heavily limit opportunities to meet people and select friends. While in smaller settlements such as small towns, villages, hamlet – despite having to deal with an extremely limited variety of people who could possibly best match your own personality – one could easily know almost everyone else.

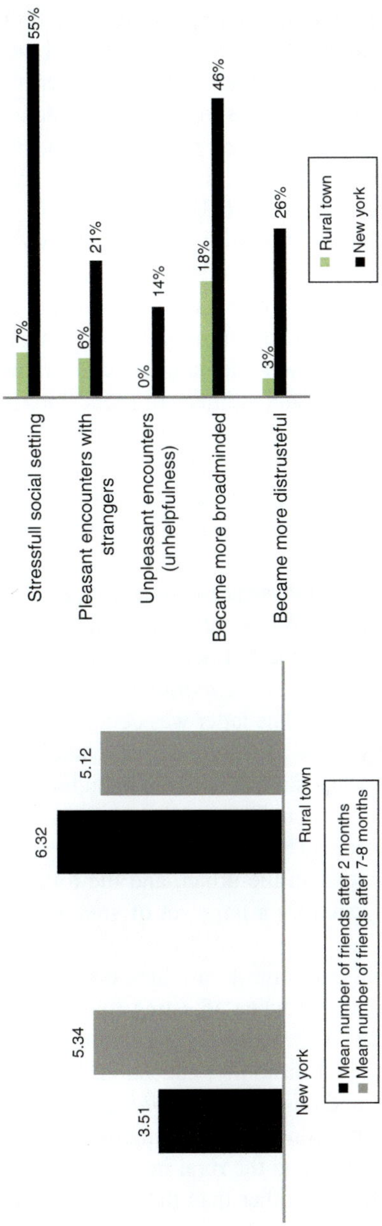

Figure 6.31 Newcomers university students in New York and a small rural town.

Source: Author's elaborations from Franck (1980).

to those shown in Franck (1980). The latter found that more urban friends invited each other at homes and more often than the rural; it also found that the number of friends is the same (even a bit more in the urban actually) between urban and rural students after the initial months. When asked about stress linked to social settings (the public, not their own friends), the urban reported much higher stress and replies to things such as "People on the street [...] are tense [...] you can see it in their faces" (Figure 6.31).

Another earlier study (Sutcliffe and Crabbe 1963) conducted in Australia among individuals (similar in education, occupation, religion, age, and sex) living in inner city, suburban, and rural areas tested the association between intimacy of friendships and urbanicity level (Figure 6.32). There were no monotonic functional relationships between urbanicity levels and intimacy of friendships nor with regular social contact. However, rural dwellers, compared with their inner-city counterpart, have 16% more regular social contact (but this difference was statistically non-significant in the model), 169% more best friends, 45% more friends, and 52% fewer superficial friends (acquaintance).

Prattley et al. (2020) analysed responses from a 11˙181 respondents aged 50+ in England and Wales and built a social exclusion index by combining 28 items from the following four domains: *Access to services and amenities*, *Civic participation*, *Cultural and leisure activities*, and *Social relations*. The latter was composed by four variables about having a "very close" or "quite close" relationship with partner, children, family, or friends. Each domain, including the overall social exclusion index, got a score between 0 and 1, with 1 indicating the most severe exclusion. The social relations seem mostly equivalent, only slightly worst in the urban, and the total social exclusion index too, once adjusted by a large set of area and personal factors (Figure 6.33).

The fact that without control variables the rural sample appears less socially excluded, but when adjusting for confounders, specifically *after* adding the *Neighbourhood deprivation* variables (income, employment, health and disability, education, housing and services, living environment, and crime) and *Individual* level variables (marital status, self-rated health, education, and employment), the social exclusion index becomes worse in the rural in relation to the urban, which might suggest that factors other than the urbanicity itself are mostly

		Urbanicity level					
		High density (city center)	Medium density	Lower density	Low density (outer city)	Rural (outside main cities - rural fringe)	Rural change (%) related to city center
		I	II	III	IV	V	(V-I)/I in %
	Regular social contact	183	183	192	179	212	16%
Intimacy	Best friends	13	65	39	59	35	169%
	Friends	109	95	122	102	158	45%
	Acquaintance	61	23	31	18	29	-52%
	Spatial distribution of friends	45% same area	60-70% same area				

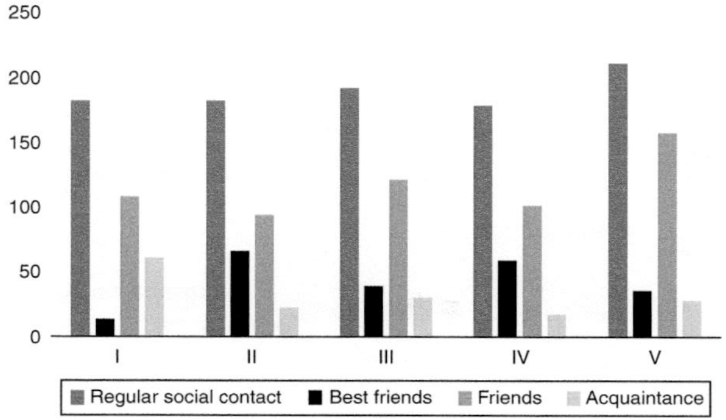

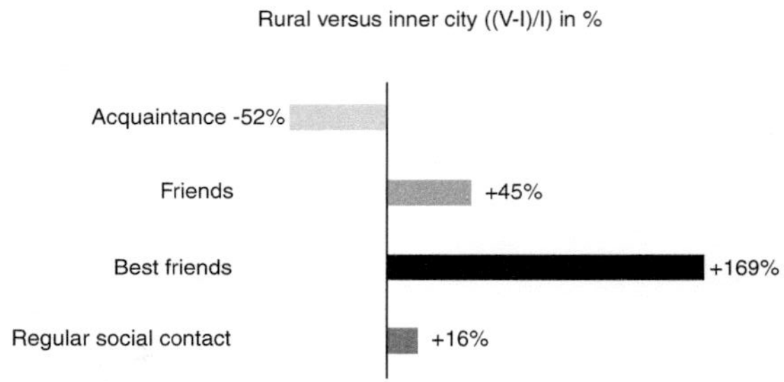

Figure 6.32 Intimacy of friendships and urbanicity level.
Source: Author's elaborations from Sutcliffe and Crabbe (1963).

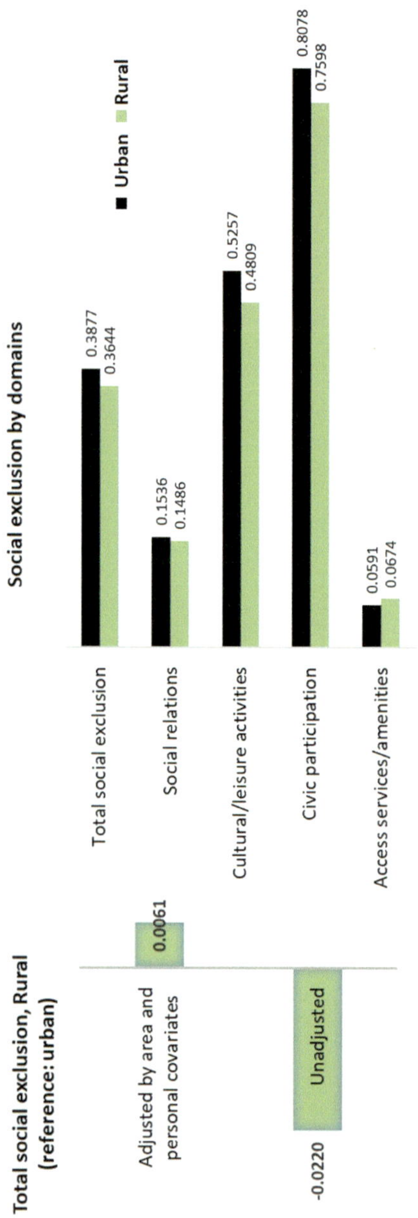

Figure 6.33 Social exclusion in England and Wales.
Source: Graphs from Prattley et al. (2020).

driving the social exclusion, even if these factors might be correlated to the urbanicity level.

A social network study (Schläpfer et al. 2014) across city sizes within same countries (UK and Portugal) used mobile phone communications data as a proxy, despite people no necessarily use mobile phones for their communications which could happen face to face, by emails, or in other ways. They found that phone calls, quantified in terms of time spent, reciprocal calls, and mobile contacts, scale superlinearly with city size with a scaling coefficient of 1.13, 1.11, and 1.11, respectively. Namely a 1% increase in population size of a city is associated with a 1.13% increase in time spent on phone calls, and 1.11% increase in both the number of mobile contacts and reciprocal calls. The scaling coefficient of time spent has also been confirmed by another study in the United States, resulting 1.14 (Calabrese et al. 2011).

A surprising result of their work was that the average "local clustering coefficient" ("fraction of connections between one's social contacts to all possible connections between them", a number from 0 to 1) remains constant across city sizes: "it suggests that even in large cities we live in groups that are as tightly knit as those in small towns or 'villages'" (Schläpfer et al. 2014). In fact, in large cities the probability that two of a person's contacts are also mutually connected would be very small if these connections were randomly created. The constancy of this coefficient however suggests otherwise: that regardless of being in small towns or big cities, around 25% of one's contacts also know each other.

6.6 Why people go to/remain in cities?

When human fluxes are voluntary, it

> has important advantages, since it brings skill and labour to places where they can best be used and people to places which they prefer. But much mobility is far from voluntary, and so moving entails serious costs, of which psychological depression is not the least.
>
> (Lynch 1984, p. 251)

For some, staying in small settlements may mean to suffer hunger, while others move voluntarily. Among the latter, some are happier in cities, but some aren't. When this is the case we wonder why they

Table 6.1 Possible reasons to move/stay in cities for the unsatisfied

<table>
<tr><th colspan="4">UNSATISFIED (1,2a, 4a) OR RELATIVELY SATISFIED (3,4b) URBANS: POSSIBLE REASONS</th><th></th></tr>
<tr><td rowspan="3">NEWCOMERS TO CITIES</td><td colspan="3">(1) overoptimistic expectations + (4b)</td><td>DREAMERS</td></tr>
<tr><td rowspan="2">(2) self-selection</td><td colspan="2">(2a) overambitious – later disappointed</td><td>AMBITIOUS</td></tr>
<tr><td colspan="2">(2b) more prone to lower happiness or extreme moods</td><td>MOODIES</td></tr>
<tr><td rowspan="4">BORN IN CITIES</td><td colspan="3">(3) unaware of better niches for them</td><td>UNAWARES</td></tr>
<tr><td rowspan="3">(4) aware but</td><td colspan="2">(4a) cannot move for habits and practical anchors</td><td>ANCHORED</td></tr>
<tr><td rowspan="2">(4b) prefer to trade-off with urban advantages</td><td>(4b1) within generation</td><td rowspan="2">CALCULATORS</td></tr>
<tr><td>(4b2) across generations</td></tr>
</table>

Source: D'Acci (2021).

voluntarily internally migrate (or, those born there, stay) to higher urbanicity levels and briefly list possible replies and some "counter-replies" (Table 6.1):

1 Newcomers' over-optimistic expectations of urban life (Cardoso et al. 2018), or an altered estimation of their *predicted utility* (Kahneman 2000) of moving to cities, which is a valuation-belief of how the future *experienced* utility is likely to be.[33]
2 Self-selection:[34]
   a Migrants to cities might tend to have personalities with higher levels of aspirations which once disappointed may mean lower satisfaction levels (Hanell 2022, Morrison and Weckroth 2017, Chen et al. 2015).[35]

33 The actual manifested choice to move to/stay in an environment of a certain urbanicity degree (a rural settlement, a village, a town, a city, a megacity) passes through another type of utility referred to as decision utility, which is influenced by many factors such as your estimation of the predicted utility and how you filter your memories from past experienced utility (remembered utility) (Berridge and O'Doherty 2013).
34 Lu and Qin (2014) and Tong and Piotrowski (2012).
35 But what about those who have been in cities for generations? Would they genetically inherit or culturally absorb these aspirations from families and the city atmosphere?

  b "Some areas attract people who are disproportionately prone to be more or less happy" (Glaser, Gottlieb and Ziv 2014, p. 2). However, as above, for those in cities for generations[36] still reporting lower happiness, this would require a strong genetic component for happiness[37] *and* capable of being passed through kin, generations, reshuffles, and mutations. Even assuming the latter possibility, dose–response studies indicate a *causal* link between mental disorders and time spent in cities.[38]
3 Those already born and raised in cities may not be aware of better overall lifestyles available at lower urbanicity levels. They are *unknowingly* less happy than they could be.
4 Or maybe some of them are aware but:
  a Even if they would like to move, it is too problematical – psychologically and practically – to move away from families, friends, loved ones, roots, and lifestyles absorbed in the first 20–30 years of life.
  b Or even if urban dwellers are [*knowingly*] "unhappier" they still *prefer* to stay for:
    i Having higher incomes, amenities, services and social status, treating subjective well-being as *one* of many variables of the utility function [if any exist, and, if so, a rational one] rather than *the* ultimate utility function itself.[39]
    ii Intergenerational social mobility.

6.7 The utility function revisited

If we decide to consider the last two above possibilities (4bi, 4bii.), the paradox of how to conciliate the urban–rural happiness gradient[40] with the continuous growth of urban dwellers might be rethought from the perspective of considering "happiness" as *part* of the final goal of our lives rather than *the* goal itself, which also somehow links:

a Spatial economically with the Spatial Equilibrium approach (our spatial location decisions are an offset between benefits and costs of any sort, Glaeser 2008);

36 Meaning being born there rather than having [self] selected them.
37 Barlow (2019) and Polderman et al. (2015).
38 van Os, Kenis, and Rutten (2010).
39 Glaeser, Gottlieb and Ziv (2014).
40 Okulicz-Kozaryn (2017), Berry and Okulicz-Kozaryn (2013), Sørensen (2014), Sander (2011), and Okulicz-Kozaryn and Mazelis (2018).

b Allometrically[41] with the power law function between city size and urban outputs (often superlinearly scaling for socio-economic outputs: creativity, GDP, crime, illness, … and for some studies for CO_2 emission and congestion; sublinearly for infrastructural: total street lengths, land area, electrical cables …) presenting benefits and costs associated with city size, where one of these costs is the lower life satisfaction probably also due to congestion, pollution, crime …, which several empirical pieces of evidence show to increase more than proportionally (superlinearly) when city size increases;

c Philosophically with the Aristotle's Eudaimonism (Aristotle 2009) where the greatest accomplishment of a person's life resides in the realisation of her potentialities, her "daimon".

6.7.1 Spatial equilibrium or **subjective** *spatial* **dis-***equilibrium?*

Point "a" refers to the Spatial Equilibrium whose logic suggests that the lower life satisfaction achievable in an urban area is somehow offset by other types of benefit, such as urban amenities, services, higher real incomes, social mobility, a chance to increase professional ambition, and so on. Vice versa for a rural (or less urban) area: higher "life satisfaction" and mental health (or "happiness"[42]) are "paid" by lower real incomes, less urban amenities, and so on. Sørensen (2014) quantified this amount, in Europe, as around €9˙000 per year: "for a

41 Bettencourt et al. (2007) and D'Acci (2025).

42 I prefer to write life satisfaction and happiness under quotation marks because one can be satisfied, or happy, with a low income but in the countryside rather than richer but in the city. Rather than see it as: "I give up a bit of life satisfaction for more accessibility to amenities and services", it would be as: "I am more satisfied in life (in the *long run*) precisely because of giving up some *daily* life satisfaction by not living in a more natural and less stressful rural environment in exchange of a better professional career". Or the other way round: "I am more satisfied in life (in the *long run*) because of giving up a professional career for a *daily* higher life satisfaction by living in a peaceful rural environment". The key is the temporal scale by which we think about life satisfaction: daily or in the long run? Or we can simply clearly define what we mean by life satisfaction. If we prefer a basket of factors (e.g. lower income, lower urbanicity, more peace, less services, lower *daily* life satisfaction…) against another (e.g. higher income, higher urbanicity, more stress, more services, higher *daily* life satisfaction…) it *might* (see next discussion in the chapter about irrational, biased decision-making and feelings) mean that we feel overall more satisfied about our life (in the long run, in a vision "from the above") by selecting the basket we prefer.

city dweller to get to the same level of life satisfaction as the rural dweller, the city dweller would need to increase his or her monthly income by €764" (Sørensen 2014, p. 1458).

However, in scenarios of radically different spatial location decisions and with long temporal implications, such as deciding to live the entire life (or a substantial part) in a megacity, a city, a town, a village, or the rural countryside, and when people are actually free to decide to stay or to move, it could be better defined as "*Subjective* Spatial *Dis*-Equilibrium": the overall utility function (U) – which a person maximises against her financial budget (i = input money: wage) and her costs (o = output money: housing costs, commuting costs, taxes …) in relation to the *subjective* advantages (a) of living in a specific location – is *not* constant (k) across *all* locations ($U(i,o,a) \neq k$); that is why she moves or stays. It might be not the case of a simple basket *variations* (trading one advantage for another within the same overall Utility level) but of actually *increasing* the *overall Utility* level.

(1) When the "subjective" equilibrium among different locations is broken (i.e. a location clearly implies an overall higher U, even at same i) she might move; (2) stay otherwise; (3) or, in the latter case, she might still move to enjoy a different basket composition of the ingredients[43] of U even if the overall U remains constant (namely when moving within the same subjective indifference curve of her own spatial utility function). In cases (2) and (3) we are in a subjective spatial equilibrium (e.g. being an entrepreneur in a city or a fisherman in the countryside, for someone might have subjectively overall roughly mutually compensatory trade-offs: very different i, o, a, but somehow equivalent U), while in case (1) we are in a subjective spatial dis-equilibrium (when one *does* prefer to be a peaceful fisherman in a superb mountain lake scenario rather than a stressed entrepreneur in a crowded urban scenario, or vice versa). To use the above Sørensen's monetary quantification, if you propose a rural dweller an extra €9˙000 per year if she moves to the city, there are cases where she is indeed undecided because both baskets (rural life *versus* urban's plus €9˙000 per year) are rather indifferent/equivalent (cases 2 and 3), while there are cases in which she is not undecided at all (case 1) and

43 Peaceful picturesque rural life, professional career, fizzy urban life, closeness to cinema, theatres, universities, museums…, freedom (or depression) of the anonymous city, clear air, blue sky, singing birds and crickets, income… .

therefore she does not decide by "heads or tails" where and how to spend her life.[44]

6.7.2 Urban allometry

Point "b" relates to empirical evidence of some sort of universal urban laws (West 2017): despite the fact that cities and regions have developed independently and remotely along unique historical paths, genius loci, and geographical environments, an empirical regularity systematically appears between population size and various urban factors. The reasons for these surprising allometric relations are still

44 From Glaeser 2008: "The key theoretical element in urban economics is the idea of a spatial equilibrium: there are not rents to be gained by changing locations" (p. 47). "[…] the hallmark of urban and regional economics is the spatial equilibrium concept – the idea that people are indifferent across space" (p. 165). "[…] people can't improve their condition by moving" (p. 205). My brother a long time ago decided to move from our mother 1-million inhabitant city, Turin, to the mountains, in a traditional Piedmont farmhouse, 10 min from a barely 6 thousands inhabitant village, and, if you ask him, he gained an incomparable higher quality of life; but the latter is not simply a *compensation* for lower services, which overall could make *comparable* staying in Turin with higher services or in the mountain village with lower; on the contrary, it is *the reason* itself to make much *higher* his own *overall utility* function associated to living in the mountains. The two options, Turin/mountain, are *not* even slightly comparable/*indifferent* for him. He literally *improved* his condition by moving. I heard the same story so many times from friends telling me how much better *overall* their lives became after moving out from the city to nearby villages or countryside. They are without doubt *not indifferent* between living in the city or in the nearby countryside or villages. They definitely improved their conditions by moving: that is ultimately *why* they moved, and if you ask all of them, they will never return to the city at all. Of course, I also heard similar stories from people who moved from villages or countryside to cities. Therefore, if we see it from a *subjective* point of view, when a person decides to move from a city to a small village in the nearby countryside (or vice versa), even if she will pay a different amount of time and money in commuting (which probably is offset by a bigger/cheaper house, and different life style) or if she will get a different income and/or job, she is *not* indifferent across spaces and she actually does *improve* her condition by moving… otherwise *why* does she move? (excluding case 3 above).

> Individual choice over locations produces the single most important concept in urban or regional economics: the spatial equilibrium. This core insight comes from the idea that if identical people are choosing to live in two different places then those two different places must be offering an equivalent bundle of advantages, like wages, prices and amenities. Essentially, there must be no potential for arbitrage across space.
>
> (Glaeser 2008, p. 4)

under investigation and hold great promise for increasing the efficiency of societies able to control the distribution of their populations' size.

6.7.3 Aristotelian daimon

Point "c." involves the realisation of "both the potentialities that are shared by all humans by virtue of our common specieshood and those unique potentials that distinguish each individual from all others" (Waterman 1993, p. 678).

A slightly similar concept of the former of the above two potentiality types is mentioned in Inglehart when he reminds us that "humans have evolved to seek meaningful patterns" (Inglehart 2018, p. 159), which might also evoke the twentieth canto of the *Inferno* of Dante Alighieri's "La Divina Commedia": "considerate la vostra semenza: fatti non foste a viver come bruti, ma per seguir virtute e canoscenza".[45]

Probably the human innate perseverance towards achieving the Aristotelian daimon's realisation as a species and individuals drives us to an urban environment pursuing better education and a higher chance of social/cultural escalation despite (particularly for some) the urban costs.

In a milestone paper, Simon describes how "A real-life decision involves some goals or values, some facts about the environment, and some inferences drawn from the values and facts" (Simon 1959, p. 273); although each of these steps (goals/values, facts and inferences) might be subject to certain degrees of – often "rationally" systematic – irrationality and biases (see recent developments from Behavioural Economics, e.g. in Dhami 2016), we can assume that most of us cultivate, mature personal life purposes which arise within

But… what criteria should we follow to define people as "identical"? Maybe some of them are under the assumption (3) that their own overall U related to these locations is indeed equivalent both across these locations and across people (therefore: "identical" people). However, if "identical" people choose such extremely different places to live (e.g. a small flat in the city centre, a large suburban house, or a cottage in nearby countryside), maybe they are not that "identical" after all and the bundle of advantages, prices, and amenities is not *equivalent* for the same locations for *different* people. Figures 6.3, 6.4, 6.6, 6.7, and 6.11 of this chapter show how small the percentage of *indifferent* people actually is.

45 Consider your origins: you were not made to live as brutes, but to pursue virtue and knowledge (Author's translation).

contextual environments surrounding us and requiring certain environments for their accomplishment.

"We have objectives in life other than being satisfied, and we may knowingly make choices that reduce happiness [...] if those choices further other aims (Luttmer Erzo 2005, Benjamin et al. 2011)" (Glaeser, Gottlieb and Ziv 2014, p. 4); seeing happiness/life satisfaction as one ingredient of the utility function rather than the function itself is in contradiction with part of the 19th-century economists (e.g. J.S. Mill) whose approach was probably being influenced by Bentham's (1789) inclination to see happiness as a determinant of behaviour. This tendency to think about happiness as the ultimate goal of individuals traces back to ancient philosophers such as Aristippus (strong hedonistic school putting pleasure as life's main goal), Epicurus (pleasure, achieved with modesty, the absence of pain, is both the end and the aim), and medieval philosophers as Augustine and Aquinas (above all, what humans pursue is 'happiness', human fulfillment or beatitudo).

A different philosophical tradition (the Stoics, Epictetus, Kant, Mandeville) rejects that what people do/should maximise is happiness. For around a century, major economists (e.g. Fisher, Stigler, Becker, and Rayo) abandoned paralleling happiness with utility: a utility-maximising individual could decide to live in a city despite knowing in advance its negative psychological influences on her happiness/life satisfaction, or in a rural village despite its lower income, professional career, and fewer services and amenities.

6.8 Urban dwellers' utility

So, why in cities?

Excluding those who *truly prefer* urban life (around one-third) for the urbanity feeling itself, who are *definitely* happier and physically-mentally healthier than living in other contexts, there might be a certain proportion of urban lovers who genuinely *believe to prefer* living in cities regardless of the objective signs of physical and/or psychological discomfort[46] they experience which are *also* related to their own urban life but that they fail to recognise, or, if they do, they fail to recognise their direct link with urban life.

We might call *truly urbans* the first who truly prefer and physically/psychologically benefit from urban life, while the second *urban*

46 Obesity, pollution-related damages ... insomnia, depression, chronic stress, inside loneliness, underground dissatisfaction... .

believers, who believe to prefer city life despite objective evidence of negative effects on them.

We focus on the latter (urban *believers*) plus the other roughly two-thirds declaring to not prefer living in cities even though they *do*, or *have to*, who we can call, respectively, *involuntary urbans* and *forced urbans* (Table 6.2). The latter are indeed *literally* forced into cities or they would die or live in extreme poverty and basic service-infrastructure deprivations otherwise.

We have also seen another category: those who prefer (truly or believing to prefer) urban life but because they never experienced other life types and if they would they could probably change their minds (or vice versa), and we can call them *unaware urbans* (Table 6.1).

Referring to observed quantified urban advantages (superlinearly scaling: by doubling city size, in terms of inhabitants, you have a roughly 15% increase in wages, wealth, creativity, … and sublinearly: around 15% saving in infrastructure), Geoffrey West (West 2011) said

> this, no doubt, is the reason why a million people a week are gathering in cities. Because they think that all those wonderful things – like creative people, wealth, income – is what attracts them, forgetting about the ugly and the bad.

This sentence contains at least three key concepts behind the words "think", "wonderful", and "forgetting", which we are going to briefly discuss, starting with "wonderful".

Usually – compared with rural areas, villages and small towns – cities offer better careers, more money, and more amenities

Table 6.2 Typology of urban dwellers

URBAN DWELLERS		
TRULY PREFER URBAN ENVIRONMENT	→ and psycho-physically *benefit* from it	**TRULY URBANS**
	→ but *unknowingly* pay a psycho-physical cost from it	**URBAN BELIEVERS**
DON'T PREFER URBAN ENVIRONMENT	→ but still *decide* for it to trade-off costs and benefits	**INVOLUNTARY URBANS**
	→ but *must* live there (or jobless and/or at life risk)	**FORCED URBANS**

Source: D'Acci (2021).

and services, which are parts of human desires whose satisfactions drive individuals' life decisions. Contrarily to the narrow utilitarian economic view of human well-being conception – seeing emotions, feelings, behaviours, and desires as metaphysically given (i.e. independent from social interactions), and the satisfactions of the latter as a source of well-being – human desires are profoundly socially determined and, as such, their satisfaction does not necessarily enhance well-being (Hunt and Lautzenheiser 2015, p. 538). This especially in the case of social status and/or material consumerism ambitions induced from socially determined desires. Someone might prefer cities because *there* is the place to get more chances (within or across generations) for higher social status and incomes which ultimately persuade you to feel more recognised and respected (both mostly socially determined feelings and desires) and to believe to feel happier by the consumptions of commodities. It might then be the case that one spends almost her entire life in a perpetual quest to consume and possess more and/or to achieve an ever higher social/power status, unaware that her aspirations change as her circumstances do; this consolidated detected evidence is referred to as *habit formation* by economists and *hedonic adaptation* by psychologists (Easterlin 2003), also called *hedonic treadmill* (Brickman and Campbell 1971) – based on the notion of *adaptation level* (Helson 1964) – somehow similar to the concept of *satisfaction treadmill* (Kahneman 2000) – based on the concept of *aspiration level* (Irwin 1944). The more you *have* the more you want; the more you *are* the more you want to become.

If aspirations arise at *the same extent* as previous ones are realised, objective well-being may increase but not the subjective, and we talk about *complete* adaptation. Research findings indicate that material aspiration, comfort, and positional goods are subject to complete adaptation effects as commensurately growing with income.

Under complete adaptation conditions, after a change in life individual subjective well-being would return to the original set point, which is the individual "baseline" level dependent on genes and personality. A major robust finding of well-being research is that life situations' contribution to "happiness" counts only very little, and far less than inherited temperament and personality.[47] This empirical evidence in psychology is known as *set point theory*.

47 Kahneman (2000), Diener et al. (1999), Lykken and Tellegen (1996), and Myers and Diener (1995).

While psychologists tend to consider the dynamic gap between aspirations and attainments as determinant of satisfaction/subjective well-being, economists typically consider only attainments, namely "more is better" and life circumstances have *enduring* effect on "happiness" (Easterlin 2003).

If we merge psychologists' and economists' views – and add a touch of common sense from experiences in our own lives and those around us – we can say that having more (health, money, power, social status, comforts) is indeed better and often has life-lasting consequences which are nevertheless largely genetically framed within an inextricable game between genes and environment/context within which the former fixes the window of manifestable possibilities mouldable by the latter. Depending on life events and environments one could express her own *full* genetic potential or not; she may live her own life at a lower "happiness" and/or satisfaction, subjective (and objective) well-being level for which she is genetically predisposed, which would be the ultimate shame.

What if one underlives his genetic potential in enjoying life and achieving virtues, because of deciding to set his life in an urban setting to pursue socially determined desires which end up resulting neither that desirable and overall valuable nor that satisfying? We need a good education to get a good job to get good money to get good material satisfaction and, by the latter three, to get good social recognition. And usually, all this is achievable in cities rather than in rural areas or small villages. We can call urban *materialists* this typology of individuals who choose the urban life for materialistic purposes.

However, there is another face of the coin: *Homo sapiens*

> evolved to leave the beaten track, to try things out, to get distracted and generally look like we're wasting time [...] the learning algorithms in our brain know that something we learnt by chance today will come in useful tomorrow.
>
> (Stafford 2012)

To get "distracted", stimulated, curious, and especially educated to treasure and elaborate information which in turn generates new knowledge and ideas, is typically boosted – and sometimes only possible – in cities, where you have schools, universities, cultural stimulus and opportunities to daily meet people carrying any sort of background, knowledge, habits, philosophies, promoting new ideas and, in a larger perspective, humanity progresses. Even though often the frenetic urban style compromises the peace necessary for the creative and contemplative process our minds need to study and produce well.

Part of those choosing cities for their lives are driven by these types of cultural goods and by the ambition to acquire more knowledge for giving their own contributions to personal and humankind advances. We call them the urban *culturalists*.

Both, urban materialists and culturalists, belonging to the *involuntary urbans* before-mentioned category, decide to trade-off a preferred life setting (natural, rural, village, town environments) for material, social and/or cultural aspirations. In this sense they "have to" live in *unwanted* physical and lifestyle settings (cities) in order to achieve other *wanted* types of goals (material, social, cultural).

After these premises, we can now ask ourselves "what is there to decide whether a particular pleasure is worth purchasing at the cost of a particular pain, except the feelings and judgment of the experiences?" (Mill 1863, p. 9): is it "more worthy" to sacrifice a peaceful picturesque rural-village life for materialist goals, or for cultural?

As long as they *quantitatively* produce the same amount of pleasures, for Bentham they are equivalently worthy, for Mill not. Benthamite utilitarianism does not invidiously compare *qualitatively* different types of pleasure. In his famous statement, Bentham indicates that "if the *quantity* of pleasure was the same, pushpin was as good as poetry" (Hunt and Lautzenheiser 2015, p. 197) while for Mill some *types* of pleasure are more desirable and valuable than others: poetry would be valued more than pushpin; and he replies to Bentham with the equally famous quote that "it is better to be a human being dissatisfied than a pig satisfied; better to be Socrates dissatisfied than a fool satisfied" (Mill 1863, p. 8). He then adds another fundamental point: if the pig or the fool holds a different opinion and thinks to be indeed happier than the dissatisfied human or Socrates, it is simply because "they only know their own side of the question. The other party of the comparison knows both sides" (Mill 1863, p. 8). Thus, we might be tempted to judge as more worthy to sacrifice a preferred natural-rural-village life type for higher education enabling us to increase our pleasure of knowledge and by that perhaps to even give our contribution to humanity advances, rather than for getting more money to buy the most expensive car and fanciest clothes or higher social status to show up and socially induced materialistic-power ambitions.

Bentham's utilitarianism considers (individual) *intensity* of pleasure, while Mill's utilitarianism (interpersonal) adds the fundamental concept of *kinds* of pleasure.

In favour of the "nobler" kind of pleasure (e.g. those motivating the urban culturalists) there is not just Mill's theoretical thought; findings (Easterlin 2003) suggest that, contrarily to pecuniary domains, nonpecuniary domains might be less subject to hedonic adaptation. Scitovsky (1976) argues that comfort goods (car, house …) are more subject to hedonic adaptation than cultural goods (arts, music, literature …), condemning the urban materialists to an endless aspiration hamster wheel. People are presumed to be the best judges of their own interests, but if they regularly make decisions ignoring hedonic adaptation and social comparison effects, this presupposition is no longer valid and we cannot anymore assume that they are able to maximise their psychological well-being (Easterlin 2003).

We saw that cultural goods are less subject to hedonic adaption: aspirations change less than one's circumstances change, therefore the actual subjective well-being increases. This is called less than complete adaptation and complements the set-point theory. Therefore, while the *urban materialists* might benefit from mostly an objective well-being increase, the *urban culturalists* might benefit *also* from a subjective well-being from the psychological profit linked to the less than complete adaptation effects associated with cultural goods and pure educational-knowledge pleasures.

The second term we underlined before in the above-mentioned West's statement, "forgetting", embraces the omnipresent pros-cons balance we make – realising it or not, rationally or not – every day in our minds for any decision. In the spatial domain decisions (e.g. deciding to live in a small village or a megacity) it refers to the spatial equilibrium we discussed in the previous paragraph. In the next paragraph, we will expose some reasoning concerning another way to look at the "forgetting the ugly and the bad" meaning coming into the game when we, rather unconsciously, are victims of the cognitive dissonance phenomena filtering and distorting our capacity to make use of objective information. We now end briefly by discussing the third term we emphasised in West's sentence: "think".

People indeed "think", in the sense that they *assume*, they *believe*, that all these wonderful things (money, creativity …) attract them to cities regardless of the negative aspects (crime, stress, congestion, pollution, lack of nature, …). It is well-established[48] that effective forecasting is a task in which people do not outclass, and when they are already living in cities we saw how cognitive dissonance biases alter people's perception and proper use of available information.

6.9 Do we choose what we prefer, and do we prefer what is best for us?

A necessary query academics should face before exploring people's preferences (revealed – typical in standard economics – or stated – typical in psychology) is the following: "is the one that a person prefers necessarily the one that is better for her?" (Broome 1991). We have already seen how people are not always aware of the forces shaping their choices and not so successful in maximising their own well-being by their decisions (Easterlin 2003).

Even assuming a person fully operating within the self-interested condition, she is defined imprudent when she still fails to do what is best for herself (Broome 1991), which appears to be an irrational behaviour – though we will see how this judgement depends on the temporal scale of view (immediate *versus* lifetime utility), and on the nature of "utility" intended (whether "positive feeling" or "greatest good" for the individual).

The notion of utility maximisation in economics, as long-standing as economics itself, has recently faced a dramatic shift from the neo-classical approach where irrational behaviour was seen as *unsystematic* and therefore impossible to model, to the behavioural sciences approach suggesting instead a *systematic* irrationality (Dhami 2016). Findings in behavioural economics show cognitive simplification processes (use of heuristic and biases when making decisions) from where generative principles can be extrapolated.

There are two main psychological information courses when we make decisions (Gilad et al. 1987):

1 What information we "allow" "in"
2 What we do with it once in

Cognitive dissonance (Festinger 1957) is one of the labels embracing behavioural processes operating within point 1, which limits

48 Kahneman (2000), Gilbert et al. (1998), Kahneman and Schkade (1999), Loewenstein and Schkade (1999), and Schkade and Kahneman (1998).

the information we actually "want" to see. At least three behavioural biases lead to less-than-full use of the available information (Gilad et al. 1987):

- I Prior hypothesis bias: prior beliefs (cities are very good for me) leading to snub disconfirming information (e.g. crime, pollution, noise, stress, no nature, no time, dirtiness, and feeling unhappy);
- II Adjustment and anchoring: early evaluations act as an anchor making subsequent adjustments too small;
- III Escalating commitment: improper discounting of undesirable information (urban life is actually revealing to be bad for me) regarding a prior commitment (I believed/invested so much in moving to/staying in the city) to a course of action and the ensuing continuation or even escalation of that commitment (I cannot change life now, let's carry on, maybe it will become better or I will start liking urban life one day).

"Selective exposure" is a type of dissonance reduction which avoids dissonant information – by completely ignoring them or by discounting their value – while seeking for confirming ones.

Under spatial equilibrium decisions we consciously "forget" the ugly and the bad (I am aware of the ugly and the bad but still prefer to live there because of other advantages), while under cognitive dissonance biases we rather unconsciously "forget" about that (I "automatically" and partially unwarily discount/filter the ugly and the bad of urban life).

However, even the most *truly urban* and *urban believer* victim of cognitive dissonance biases might forget about the ugly and the bad … but up to a point. In fact, the dissonance function is not monotonically increasing but curvilinear (Frey 1982) where dissonance information is filtered out at low levels of dissonance, while when the latter becomes too large the information blocked off reverses, allowing to correctly revise the initial decision rationally in line with the objective external evidence.

Neoclassical theories assume that decision-makers instantaneously and fully realise any change in the exogenous parameters that in turn might determine a change in their behaviours; conversely, cognitive dissonance evidence made clear that this updating of exogenous parameter changes is imperfect (neither instantaneous nor full). It seems that only after a certain threshold (k) of discrepancy between expected utility, E_U, (city life is/will be great for me [or vice versa]) and experienced utility, Ex_U (after years living in cities I have to say that it is not actually that great [or vice versa]) the updating would take place and a new behaviour (living in cities or not?) emerges; k is a 'choice' variable which is part of the utility function together with the traditional arguments ($U=f(...., k)$) and is proportional to individual differences in personalities (Gilad et al. 1987). If we call S the level of surprise (in a negative sense) between expected and experienced utility ($S= E_U - Ex_U$), when $S > k$ the update of the information takes place.

Dissonance reduction, along with self-selection, would predict rather high subjective happiness in those who voluntarily decided to move to a certain place (e.g. cities), while treadmill effects would predict a return to their characteristic level of subjective happiness mostly pre-determined from genes and personalities (Kahneman 2000).

Coming back to our main question of this paragraph: do we choose/prefer what is actually best for us?

Kimball and Willis define the concepts of baseline mood (M) and elation (e) (Kimball and Willis 2006): the baseline mood (M) is the level of "happiness" (H) which would prevail in the absence of surprises, while elation (e) is the contribution that surprises make on "happiness" (H), and the latter is the sum of them (H=M+e).

Elation is closer to the Morris' definition of happiness as an intense transient sensation (Morris 2006) and is what Kimball and Willis consider as a noise acting as a distraction when people try to find out the right determinants for increasing their M, even though the latter is only one argument of the flow utility function.

M depends on genes (therefore beyond individual control) but also on individual's choice in life, both long- and short-term choices such as those related to factors like sleep, exercise, eating habits, social relations, friends, type of work, and hobbies, which are at least partially under one's own control. However, because of several biases already shown and because of the noise from elation (e.g. the intense yet ephemeral exciting feeling after buying/obtaining something new), people are often not aware of what might truly raise their baseline mood. This may perhaps have a role in explaining the Easterlin paradox (people are not *as* happier *as* they are richer) and the urban dwellers not as happier as they could be compared to their non-urban counterparts.

As Mill, one and half centuries ago wrote,

> the individual who is presumed to be the best judge of his own interests may be incapable of judging for himself. [...] the person most interested is not [always] the best judge of the matter, nor a competent judge at all.
>
> (Mill 1874, Vol 3, p. 957)

6.10 Happiness, life satisfaction, and short- and long-term utility

Often the terms "happiness", "subjective well-being", "utility", "welfare", and "life satisfaction" are used interchangeably, generating confusion and fundamental mistakes.

The meaning of utility in plain English is *usefulness*. But, usefulness for what?

Bentham's idea that happiness is the determinant of behaviour is rooted in his famous note about mankind placed "under the governance of two sovereign masters, pain and pleasure. It is for them alone to point out what we ought to do, as well as to determine what we shall do" (Bentham 1789), and in his even more famous motto "the greatest happiness of the greatest number that is the measure of right and wrong" (Bentham 1776) which probably was the English translation of the Italian Enlightenment thinker Cesare Beccaria's "Dei delitti e delle pene" (Beccaria 1764) when in the introduction we read: "la massima felicità divisa al maggior numero" (the greatest happiness distributed to the greatest number).

The idea of Bentham's utility linked with the concept of happiness entered in economics with Jevons' theory of political economy (Jevons 1871), where he quoted his expression as "perfectly reflecting the meaning of utility in economics". Since then, the utilitarian social philosophy seeing all human activities strictly aiming to maximise pleasure (intended as utility) became the philosophical foundation of neoclassical economics in the second half of the 19th century.

Also Senior in his "An Outline of the Science of Political Economy" associates the term *utility* with *pleasure*: "of the [...] qualities which [...] give it value, the most striking is the power, direct or indirect, of producing pleasure [...] *Utility* [...] come nearest to [expressing this quality]" (Senior 1938, p. 6).

However, a better reading of Bentham reveals a slight but crucial variance in his meaning of utility: in his first definition, he wrote: "utility [...] is that principle which approves or disapproves

[…] action […] according to the tendency […] to augment or diminish the happiness", where the latter is seen as a balance of pleasure over pain; but in his subsequent paragraph he provides a more comprehensive idea: "By utility is meant that property in any object, whereby it tends to produce benefit, advantage, pleasure, good, or happiness" (Bentham 1789). Where if we read "or" as a disjunctive conjunction, it suggests that the notions of "benefit", "advantage", "pleasure", "good", and "happiness" are not interchangeable. Bentham tempts to clarify it in a footnote which appeared in the second edition (1823) of the same book (*An Introduction to the Principles of Morals and Legislation*) in which he added: "The word *utility* does not so clearly point to the ideas of pleasure and pain as the words happiness and felicity do".

This opens the road to a separation of two clearly distinct concepts:

1 The greatest good for an individual
2 The positive feeling felt from an individual.

We might prefer to use the first for the term *utility*[49] – as usually economists over the last century (excluding earlier traditions) did – and the second for the term *happiness* – as typically adopted by psychologists.

Economists seem to prefer using people's choices as reflections of their utility, while psychologists prefer to use people's felt experiences (feelings) as reflections of their happiness.

Whatever we decide to define and use for the terms "utility" and "happiness", the type of reasoning we conduct depends on the temporal angle we consider: long or short term.

In economics lifetime utility is the individual's whole objective function including things subsequent to her death valued important by the individual; the extent to which she gets what she wants and has been revealed by her choices which often suggests a valuation of goods not traded in markets such as freedom, gratification, respect, unpolluted environment, lively community … or partially traded such as free time, health, and longevity (Kimball and Willis 2006).

Lifetime utility is sometimes interpreted as a discounted sum over time of flow utility which is somehow a similar notion, although in a different scale of thinking, to Kahneman's proposal to quantify

49 As Kimball and Willis (2006).

individual welfare as a discounted sum of "instant utility" (Kahneman 1999), also called current effect (how positive our feelings are at a particular time). However, this interpretation is not entirely correct because it associates two different levels of utility which often run in parallel independent non-communicating paths, and at different "speeds". You may have a very quotidian happy life every single day of your life regarding daily habits (friends, sport, free time, relaxing life pace …) and scenarios (bucolic environment, location with wonderful weather, frequent holiday trips …) but an unsatisfactory one if your life goal was to become a renowned professor or to win a Nobel Prize and you didn't achieve it … or vice versa: a very satisfactory life when seen as your own career achievements (you won the Nobel Prize at 81 years old) but at the price to live a poorly happy daily life (not much time for family, friends, sport, hobbies, stressful fast pace, unrelaxed mind …), so that if you would calculate your global utility (lifetime utility) as the strict summary of your daily utility (current utility) in the first case you might obtain a much greater value than in the second, even though if you would calculate it by considering your lifetime career achievements, the result could be opposite. Unless a kind of anticipatory hedonic inertia (D'Acci 2013) increases also your daily life current utility because of being aware that you are professionally-culturally growing and on the right path to achieve your lifetime utility goal; the same is true if your professionally-culturally daily growth is a source of joy and "happiness" on its own.

Excluding the fortunate case where daily actions repeated over the life "only" merely promoting current effects perfectly match the farsighted lifetime utility too, people often have to make compromises between current effect and lifetime utility decisions, partially exemplified in the Cicada and the Ants fable and, for some aspects, the Hesse's Narcissus and Goldmund.

One's strategy may be to achieve lifetime utility (e.g. a professional career) by sacrificing some daily life pleasures (e.g. free time, rural life, quietness …), while another's strategy may be to achieve her lifetime utility by structuring daily life with plenty of current-affect pleasures, or a middle way (Figure 6.34).

Therefore, you might decide to live in a city, even if you don't like it, because it's the only way to get a higher education and a professional career (long-term utility), or you might decide to live in a rural, village, town area to enjoy your daily life moments in a peaceful lifestyle, without pollution, crime, congestion … but at the price of your

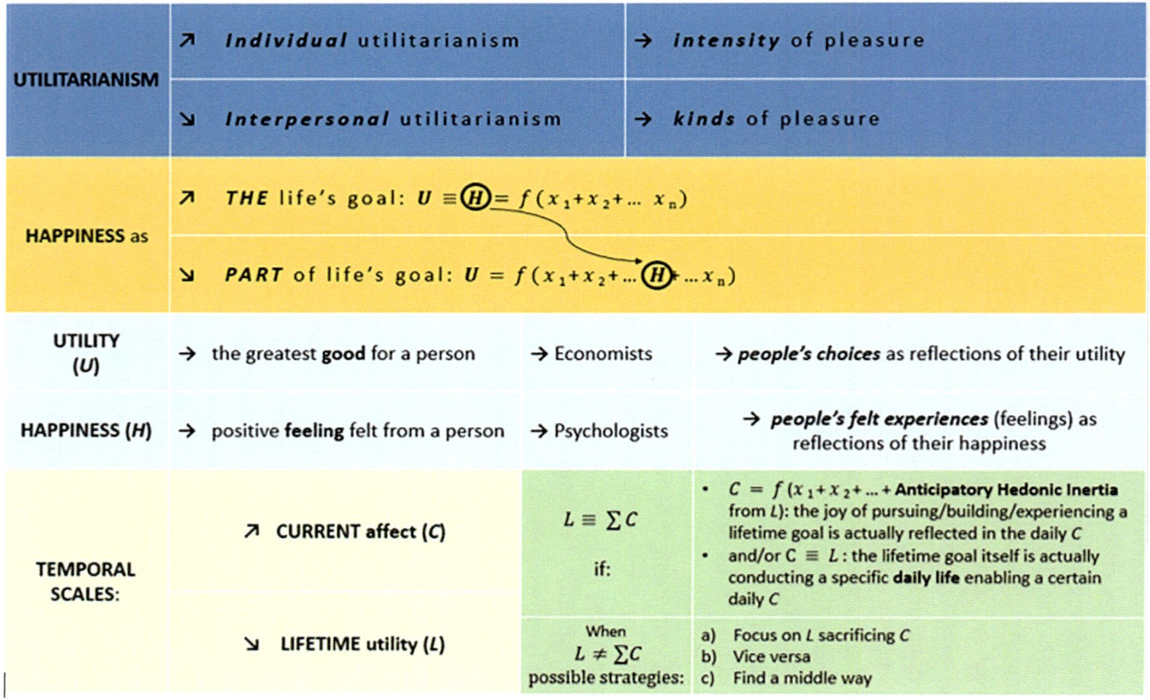

Figure 6.34 Utility (U), happiness (H), and temporal perspectives.
Source: D'Acci (2021).

professional satisfaction. Some are lucky enough to have their long-term utility ambitions in line with their short-term ones.

Probably in the medium-long term future the combination of advances in artificial intelligence, robots (Graetz and Michaels 2018), telework (Chung and van der Lippe 2020), falling working hours (Dolton et al. 2016), hologram communication, transports, teleservices, and in the design and governance of cities and territories (D'Acci 2019, 2025, D'Acci and Voto 2023, D'Acci et al. 2024) will revolutionise our cultural-socio-economic systems and liberate our residential choices,[50] no longer under hard compromises (e.g. a better job and richer but in a high urbanicity context which one doesn't like) but guided purely by our true preferences: megacity, city, town, rural lifestyle.

When this will happen, based on current preferences seen, probably the world's urban dwellers would become only 1/3 (those preferring cities no matter what); or perhaps by that time we will design and manage our cities so nicely that they will become more attractive on their own and be chosen as the best place to live regardless of their better educational, professional, service opportunities, but because they will be a beautiful place to live.

We would live in cities not because we have to but because we want to.

6.11 Conclusions

Scientists have known for a long time that

> just as social isolation is well known to have harmful effects (Harlow, Dodsworth and Harlow 1965), so does the opposite extreme: overcrowding can induce stress and illness in species ranging from insects to rodents (Calhoun 1950) to primates, including humans (Hall 1966).
>
> (Kennedy and Adolphs 2011, p. 452)

An empirical proof that something psychologically "wrong" happens to humans in cities came from numerous studies showing links

50 As Martinotti (1996) reminds us, urban forms are linked with how different populations (aggregate of individuals with common traits) gravitate around metropolitan centres: inhabitants, workers, and city users. Or as Geoffrey West (2011) says, that cities are just a physical manifestation of our interactions.

(often also causal as demonstrated by longitudinal studies) between urbanicity levels and mental health as well as life satisfaction and subjective well-being.[51] In line with these pieces of evidence, surveys about self-declared life satisfaction and stated preference for places to live indicate that only around one-third actually prefer an urban environment. Despite this, more than half the world's population live in cities and this proportion is predicted to become nearly 70% by 2050.

There are several reasons as to why people still decide to live in cities; among them, we discussed a few types of utilities that individuals could get from city life and concluded that someone might prefer to sacrifice her preferred environment (and linked "happiness") in order to achieve other types of advantages such as social mobility, money, culture, and professional satisfaction. "Happiness" should be seen as part of the utility function rather than the function itself and traded off against other arguments in the utility function such as virtues, talents' realisation, cultural-knowledge development, career, money, services, and social status.

51 Someone might advance the hypothesis that people are mentally worse off in cities rather than in smaller, natural villages also (or even largely) because of cultural ideology, which biases perceptions and feelings by idealising bucolic, small settlements and natural environments. However, cross-cultural, cross-age (even in very young children, i.e., at a pre-ideological stage), and cross-temporal studies suggest that this may not be such a strong case – even if cultural ideology plays some influence which is difficult to scientifically prove/disprove. Also, based on personal experience, among the few hundred people I have somehow known so far, almost the majority were biased the other way around, with the ideology that city life is much better than the isolated, sad country life (unless my social network is a strong outlier, but I don't think so, as it is very varied in any factors). Also among many academics it seems to me that the reverse is true: there is an "admiration" for the big cities – even acknowledging their limits – rather than the smaller settlements and the countryside. Regardless of this, there is not much spillover between the academic world and the population, namely this supposed (by some) ideological collective bias against cities in favour of the countryside, it should come from the population itself or the politicians. On occasions, the latter however might probably have an interest in promoting big cities as it would be easier to manage population and infrastructure rather than spread here and there in scattered population across the territory. Finally, even assuming that it is true that most of the population is ideologically biased against the cities, it is not easy and long-lasting convincing people that, for example, living at 45 degree Celsius is great. You can certainly bias the mass, but up to an objective point, especially in democracies and sufficiently educated societies.

Definitions of happiness, utility, and satisfaction are required to properly reason about people's life strategies and decisions. We distinguished lifetime utility and current utility, as well as the "greatest good" and "positive feeling felt" and discussed the implication of one's compromises/sacrifices between her utility function's arguments.

In the future, technological changes such as robots, hologram communication, telework, teleservices, hyperloops and sky trains, plus new (consequent) urban-territorial design, will radically transform our socio-economic system, freeing us up to truly decide to live where we *prefer* rather than where we *need*. We will no longer need to trade off part of our daily happiness by living in undesired environments/lifestyles in order to achieve other lifetime utility goals, express our talent and develop virtues: "society is [...] likely to flourish to a greater extent with happy citizens than with unhappy ones" (Veenhoven 1988, p. 351).

7 Genetic perspectives

Abstract

We belong to one of the approximately 200 species of the order Primates; as such we were tree-dwellers living in forests for circa 80 million years and in savannah-like habitats for the last 4 million years, excluding the past 8–10 thousand years when we started our rural and urban journey, and, for some, the last century of mega-urban living. This information is somehow still embedded in our DNA, but probably not the one changed a century ago.

The 1920s were characterised by a radical behaviourism which predominantly looked *outside* the mind (external contingencies of reinforcement, e.g. the work of J.B. Watson about classical conditioning, and of B.F. Skinner about reinforcement) under the assumption of a domain-generality, a single all-purpose learning human brain (genetically) designed for a general ability to *learn* by reinforcement according to specific environments and external inputs: *any* behaviour could be shaped (Buss 2019).

This school of thought lasted until the 1970s when empirical evidence made radical behaviourism indefensible. In fact, the experiments of H. Harlow (with monkeys) and J. Garcia (with rats) showed empirical violations of "laws" of *learning*, which, together with the studies of M. Seligman about predispositions, signed the decline of behaviourism.

Based on this, and pushed by the universal language concept of N. Chomsky, plus the rise of computers and related information-processing metaphor seeing the human mind as a summary of programs processing information, the *cognitive revolution* came. It

DOI: 10.4324/9781003355014-7

was actually a kind of return to the Freud's psychology of instincts predating the radical behaviourism emergence. Freud, somehow similarly to Darwin, proposed an instinctual system, also developed by W. James' book *Principle of Psychology* from the 1890. They looked *inside* the mind, rather than *outside* as the behaviourists.

The mind was not anymore seen as a domain-general machine, but as a series of cognitive mechanisms explicitly designed to process *certain* information, as computer programs for different tasks.

In the same spirit, K. Lorenz and N. Tinbergen founded the discipline of *ethology*.

This overall return to the psychology of instincts, culminated in evolutionary psychology and akin fields: human behavioural ecology, and evolutionary anthropology.

"Everything about an animal [...] including its inherited behaviour [...] is a coded message about the worlds in which its ancestors survived" (Dawkins and Wong 2017, p. 22). This code is written in the DNA, whose "information in all living creatures has been handed down from remote ancestors [...] copied for millions of years" (Dawkins and Wong 2017, pp. 19, 20).

We belong to one of the approximately 200 species of the order Primates; as such we were tree-dwellers living in forests for circa 80 million years and in savannah-like habitats for the last 4 million years, excluding the latest 8–10 thousand years when we began our rural and urban journey, and, for some, the last century of mega-urban living. This information is somehow embedded in our DNA.

Given these time periods, humans' environment of evolutionary adaptedness[1] (EEA) was mostly the pre-industrial and pre-agricultural one, millions of years ago.

According to Wilson E.O., humans had two main stages of acceleration in mental evolution: the first for around 10 million years when transitioning from a large arboreal primate to a first man-ape (probably *Australopithecus*); the second, much more rapid, started around 100˙000 years ago, was primarily a cultural evolution phenotypic type, "building upon the genetic potential in the brain that had accumulated over the previous millions of years" (Wilson 2000, p. 565). However, he later in the chapter opened the way to genetic evolution too when talking about the rapid growth in population density subsequent to the agricultural revolution 10˙000 years ago and the exponential growth in knowledge and technology during the last few thousand years:

1 Selection pressures shaping adaptations during an adaptation period.

> there is no reason to believe that during this final sprint there has been a cessation in the evolution of either mental capacity or the predilection toward special social behaviors. The theory of population genetics and experiments on other organisms show that substantial changes can occur in the span of less than 100 generations, which for man reaches back only to the time of the Roman Empire.
> (Wilson 2000, p. 569)

The assumption that humans stopped evolving 50˙000 years ago (Gould 2000) has been corrected by evidence accumulated during the past few decades indicating human evolution over the last few millenniums (Voight et al. 2006, Mathieson et al. 2015, Pickrell et al. 2009, Tishkoff et al. 2007, Kwiatkowski 2005, Yi et al. 2010, Turchin et al. 2012, Beauchamp 2016, Bloom 2001).

Aside from the latest innovative genetic technologies and statistics allowing increasingly quantified facts, there are also hypotheses such as in Cieri et al. (2014) based on fossil records suggesting a human temperament shift towards less aggressiveness and more social tolerance and cooperation, started in the late Pleistocene, associated with population size and density (Jacobs and Roberts 2009, Richerson et al. 2009).

The time necessary for selective pressures to alter DNA depends on the magnitude of the former. Combining field and lab experiments, it appears that a time between 30 and 60 generations is required, which for humans means 600–1˙200 years (Reznick and Endler 1982, Reznick, Bryga, and Endler 1990, Reznick et al. 1997, Bloom 2001), although evidence suggests that, in only 2–10 generations, humans could evolutionary adapt their genome to changed environments (Milot and Stearns 2020), and evolution, in general, could even happen in only two generations (Kinnison and Hendry 2001, Johnson and Munshi-South 2017).

There are several types of selection: natural (survival), sexual (mating), and genetic drift (random changes: mutations, founder effects, and genetic bottlenecks).

Natural selection is not intentional and cannot look into the future; it can be gradual and slow, or a sudden change (punctuated equilibrium) might happen; even in the latest circumstances, it is usually still occurring in tiny increments in each generation (Buss 2019).

Whatever ways such evolutionary adaptations happen, they are far from optimal when environments change too quickly (evolutionary time lags) and/or when adaptations are too costly.

Constructed niches since the Neolithic likely created the human genome selective pressure (Downey 2016, Barnes et al. 2011, Fumagalli et al. 2011, Harris and Meyer 2006, Hawks et al. 2007, Lachance and Tishkoff 2013), which might still occur in our ever-changing urban creations.

Niche constructions (cities, economies, social norms …) are a kind of culture-gene co-evolution: culture creates selection pressures which induce new adaptations. Culture-gene co-evolution is one of the most dominant forces in recent human evolution (Henrich 2015).

A vast list of recent evolutions in humans are accurately described in Williamson et al. (2007) and Balter (2005), and some specific features appear in Kendal et al. (2011), Laland et al. (2010), Richerson et al. (2010), Hill et al. (2009), Hare and Tomasello (2005), Hare et al. (2012), and Réale et al. (2007).

Selective sweep evidence was found more in European-Americans and Chinese than in African-Americans, supporting the hypothesis of new selective pressures from novel environments faced by modern humans who migrated out of sub-Saharan Africa, influencing such higher selective sweep rates (Williamsons et al. 2007, Kayser et al. 2003, Storz et al. 2004, Stajich et al. 2005).

This suggests how novel environments – such as the current urban habitats in which most of us are already living and more will join during the next decades – are still a source of selection in our genome besides cultural evolutions. Another result backing this indication comes from the observation of more selective sweeps within subpopulations than in cosmopolitan samples, suggesting adaptation to local environments in recent human evolution (Williamsons et al. 2007).

"Local" environments in the case of cities are represented, with obvious precautions and limitations, by "any" urban areas. In fact, biotically and abiotically, cities are far more similar to each other than to their nearby nonurban environments (Groffman et al. 2014, Rivkin et al. 2019): air–light–noise pollution, paved surfaces, density, life speed, and population size.

Referring to the latter – size – mounting observations are investigating whether a universal law of urban phenomena (e.g. crime, GDP, emissions, surface, creativity …) exists by which, it doesn't matter where, cities always behave similarly and according to their size (D'Acci 2025, West 2017, Bettencourt et al. 2007).

From this perspective, some common aspects of urban life could be like mountain altitudes: regardless of where a specific mountain is, its altitude is the same. Subsequently, even if organisms are living in different mountains, they would convergently adapt to high-altitude life.

The degree to which species living in similar habitats develop similar adaptations is a central question within evolutionary biology and is called convergent evolution.

In plants and animals, a genetic difference often exists between urban and nonurban populations, caused by adaptive (natural and sexual selection) and nonadaptive (genetic drift and gene flow) evolutions, which for some species has happened rather rapidly in a few generations (Johnson and Munshi-South 2017).

Examples of convergent human evolution in recent times occurred around 12˙500 years ago when Andeans, as well as independently Tibetans and Ethiopians, genetically adapted their haemoglobin to fix more oxygen, allowing them to live at high altitude, or the resistance to tuberculosis and leprosy observed in higher frequencies in older cities, where exposure to such infections has a longer history too (Barnes et al. 2011).

Is the same valid for a variety of psychological-physical traits of urban inhabitants, genetically (alongside ontogenetically) adapting to happily-healthily living in contemporary urban habitats? This is a question challenged by the nascent field of urban evolutionary ecology (Rybski et al. 2019, Sukopp 1998, McDonnell 2011).

If such evolution is ongoing in response to urban living, it is likely that it will result from pre-existing mutations within current populations' genetic variation rather than from new mutations; the latter in fact require a longer time than urbanisation speeds, even though urbanisation can alter mutation rates themselves (Barrett et al. 2008, Johnson and Munshi-South 2017).

Human Sociobiology, or Human Evolutionary Psychology, seeks to interpret the psychological and cultural life of *Homo sapiens* in terms of their genetic inheritance and from an evolved species point of view. Evolutionary psychology extends the Darwinian implications to the human psyche. The vision of the tabula rasa mind at birth is replaced by the existence of an innate nature processed over millions of years of natural selection. This has several implications for the understanding of social science and behavioral processes.

Misinterpretations about sociobiology and genetic determinism together with the long-held view in the social sciences that human behaviour is the product of cultural forces alone rather than biological too cause occasional controversies.

While genes capture the evolutionary responses of prior populations to behaviour selection, a certain environmental flexibility allows us some adjustment, at least within a margin, during our lifetime. It is an inextricable game between ***genes*** and ***environment*** within which, in the short term, the *former*[2] fixes the window of manifestable possibilities mouldable by the *latter*,[3] while in the long term (evolution) the latter shapes the former.

Humans' common genome is indeed expressed in extremely various environments creating a gene–environment interaction and a related very large range of cultural forms.

It has been established from an increasing number of studies how aspects of behaviours, temperaments, psychological predispositions, even if influenced by the environment (Persson 2020, Tikhodeyev and Shcherbakova 2019, Kiive et al. 2017, Laas et al. 2014, Freund et al. 2013, Bendesky and Bargmann 2011, Champagne 2010, Belsky, Bakermans-Kranenburg, van IJzendoorn 2007 (figure 1); Weaver et al. 2004, Caspi et al. 2003, Turkheimer and Waldron 2000) – activating, inhibiting, amplifying, mitigating, or directing them towards diverse real-life manifestations – are genetically coded (Niepoth and Bendesky 2020, Pulver et al. 2020, Franke and Reif 2020, Fernàndez-Castillo et al. 2020, Duque-Wilckens et al. 2020, Zwir et al. 2020, O'Leary et al. 2019, Harro et al. 2019, Tyree et al. 2018, Røysamb et al. 2018, Sanchez-Roige et al. 2018, Baran et al. 2017, Tielbeek et al. 2017, Plomin et al. 2016 (figure 1); Fernàndez-Castillo, Cormand 2016 (figure 1, tables I, II); Jones and Norton 2015, Bouchard 2014 (table 1); Blouin et al. 2013, Heinz et al. 2011, Katz 2011, Robinson, Fernald and Clayton 2008, Donaldson and Young 2008, Caspi et al. 2002, Baker et al. 2001, Lesch and Merschdorf 2000).

Around two-thirds of findings in psychology failed to be replicated (Open Science Collaboration 2015), while findings in behavioural

2 See, among many, figure 1 in DeFries et al. (1978); figure 1 and tables 1–2 in Fernàndez-Castillo and Cormand (2016); table 1 in Bouchard (2014); figures 2–3 in Chang et al. (2018); figures 1–2 in Lo et al. (2017); figure 1 in Cornelius et al. (2013); figure 1 in van den Berg et al. (2016); figures 1–2 in Pearce et al. (2017); figure 1 in Tomson et al. (2016); figures 1–3 in Garcia et al. (2010); figure 1 in Hu et al. (2016); figure 2 in Kubinyi et al. (2012); and figure 2 in Donaldson and Young (2008).

3 Figure 11 in Rice and Barone (2000); figures 1–4 in Kaufman et al. (2004); table 3 in Holt-Lunstad et al. (2015); figure 2 in Freund et al. (2013); figure 1–3 in Caspi et al. (2003); figures 1–4 in Griffiths and Linquist (2024); figure 1 in Weaver et al. (2004); figures 1–2 in McGowan et al. (2009); and figure 1 in Belsky et al. (2007).

genetics are large in magnitude, based on six- and seven-figure samples, and have been replicated in many decades and countries (Plomin et al. 2016).

By searching on ScienceDirect (March 2026) "gene behaviour" as words co-occurring present under "title", 1˙476 results appear.

Starting from this genetic evidence, although within an ongoing debate regarding the relative contributions of Nature and Nurture to mental characteristics, and taking into account the recent epigenetic revelations (Berretta et al. 2011, Herrel, Joly and Danchin 2020, Doherty and Roth 2020, Silva and Steffen 2019, Bollati and Baccarelli 2010, Bird 2007, Goldberg, Allis and Bernstein 2007, Weinhold 2006) and mental plasticity surprise (Zerilli 2020, Valk et al. 2017, Ghalambor et al. 2015, Chattarji et al. 2015, Dulac 2010, Dingemanse and Araya-Ajoy 2015, Dingemanse et al. 2010), we ask ourselves the following three questions:

1 Are we currently genetically equipped to live most of our lives under a neon, seated on a chair, in an enclosed space, facing a monitor, with artificial light and air, in a polluted mega-urban box of cement and cars where congestion, noise, thousands/millions of strangers, and social stress are the daily norm and the contact with nature a fantasy? Is our brain already prepared since previous evolutionary selection processes, or sufficiently plastic[4] to behaviourally equally adapt to such different types of life which one can experience in a rural, village, town, city, and the very recent megacity, conurbation daily context?
2 If not, is the behavioural selective pressure of contemporary urban environments strong enough to induce genetic adaptation?
3 And if so how fast?

There could be various scenarios:

1 Despite the urban socio-economics advantages and pleasant aspects (such as cultural stimulus, accessibility to services, dynamic spirit, enormous range of potential fitting personalities and inspiring people, freedom due to the anonymity or large numbers, often

4 Or – in relation to the population size – *dual* enough, referring to our ancestral orientation towards the larger community rather than groups discussed in chapter 2.

attracting skyline aesthetics), if cities are experienced predominantly as stressful for some, they might not be adapted and the following sub-scenarios could appear:

- a Sooner or later, across generations, our brains will properly adapt to the new urban environment because the related neuropsychological selection pressure for the urban psychological stress is affecting a majority and is strong enough to influence reproductive success.
- b The selection pressure is minimal or near-zero, either because:
  - i Suffering from mental health issues doesn't significantly impact the number of children (and rise them to be "reproductively successful") in relation to the non-affected counterparts
  - ii The mental health issues are negligible or more than compensated by the positive psychological aspects which cities bring.
  - iii It only affects a minority of the population.

Therefore, we will not adapt and (at least those more susceptible) carry on suffering the odds of choosing to enjoy the benefits which urban life offers.

2 We are already sufficiently adapted due to:
- a The plasticity of our brains which natural selection sculpted to allow our astonishing capacity of adaptation to diverse environments despite their differences (at least within certain limits).
- b The recent evolutions in earlier forms of urban life starting since the previous millennium (even if lighter and for a trifling percentage of world population). And actually we, as a species, are expressing ourselves at the best in cities which, rather than seen as a negative niche, could be seen as a sociocultural system whose scientific and technological progress freed us up from the constrains of small population sizes of the pre-agricultural revolution (around 10˙000 years ago), and the pre-industrial one (around two centuries ago).

Some hypothesise that *modernisation* – the wider process within which *urbanisation* is inserted – will involve a decline or even an end of natural selection on humans,[5] however they contradict empirical evidence from data: "there is mounting evidence that phenotype and fitness covary in modern human populations (e.g. Byars et al. 2010, 2017, Stulp et al. 2015, Beauchamp 2016, Kong et al. 2017)" (Milot and Stearns 2020).

A limited number of studies have tried, via evolutionary quantitative genetics methods, to investigate urban selection on human genome, probably also because multigenerational longitudinal genetic data were lacking (Tropf et al. 2015, Beauchamp 2016, Byars et al. 2017). "Quantifying the contribution of urban factors, including physical attributes of the habitat, stressors, and cultural norms, has yet to be done" (Milot and Stearns 2020).

The advent of agriculture (12˙000 years ago) created, among other changes, settlements and densification which altered our human nature previously adapted to foraging societies; "behaviour" was "likely among the traits most impacted by the shifts in selective pressures" (Milot and Stearns 2020).

Looking at the past, we can draft a multi-timescale human genetic response to change in the environment (Milot and Stearns 2020):

5 Such arguments are mostly encountered on popular media rather than in academic articles. ***Promethean*** arguments state that technological and cultural progress are isolating humans from natural selection: in developed societies, "nearly everyone reaches sexual maturity and can reproduce […] Following this logic to its end, full escape from natural selection in the future would be conceivable with the progress of individual medicine and the rise of transhumanism"; ***Limitative*** arguments reason around these points: (1) "genetic inertia is too large in a population of billions of humans for either selection or genetic drift to have any significant impact on our species in the near-term future"; (2) "as the mobility of individuals – and hence of their genes – increasingly produces global mixing, the potential for local adaptation should shrink, particularly in cities that receive continuous migratory influx"; (3) "Low fertility could further locally restrict the appearance and spread of new beneficial mutations"; ***Ontological*** arguments "consider that cultural evolution has replaced biological evolution" (Milot and Stearns 2020). Various critics to the above arguments are frequent, among them:

> in large populations, selection is more efficient and more mutations occur, while large-scale mobility can help to spread beneficial ones. Ontological and degenerative arguments neglect the complex interplay between culture and biological evolution. Culture evolves continuously and rapidly and may keep phenotypes away from their fitness optimum, and hence maintain selective pressures over the long term.
>
> (Milot and Stearns 2020)

I **Thousands or tens of thousands of years**: rare alleles rapidly increasing their frequency for selection response in one or few genes whose function is known (e.g. malaria resistance, lactase persistence, skin pigmentation to reduced ultraviolet light, adaptation to high altitude reduced oxygen).

II **Tens or hundreds of years**: it appears that small changes in the frequencies of many genes, instead of big change in the frequencies of one or a few genes, could involve a quick selection response in traits which are polygenic (e.g. blood pressure, blood lipid levels, glucose tolerance, and risk of coronary artery disease, body mass index, age at menarche, and height) (Pritchard and Di Rienzo 2010, Jain and Stephan 2017).

III **Contemporary times**: genomic changes of contemporary selection are starting to be identified related to, e.g. extended life and delayed maturation in the UK population (Mostafavi et al. 2017).

Having a genetic response to the recent environmental change of most humans who now live in an urban area rather than the rural lived till then is therefore possible. However, its occurrence, rapidity, and measurability depend on the following questions, as listed in Milot and Stearns (2020):

1 Are we checking genotypic or phenotypic traits?
2 If the former: a single gene or polygenic trait?
3 How much this gene(s) effect the traits?
4 How much is the selection pressure of the environmental change in relation to:
   a Reproduction;
   b Traits' expression;
   c The link between reproduction and such trait(s)?

Milot and Stearns (2020) discussed about urban selective factors on humans[6] such as stressors (pollutions …) and sociocultural ones.[7]

6 Also social scientists – some even before Wilson's *Sociobiology* (1975) – biologically approached human social behaviour, such as the "Zoological perspective in social science" of the sociologist/anthropologist Tiger and the anthropologist Fox (1966); the Biosocial approach of the sociologist van den Berghe (1975); the sociologist Lopreato in his *Human Nature and Biocultural Evolution* (1984).

7 See also Kaplan (1996), Gries and Grundmann (2018), Stulp and Barrett (2016), Alvergne and Lummaa (2014), Mace (2008), Bor et al. (2017), Pepper and Nettle

This book is mostly related to the latter and psychological ones.

It ultimately questions if our norm of reaction[8] regarding living in contexts extremely different ranging from rural hamlets to megacities is rather narrow (as e.g. the possible number of chambers in our heart) and then generates various discomforts (physical and, as the subject of this book, mental), or broader (as e.g. the fat in our bodies which depends also on diet, exercise, temperature …), and therefore does not generate discomforts.

Van Vugt (2018) defines a "dramatic clash" the one between our biological and cultural evolution started 12˙000 years ago with the advent of villages, towns, and cities. Our minds evolved for life as hunter-gatherers on open grasslands, but today we live in multi-level homes within complex urban societies. How does this shift impact us as we navigate life in modern cities[9]?

Cultural evolution proceeds at a far more rapid pace than biological evolution. It is through our cultural capacities that humans have come to dominate the planet. However, not all modifications we make to our environment serve our well-being,[10] either in the short term or the in the long term. Evolutionary mismatches can occur when a species is no longer well-adapted to its surroundings – this includes environments of its own making (Longman and Shaw 2026), such as cities. This can happen when environments change too quickly for genetic adaptation. Once we have a clearer understanding of evolutionary mismatches, we are better equipped to design environments [including cities] that align more closely with human nature (van Vugt and Giphart 2018, p. 6).

Some of the ideas I draw from evolutionary psychology are less firmly supported than those drawn from neurobiology, so certain conclusions remain tentative.

At a different level of reasoning, we can draw on the concept of the supernormal cue – a term introduced by Nobel laureate Nikolaas

(2014), Adams et al. (2014), Zagorsky and Smith (2017), Nunn et al. (2016), Bolund et al. (2015), Burger and DeLong (2016), and Pelletier et al. (2017).

8 The total variation in the trait in all survivable environments (Wilson 1998).

9 Most ideas about our hominid ancestors' behaviour are speculative because the fossil record is very sparse – just like some evolutionary-psychology claims about why we behave as we do today.

10 For example, a comfortable healthy mattress is a positive mismatch. Probably cities, overall and for many, too. But with some negative mismatches within the overall output picture.

Tinbergen (1951) – which refers to an exaggerated signal that powerfully activates an evolved instinct but may ultimately work against our well-being. Examples include our craving for sugary foods, our attraction to brightly coloured confectionery, or a moth fatally drawn to a patio heater, mistaking it for the moon. This prompts a provocative question: could the glittering appeal[11] of modern cities and megacities act as a supernormal cue, luring us in much like mosquitoes to a bug zapper?

11 At least for some, see 6.1.

8 Niche construction and niche picking

Ontogenetic inheritance, economic geography and geographical psychology perspectives

Abstract

As some other few species, we have the capacity to actually build our own habitats (i.e. villages, cities) which we inherited and transmit across generations. When organisms select their preferred niche, a gene–environment correlation may arise, namely a correlation between genotype frequencies and environment types. Geographical psychology reports a significantly recurrent spatial pattern of psychological traits distribution. The role which individual behaviour-decisions play when they aggregate emerging in spatial distribution patterns has been recognised also in economic geography.

8.1 Ontogenetic inheritance perspectives: niche construction

Different niches mean different ways of life, belonging to the study of behavioural ecology (West et al. 1988, Stotz 2017).

Niche construction (NC) is the environment modification by organisms and its legacy over generations (Flynn et al. 2013); an ecological inheritance which, according to many, represents an actual evolutionary process (Lewotin 1983, Rubin, Bukowski and Panker 2006).

Niche construction theory (NCT) studies NC as a reciprocal causation phenomenon: product and cause of evolution. It incorporates biological and social knowledge of the human sciences (Kendal, Tehrani and Odling-Smee 2011).

NC is a type of extra-genetic heritance previously called "exploitive system" (Waddington 1959), "ontogenetic inheritance" (West et al. 1988), or "ecological inheritance" (Odling-Smee 1988, Odling-Smee, Laland and Feldman 1996).

DOI: 10.4324/9781003355014-8

There are two time scales of phenotypes optimisation: ontogeny and phylogeny.

Developmental niche construction (DNC) ontogenetically acts via feedback between organisms and the resources of their own niches (examples of ontogenetic niches are culture and parents); selective niche construction (SNC) phylogenetically acts with natural selection by modifying selection pressures via feedback across generations (e.g. ecological inheritance) (Constant et al. 2018).

SNC refers to ecological niches (environmental factors produced by organisms) casually influencing inclusive fitness (survival and reproduction rate), while DNC refers to inherited epistemic, social, and physical resources enabling the "reconstruction of the species-typical developmental trajectory" (Constant et al. 2018).

Cities, as the quintessential examples of niche construction, are "ecosystem engineering" (Odling-Smee et al. 2013) representing a selective pressure in the form of "heritable information" acting "on behavior, cognition, and health" (Downey 2016).

In this sense, niches are both environmental and behavioural (Marlowe 2005).

Odling-Smee (1995), when comparing NC with epistasis (phenotypes resulting from genes interaction at different loci), suggests NC as potentially more significant than epistasis in evolution. NC in fact provides an external (rather than internal) route for the gene interactions at different loci. This happens via the modification of selection pressures which NC (expression of genes extended phenotypes) induces. The latter persists as long as NC remains, contrarily to genetic recombination via sexual reproduction which broke epistasis.

Mathematical population-genetic studies (Odling-Smee et al. 2003, Laland et al. 2000, 1999, 1996, Ihara and Feldman 2004, Borenstein et al. 2006) have explored NC feedback loops, demonstrating relevant micro-evolutionary dynamics (Flynn et al. 2013, Kylafis and Loreau 2008, Laland et al. 1996, 1999, Odling-Smee et al. 2003, Silver and Di Paolo 2006). Their results are in line with quantitative genetic studies (Wolf 2000), revealing momentum effects (direction of evolution continues even after selection ends), time lags (when selection is not as fast as environmental changes), inertia (tendency to resist current adaptive pressures), and abrupt catastrophic responses to selection (Laland et al. 2009, 2001, 1999, 1996, Robertson 1991, Feldman and Cavalli-Sforza 1976).

Equation 8.1 simplifies the evolutionary change in organisms where the organism state (O) changes (dO) over time (dt) in response to O and environmental states (E), determining the evolutionary change in organisms (dO/dt). In standard evolutionary theory, the change in E over time depends only on E itself (Eq. 8.1b), while in NCT it depends also on the organism (Eq. 8.1c) (Kendal, Tehrani and Odling-Smee 2011, Lewontin 1983):

$$(a)\ \frac{dO}{dt} = f(O,E); \quad (b)\ \frac{dE}{dt} = g(E); \quad (c)\ \frac{dE}{dt} = g(E,O) \quad (8.1)$$

When NC creates environments lasting multiple generations, it becomes an external heritable environment, or, as Dawkins (2004, 1982, 1976) calls it, a form of extended phenotype.

For humans NC depends considerably on social behaviour and culture, which in this perspective are seen as a type of epigenetic transmission.

Culture – for which Dawkins coined the term "meme" in his parallel with genes – replicates, mutates, and evolves. Similarly named as "group-level cultural traits for direct environmental control" (Waring et al. 2024), what ultimately creates cities and their typologies is culture, which in turn is promoted and constrained by our species' genome in an inextricable dynamic interplay between genes and culture: gene-culture coevolution (Richerson and Boyd 2004), the application of sociobiology (Gintis 2011).

8.2 Economic geography and geographical psychology perspectives: niche picking

NC alters social, biotic, and abiotic environments, which individuals are to some extent free to choose, though not always. When organisms select their preferred niche, gene–environment correlation can appear – namely a correlation between genotype frequencies and environment types (Saltz and Nuzhdin 2014).

Intrapopulation genetic variation in traits determining NC has been observed for animals' genome variation in habitat preferences (Jaenike and Holt 1991), plant genotypes variation in the habitats they choose to germinate in (Donohue et al. 2005a,b), and genetic differences in group size preferences among birds (Brown and Brown 2000) and fruits flies (Saltz 2011).

Theories of heterogeneous environment (Gillespie and Turelli 1989) embrace the vision that environment variations are random in relation to genotype, and eventual gene–environment correlations might be caused by the fact that individuals first randomly experience environments, *then* some genotypes get selected. This vision is in contrast to *active* gene–environment correlations, seeing genotype differences as the original cause determining the systemic experience of specific environments.

Human behaviours and the formation of preferences are more complex than those of fruit flies, nevertheless geographical psychology – the study of spatial organisation of psychological phenomena – reports a significantly recurrent spatial pattern of psychological traits distribution.

In active gene–environment correlations, individuals seek out environments fitting their personalities, abilities, and/or needs. For the lucky ones these four factors (environment – in its wider meaning – personality, abilities, and needs) combine; for many, pay-off evaluations occur; and for others, in various degree constrained in their preferred choices, pay-off evaluations cannot even occur, or if so into a very limited extent.

If the variety of environmental typologies is sufficient to suit everyone's desired niche, a stabilised balancing selection might occur (Penke and Jokela 2016).

Various studies have reported associations between extroversion-creativity-sociability and migration propensity (Oishi 2010, Rentfrow et al. 2015, Jokela 2009, Boneva et al. 1998), especially from isolated locations such as islands and rural areas (Camperio and Capiluppi 2011, Jokela et al. 2008). The same was found for intelligence (Jokela 2014), while agreeable personalities tend to stay in their own hometowns (Rentfrow et al. 2015, Jokela 2009, Jokela et al. 2008, Boneva et al. 1998).

People with higher openness and extroversion are also associated with higher life satisfaction when they live in greater population rather than isolated rural areas (Murray et al. 2005).

Studies in the US and UK have linked higher agreeableness with rural regions and low density, higher openness with urban denser regions, and lower neuroticism with warmer regions (Rentfrow et al. 2015).

Such empirical geographical differences in personalities might be due to three phenomena (Rentfrow et al. 2015):

1 Social influence,
2 Ecological influence,
3 Selective migration.

Social influence refers to traditions and lifestyles (social norms) which impact people's attitudes and their behaviours. Ecological influence refers to the physical environment impacting people's behaviours, feelings, and thoughts. Selective migration considers people migrating to environments in line with their own psychological features (Rentfrow et al. 2015, see also introversion, Cain 2012).

In which measure these three factors affect regional personality differences is still partially an open question and there are currently no longitudinal studies apart from those related to psychological disorders linked with urbanicity levels (D'Acci 2020).

Some studies tend to suggest selective migration (Jokela 2009, Jokela et al. 2008, Boneva et al. 1998, Oishi 2010), while social influence could impact mood and emotions, and ecological influence has an effect on lifestyles and type of activities (e.g. stimulating environments could boost curiosity and open-mindedness, Rentfrow et al. 2015).

The role which individual behaviour-decisions play when they aggregate emerging in spatial distribution patterns has been recognised also in economic geography since the 1970s (Pred 1967).

In this field we are recently assisting an emergence/resurgence of psychological and behavioural approaches in studying decision-making processes of individuals. The latter are seen as somehow affected by the environment in which they evolved (Kahneman 2003, Huggins and Thompson 2019).

Economists are rethinking utility functions in behavioural and psychological terms when studying people's trade-off utility function arguments, as happiness, in their spatial decisions (D'Acci 2021, Frey 2020, Cardoso et al. 2018, Glaeser et al. 2014). The "central premise" of evolutionary anthropology itself is understanding behaviour as a function of costs and benefits of actions, similarly to the utility maximisation in economics (Gibson and Lawson 2015, Nettle et al. 2013).

The study of individual behaviours and related spatial culture and spatial personality psychology assembling in collective emergence is discussed within the urban and regional sciences too (Sachs

2000, Tubadji and Nijkamp 2015, Clark 2018, Obschonka et al. 2013, Huggins and Thompson 2019).

Subareas of geographical psychology (Rentfrow 2013) include spatial distribution of psychological features, psychological foundations of residential mobility, and physical environment influence on behaviours (Rentfrow et al. 2013, 2009, 2008, McCrae et al. 2005).

9 Future of urban living?

Abstract

Excluding cyborgs and genetically modified humans designed to live in any chosen habitats, and rejecting the possibility for human evolution to promptly catch up with their recent rapidly transforming niche constructions, a pragmatic solution would be to build our niches in a way that accommodates as much as possible our, even though plastic, nature: a gregarious animal needing: a certain level of social life; a few in-depth quality relationships; enriched environments to fulfil-fuel our creativity and intelligence, but not too enriched to avoid overloads; regular natural experiences in open air, parks, woodlands, lakes and the likes.

9.1 Balancing decisions

How many of us are lucky enough to say that they live in their truly preferred place?

It would be a fortunate scenario to have your residential location in your ideal place coinciding with the place of your work and main family activities.

As in most decisions, deciding where to live is a compromise. One desires a coastal town but cannot find the job she wants; one a mountain village but no cultural amenities he likes are nearby; one a rural hamlet but no colleges and universities for her children are nearby; and so on.

Among the main factors in the decisional process of internal migration (an adjustment process following variable priorities during

DOI: 10.4324/9781003355014-9

a lifetime) there are housing costs, wages, social capital, life style, commuting costs, and family.

These types of compromises have been formalised modelling cities between spatial benefits and costs for decades (e.g. Fujita, 2009, Glaeser 2008).

Bigger cities are usually attractive for their higher wages (Bettencourt 2013, Batty 2008) – though not always for the poorest (Heinrich Mora et al. 2021) and the less skilled (Autor 2019) – but also for their amenities, aesthetics, and public services (Florida 2004). However, it is typically in smaller settlements where the majority seems happier, more satisfied, and with lower rates of mental issues (D'Acci 2021).

Even dismissing risks and uncertainties, namely assuming one has all the information of present and future scenarios linked with locations, it appears clear how subjective the balancing process is and how difficult it is to evaluate benefits and costs.

Such difficulty is exacerbated by the fact that it is a life-changing decision often rare if not unique, such as decisions about life partner, education, and emigration, thus offering little chance to learn from past experiences and carrying enormous consequences for one's life path and, partially, that of one's descendants. One can still change her locational decision, but not without relevant costs, monetary and not.

9.2 New urban functional forms

Decisions about where to live are getting more relaxed through faster and cheaper mobility opportunities altering the patterns of proximities to workplaces, services, and amenities.

New forms of urban living have been known since Martinotti's "new social morphology of cities" (1996) where he described new forms of urban dwellers-users, or of "populations" (intended as an aggregate of individuals with one or more common traits).

Departing from the traditional city in which city *inhabitants* and city *workers* largely coincided and lived in the same spatial unit, from the 1920s in the USA and after the Second World War in Europe, a growing differentiation between inhabitants and workers occurred due to the daily commuting capacity of the latter. The first generation of metropolis, or *early metropolis*, appeared. When subsequent times allowed increased mobility, income, and leisure, a new type of urban population arose: the city *users* – those who go to the city only to use its services (shops, cinemas, theatres, libraries, restaurants, historical monuments, museums …). These were the times of the second generation of metropolis, or *mature metropolis*, characterised by a *functional urban system* or a *daily urban system*. The last type of population is a small (although growing), specialised class of *metropolitan businessmen* who go to various central cities for business. It is a transnational [but could also be national] middle-class living between cities, defining the third generation of metropolis, or *late metropolis*.

Lenzi and Perucca (2021) linked these relatively new urban functional forms with subjective well-being and life satisfaction, emphasising how the cost–benefits trade-off of urbanicity levels changes when we consider the above non-traditional city and population definition, as spillover effects spread outside the large city reaching smaller cities, villages, and rural settlements around, in a kind of "borrowed-size" effect. People can somehow enjoy the benefits of both lower and higher urbanicity levels: a concept which is also called the "pseudo-countryside" (in its *hybrid* lifestyle use): living in a rural settlement, but within commuting distance from an urban labour market (Booi et al. 2020, Heins 2004, Green 1997).

9.3 Means and proxy of residential location preferences: telework/services, internal migration, and house prices

Counter-urbanisation[1] processes in rich countries started many decades ago, often not "just" for cheaper life and housing issues, but for lifestyle preferences alone,[2] facilitated by work flexibility coupled with improvements in transportation, information, and communication technologies.[3]

Being the workplace one of the most significant factors affecting the decisional process of an individual when having to make a trade-off calculation of pros and cons among locations where to live, when it is relaxed by various degrees of flexibility – from partial to full

1 Zhang et al. (2025), Scott et al. (2025), Berry (1976).

2 Argent and Plummer (2022), Dilley et al. (2022), Anastasiou and Duquenne (2020), Karsten (2020), Bosworth and Bat Finke (2020), Sandow and Lundholm (2019), Hansen and Aner (2017), Aner (2016), Eimermann (2015), Benson and Osbaldiston (2014), Benson and O'Reilly (2009), Mitchell (2004).

3 Vilhelmson and Thulin (2013).

telework[4] – all the residential location patterns profoundly change and with that, giving enough time, the entire region's physical, social, economic, and infrastructural systems.

The recent pandemic (Covid-19) period boosted the earlier mentioned new functional forms of urban living, enhanced by the opportunity of remote working and teleservices and by the greater attention that individuals are increasingly giving to quality of life when balancing their spatial location decisions to optimise their personal overall utility functions.

If it is true that a certain majority of people would prefer to live in smaller settlements provided the same income and career prospects and sufficient access to services, we would expect to see a migration from bigger cities to smaller ones if teleworking and teleservices are a valuable option.

This is what actually often happened around the world during the pandemic period: bigger cities lost population in favour of smaller ones that gained it.[5]

If infrastructural and social urban forms are polarising people into cities, it is expected (*ceteris paribus*) to see higher house prices there rather than in smaller settlements, as a basic principle of the demand and supply equilibrium price, especially when the demand is growing against supply constraints.

However, the above-mentioned new ways of urban living, enhanced by the sudden teleservices and telework of the Covid-19 times, are already reflected in changes in housing prices across settlement sizes: smaller settlements such as towns, villages, and countryside reported an increase in housing price against a decrease in the bigger ones.

4 Versigghel et al. (2026), Bosworth (2026), Vilhelmson (2026), Kuzmar et al. (2026), Sánchez-Moral et al. (2026), Clarke (2025), Alexander et al. (2021).

5 Such behaviour, although to some extent probably temporary, of post COVID-19 pandemic weakening population in urban contexts (Florida et al. 2021) has been reported in Scotland (BBC, 2022), Germany (Stawarz et al 2022), Japan (Fielding and Ishikawa 2021), Sweden (Vogiazides and Kawalerowicz 2022), Spain (González-Leonardo et al. 2022), United Kingdom (Rowe et al. 2023), Australia (Borsellino et al. 2022), United States (Whitaker 2021), and in many other countries around the world we read newspaper titles (although sometimes speculative and too journalistic) about people finally being free to "escape" from big cities towards smaller settlements or rural villages (*The Economist* 2021; *The Globe and Mail* 2021, *The Guardian* 2020; *The Sydney Morning Herald* 2021; *The New York Times* 2020).

This house price change pattern seeing rural outperforming urban demand and related prices has been consistently reported in various world regions.[6]

It seems that remote work and remote services are enabling some people to reside in their preferred lower urbanicity levels, whose effect is to invert the typical association between urban size and house prices. House price and internal immigration rates when teleservices and remote working became the norm both exhibited a rise in smaller settlements and a decline in bigger ones. If this was a mirror of people locational preferences, it could anticipate a future trend.

It is challenging to disentangle the actual contribution that teleworking and teleservices alone played in the "escaping" from the cities towards smaller settlement sizes. It might equally be an escaping from lockdowns and mandatory teleworking and related need for bigger *houses* rather than an escaping from the *cities*.

9.4 Future urban living?

Technological improvements in industries, workplaces, transport and communications, plus new (consequent to the formers) urban-territorial design, could profoundly transform our socio-economic system, freeing us up to decide to live where we prefer rather than where we need. We will be able to relax trade-off compromises in our residential location decisions.

Probably cities will exist until agglomeration economies, in their broadest sense, exceed or at least balance – subjectively, objectively, or in the expectations (D'Acci 2021) – agglomeration diseconomies. The traditional way to achieve agglomeration economies is by proximity.

Some, since the 1980s–1990s (e.g. Naisbitt 1995, Negroponte 1995, Knoke 1996, Toffler 1980), think that we will not live in cities due to the new technology in telecommunications, while others believe that "telecommunications may be a complement to, or at least not a strong substitute for, cities and face-to-face interactions" (Gaspar and Glaeser 1998, p. 136).

6 Ziemann et al. (2023), Gupta et al. (2021), Biljanovska and Dell'Ariccia (2023, 2024), McCord et al. (2022), Aliefendioğlu et al. (2022), Choudhry (2022), Zhai and Peng (2021), Duca et al. (2021), BBC (2021), Peachey (2021), Defra (2021), Booth (2021).

The need for face-to-face interaction is an atavistic reminiscence in our DNA as we are (still) social primates, so a better question might be: in what *type* of settlements will we prefer to live?

A near global real laboratory to test what could happen if people are free to work, consume, and use services remotely took place during the Covid-19 lockdowns. It has been consistently reported that people moved away from bigger cities towards smaller settlements and countryside, also indirectly mirrored by increase of house pricing in the latter versus a decrease in the former.

If this internal migration was indeed motivated by locational preferences alone, it offers an indication of what could happen in the future if most daily life activities could occur online. This is also evident from people who expressed residential preferences, happiness, and life satisfaction in richer countries, where they are in fact abler to decide where to live in relation to their poorest counterparts due to better diffused infrastructures, services, and capacity to commute.

"The clustering of like activities – agglomeration economies – inside the city and between them may well loosen. In fact much will depend on what we value as to where we locate" (Batty 2023). In this regard, the literature rather consistently shows that most people,[7] roughly two-thirds, value more to live not in the city (D'Acci 2021). I wonder if these two-thirds would change their mind if next generations of cities would be radically different (e.g. Isobenefit Urbanism), removing their negative aspects (e.g. congestions, pollution, life speed, stress, lack of nature ...) while enhancing their positives such as vibrancy, freedom-privacy for anonymity, face-to-face encounters, and variety. Or perhaps even that one-third would escape from cities to the countryside if the latter gained easy access to all the services, amenities, and encounters typical of the bigger city. Or maybe, because of both the above points – cities getting more attractive and countryside and smaller settlements getting more access (virtually and physically) to quintessentially urban elements – we might easily enjoy the wide spectrum of urbanicity levels living, e.g. in a rural cottage, daily visiting the adjacent village, weekly the nearby towns and cities, and monthly the closer megacity. Or vice versa.

7 In the non-poorest regions. In the poorest, cities are preferred probably for lack of basic infrastructure and services in the countryside, and/or people not rich enough to commute to the closest bigger city.

Past and recent evidences show that life satisfaction is higher in smaller settlements neither too close nor too far away from big cities (Lenzi and Perucca 2021, Fuguitt and Zuiches 1975).

I don't think we need to denaturalise the actual spirit of each urbanicity level which settlements have according to their sizes, densities, and typologies. Bucolic rural villages, intimate towns, anonymous cities, effervescent megacities should keep their own essence without attempting to ruralise cities or urbanise villages with the benevolent intention to make them more attractive to live in.

Contrarily, we should maintain the rich variety of urbanicity levels and settlements typologies so that each of us can pick the best lifestyles whished for. This would be also in line (by cautious analogy) with our atavistic landscape preferences which were found to be towards landscape mosaics rather than uniform environments.

Once voluntary remote working services become the norm, and improved transport technologies and management enable fast, cheap, comfortable trips, there will probably be a spontaneous spatial distribution of residents only following their own locational desires. If we rely on the literature about residential locational preference, we could see how even roughly half of current urban dwellers would be happy to move to smaller settlements, while the opposite is not the case.[8]

If this is true, while keeping on enhancing megacities efficiency and liveability, we should also focus our attention on smaller settlements, facilitating this spontaneous process that could happen soon based on people's locational true preferences.

Using the concept of *morphospace* of evolutionary biology – all *possible* forms that an organism could have – we can extend it to societies (Christakis 2019), and settlements (from isolated cottages to megacities): within the *Urban Morphospace*, what type(s) of *possible* settlement *best* fit our human nature while also allowing us to progress as much as we can towards our cumulative, ever-increasing societal/personal betterment? Or, given our species' (epi)genetic makeup and cultural variations, assuming related kind of "universal" basic bricks across settlement types offering elements of liveability – defined according to our species features[9] – and calling such bricks

8 Unless the future types of settlements along their population size spectrum change in a way to alter such preferences.

9 That is, proximity to proper green spaces, services, and centralities (e.g. pleasant pedestrian squares, promenades, amenities), fostering connectedness, yet avoiding

urban (or more generic, settlement) DNA, or urban genetic code:[10] what are the norms of reactions[11] of our settlement's DNA allowing us to live healthy, efficiently, and happily? The morphospace is the map of all possible settlement types; if we normatively fix (settlement DNA) some basic and near-universal (human nature) requirements which such types should have (even if taking into account cultural and adaptation variabilities), what are all the potential settlement's making us fully flourishing? I believe they are numerous, particularly if this typological spectrum is interpreted flexibly and allows frequent and promiscuous mobility within it.

widespread overcrowding, pollution, congestion, and so on. See, for example, Isobenefit Urbanism or other approaches aiming at such settlement outcomes.

10 For example Isobenefit urbanism genotype (D'Acci 2019a, 2025a).

11 See Chapter 7. In this urban metaphor it is to be intended as all the possible settlement phenotypes, "traits" (see D'Acci 2019a, 2025a) expressing their settlement common genotype: namely, fixing certain required features our settlements should have in order to be liveable and efficient, in how many forms can such features still be expressed?

Afterthoughts

I almost entirely wrote this book between 11 and 7 years ago, mostly when I was the Head of Urban Environment at the Erasmus Universiteit Rotterdam and during my affiliation at the Erasmus School of Social and Behavioural Sciences where I also developed a PhD course titled "Nature and Nurture – *Homo sapiens* in cities". But I never finished the last chapter and the conclusive thoughts until this summer, when I also updated the overall literature.

I tried to write this book without being biased by my preferences and beliefs.[1] I hope to have succeeded in this and maintained a neutral view by directly reporting and combining research outputs across disciplines.

We saw[2] that comparisons with our closest apes and our ancestors' lives – until not many generations ago – suggest that humans, despite behaviourally genetically able to also reckon larger social structures than the group, preferred to daily live in small groups. Even if these groups had not permanent members, they still permanently lived in groups, and within a much larger community which was occasionally but regularly met.

1 I love both village and megacity life as long as they are healthy, beautiful, and interesting places. However, I would prefer a daily countryside/village life with regular contact with a near town (twice a week), and a near big/megacity (twice a month), or the other way around with a few days per week (plus a few months per year) in the countryside/village. I think this is a good balance for a good life, taking the best of each environment in a proportion, which, interestingly, seems in line with our evolutionary tendency.

2 Chapter 2.

Despite this genetic inheritance suggesting that it enables us to reckon and deal with strangers of greater populations, when obliged[3] to *daily* live in big cities rather than smaller settlements, mental issues rate increases and happiness, life satisfaction, and residential preference worsen.[4] Many scholars across disciplines – and common-educated-sense – suggest that our big cities emerged too quickly[5] for our genetic makeup to catch up with their polluted, noisy, indoor, crowded, congested, nature-deprived,[6] estranged, overstimulated, and hectic daily lifestyles. This might be a reason for the empirical evidence of worse mental aspects in urban living.

However, cities are not imposed by aliens; we created them over time (even if short regarding megacities) and, often, rather "spontaneously" people decided to live in them. For this aspect big cities are still natural to us. This doesn't mean that they are our ideal habitats and the only option we have to prosper and progress. We now have the technology and management capabilities to depend less on physical proximity to enjoy the economies of scale and of agglomeration, which were/are the main reason for the (big) cities existence… at least for most[7] of us. We also have the tools and skills to make liveable and pleasant the big cities for those who prefer living there either permanently or occasionally.

Big cities are not the result of explicit enforcement of people to live there letting them grow into larger settlements. Cities are the unplanned outputs of cumulative cost-benefit alike decision-making over generations; they are a side effect of our human progress. Nobody one day woke up saying "let's build unnatural megacities". It was an irreversible (so far) chain reaction mostly driven by economies of scale/agglomeration. Once certain groups gained advantages through urban scale, others had to follow or fall behind. Humans walked this urban path which wasn't designed or planned, but (if we don't like it) we can start stepping away from it due to the new non-physical ways to achieve economies of scale/agglomeration, as well as to enjoy services and earn money. Humans are not victims of cities and megacities; they are the authors of a story none wrote. But today

3 Chapter 4.
4 Chapters 5 and 6.
5 Chapters 7 and 8.
6 Chapter 3.
7 We saw that roughly one-third *love big* urban life regardless.

we can rewrite this story *if* it is not the one we want, by (re)valorising smaller settlements and making big cities more pleasant.

The shimmering allure of cities should draw us as bees to flowers, not as mosquitoes to zappers.

We are already going towards that direction as we see increasingly more often a beautification process of cities, and I am certain that this betterment route will create cities and settlements so attractive and agreeable as to proudly epitomise one of the greatest physical manifestations of human intellect.

Luca S. D'Acci
Hampshire, England, August 2025
Piedmont, Italy, March 2026

References

Abbott A. (2012). Stress and the city: Urban decay. Scientists are testing the idea that the stress of modern city life is a breeding ground for psychosis. *Nature*, 490(7419):162–164.

Abernethy K.A., White L.J.T., Wickings E.J. (2002). Hordes of mandrills (*Mandrillus sphinx*): Extreme group size and seasonal male presence. *Journal of Zoology*, 258:131–137.

Abrahamyan Empson L., Baumann P.S., Söderström O., Codeluppi Z., Söderström D., Conus P. (2020). Urbanicity: The need for new avenues to explore the link between urban living and psychosis. *Early Intervention in Psychiatry*, 14(4):398–409.

Abshire D.A., Graves J.M., Amiri S., Williams-Gilbert W. (2022). Differences in loneliness across the rural-urban continuum among adults living in Washington State. *Journal of Rural Health*, 38(1):187–193.

Adams J., Stamp E., Nettle D., Milne E.M.G., Jagger C. (2014). Socioeconomic position and the association between anticipated and actual survival in older English adults. *Journal of Epidemiology and Community Health*, 68:818–825.

Adams R.E. (1992). Is happiness a home in the suburbs? The influence of urban versus suburban neighborhoods on psychological health. *Journal of Community Psychology*, 20(4):353–372.

Adli M. et al. (2016). Neurourbanism—a joint methodological approach between urban planning and neurosciences. *Die Psychiatrie*, 13:70–78.

Adli M. et al. (2017). Neurourbanism: Towards a new discipline. *The Lancet Psychiatry*, 4(3):183–185.

Adli M., Schöndorf J. (2020). Does the city make us ill? The effect of urban stress on emotions, behavior, and mental health. [Macht uns die Stadt krank? Wirkung von Stadtstress auf Emotionen, Verhalten und psychische Gesundheit] *Bundesgesundheitsblatt – Gesundheitsforschung – Gesundheitsschutz*, 63(8):979–986.

Aguilar-Melo A.R., Calmé S., Pinacho-Guendulain B., Smith-Aguilar S.E., Ramos-Fernández G. (2019). Ecological and social determinants of association and proximity patterns in the fission–fusion society of spider monkeys (*Ateles geoffroyi*). *American Journal of Primatology*, 82(1):e23077.

Alcock I., White M.P., Wheeler B.W., Fleming L.E., Depledge M.H. (2014). Longitudinal effects on mental health of moving to greener and less green urban areas. *Environmental Science and Technology*, 48:1247–1255.

Alcock J. (1989). *Animal behavior: An evolutionary approach* (4th ed.) Sinauer Associates, Sunderland, MA.

Alexander A., Cracknell R., De Smet A., Langstaff M., Mysore M., Ravid D. (2021). *What executives are saying about the future of hybrid work*. McKinsey & Company, New York.

Aliefendioğlu Y., Tanrivermis H., Salami M.A. (2022). House price index (HPI) and covid-19 pandemic shocks: Evidence from Turkey and Kazakhstan. International Journal of Housing Markets and Analysis, 15(1):108–125.

Allardyce J., Boydell J., van Os J., Morrison G., Castle D., Murray R.M., McCreadie R.G. (2001). Comparison of the incidence of schizophrenia in rural Dumfries and Galloway and urban Camberwell. *British Journal of Psychiatry*, 179:335–339.

Altman I. (1975). *The environment and social behavior: Privacy, personal space, territory, and crowding*. Brooks/Cole, Monterey, CA.

Alvergne A., Lummaa V. (2014). Ecological variation in wealth-fertility in Mongolia: The ‘central theoretical 0004657711.INDD 283 Dictionary: NOSD problem of sociobiology’ not a problem after all? *Proceedings of the Royal Society B: Biological Sciences*, 281:20141733.

Anastasiou E., Duquenne M. (2020). Determinants and spatial patterns of counterurbanization in times of crisis: Evidence from Greece. *Population Review*, 59(2):85–110.

Aner L.G. (2016). Dwelling habitus and urban out-migration in Denmark. *European Urban and Regional Studies*, 23(4):662–676.

Appleton J. (1996). *The experience of landscape*. Wiley, New York.

Aristotle (2009). *Aristotle the nicomachean ethics*. Oxford University Press, New York.

Argent N., Plummer P. (2022). Counter-urbanisation in pre-pandemic times: Disentangling the influences of amenity and disamenity. *Australian Geographer*, 53(4):379–403.

Aureli F. et al. (2008). Fission-fusion dynamics new research frameworks. *Current Anthropology*, 49(4):627–654.

Autor D. (2019). *Work of the past, work of the future*. Working Paper 25588.

Baker B.S., Taylor B.J., Hall J.C. (2001). Are complex behaviors specified by dedicated regulatory genes? *Cell*, 105(1):13–24.

Balling J.D., Falk J.H. (1982). Development of visual preferences for natural environments. *Environment and Behavior*, 1:5–28.

Balter M. (2005). Are humans still evolving? *Science AAAS* New Series, 309(5732):234–237.

Baran N.M., McGrath P.T., Streelman J.T. (2017). Gene regulatory network logic and social behavior. *Proceedings of the National Academy of Sciences of the United States of America*, 114(23):5886–5893.

Barlow F.K. (2019). Nature vs. nurture is nonsense: On the necessity of an integrated genetic, social, developmental, and personality psychology. *Australian Journal of Psychology*, 71:68–79.

Barnes I., Duda A., Pybus O.G., Thomas M.G. (2011). Ancient urbanization predicts genetic resistance to tuberculosis. *Evolution*, 65(3):842–848.

Barrett R.D., Schluter D. (2008). Adaptation from standing genetic variation. *Trends in Ecology & Evolution*, 23:38–44.

Batty M. (2008). The size, scale, and shape of cities. *Science*, 319(5864):769–771.

Batty M. (2018). *Inventing future cites*. MIT Press, Cambridge, MA; London.

Batty M. (2023). The post-pandemic world: Are big cities hollowing out? *Environment and Planning B: Urban Analytics and City Science*, 50(6):1409–1412.

Baxter A.J., Scott K.M., Vos T., Whiteford H.A. (2013). Global prevalence of anxiety disorders: A systematic review and meta-regression. *Psychological Medicine*, 43:897–910.

BBC (2021). Urban flight' raises house prices in villages. *BBC News*, London. www.bbc.co.uk/news/business-56945217

BBC (2022). More people in Scotland swap cities for rural life. *BBC News*, London. www.bbc.co.uk/news/uk-scotland-62149061.

Beauchamp J.P. (2016). Genetic evidence for natural selection in humans in the contemporary United States. *Proceedings of the National Academy of Sciences of the United States of America*, 113:7774–7779.

Beccaria C. (1764). *Dei delitti e delle pene*. Coltellini Press (Giuseppe Aubert), Livorno.

Bedrosian T.A., Nelson R.J. (2013). Influence of the modern light environment on mood. *Molecular Psychiatry*, 18:751–757.

Beer A., Faulkner D., Law J., Lewin G., Tinker A., Buys L., … & Chessman S. (2016). Regional variation in social isolation amongst older Australians. *Regional Studies, Regional Science*, 3:170–184.

Bell D.H. (1992). The law clinic as a regional center: Looking for solutions to rural southern housing problems. *The Washington University Journal of Urban and Contemporary Law*, 42:101–126.

Bell P.A., Greene T.C., Fisher J.D., Baum A. (2001). *Environmental psychology*. Taylor & Francis, New York.

Belsky J., Bakermans-Kranenburg M.J., van IJzendoorn M.H. (2007). For better and for worse: Differential susceptibility to environmental influences. *Current Directions in Psychological Science*, 16(6):300–304.

Bender B. (1993). *Landscape: Politics and perspectives*. Berg, Oxford.

Bendesky A., Bargmann C. (2011). Genetic contributions to behavioural diversity at the gene–environment interface. *Nature Reviews Genetics*, 12:809–820.

Benjamin D.J., Heffetz O., Kimball M.S., Rees-Jones A. (2011). What do you think would make you happier? What do you think you would choose? *American Economic Review*, 102(5):2083–2110.

Benson M., Osbaldiston N. (Eds.) (2014). *Understanding lifestyle migration*. Palgrave Macmillan, London.

Benson M., O'Reilly K. (2009). Migration and the search for a better way of life: A critical exploration of lifestyle migration. *The Sociological Review*, 57(4):608–625.

Bentall R.P., Fernyhough C. (2008). Social predictors of psychotic experiences: Specificity and psychological mechanisms. *Schizophrenia Bullettin*, 34:1012–1020.

Bentham J. (1776). *A fragment on government*. Reprint: Harrison R. (Eds) (2012). *Bentham: A fragment on government*. Cambridge University Press, Cambridge; New York; Melbourne, VIC.

Bentham J. (1789). *An introduction to the principles of morals and legislation*. Reprinted: Dover Philosophical Classics (2007), New York.

Benton J.R., DiYanni R. (2012). *Arts and culture: An introduction to the humanities*. Prentice Hall, Englewood Cliffs, NJ.

Berghe van den P. (1975). *Man in society: A biosocial view*. Elsevier, New York.

Berman M.G, Jonides J., Kaplan S. (2008). The cognitive benefits of interacting with nature. *Psychological Science*, 19(12):1207–1212.

Berman M.G., Kross E., Krpan K.M., Askren M.K., Burson A., Deldin P.J., Kaplan S., Sherdell L., Gotlib I.H., Jonides J. (2012). Interacting with nature improves cognition and affect for individuals with depression. *Journal of Affective Disorders*, 140(3):300–305.

Berretta E., Cutuli D., Laricchiuta D., Petrosini L. (2011). From animal to human epigenetics. Developmental human behavioral epigenetics. Principles, methods, evidence, and future directions. *Translational Epigenetics*, 23:27–58.

Berridge K.E., O'Doherty J.P. (2013). From experienced utility to decision utility. In: Glimcher P.W., Fehr E. (Eds.), *Neuroeconomics* (2nd ed.) (pp. 335–351). Academic Press.

Berry B. (1976). *Urbanisation and counterurbanisation*. Sage Publications, Beverly Hills.

Berry B.J.L., Okulicz-Kozaryn A. (2009). Dissatisfaction with city life: A new look at some old questions. *Cities*, 26:117–124.

Berry B.J.L., Okulicz-Kozaryn A. (2013). An urban-rural happiness gradient. *Urban Geography*, 32(6):871–883.

Berto R. (2005). Exposure to restorative environments helps restore attentional capacity. *Journal of Environmental Psychology*, 25:249–259.

Besteher B., Gaser C., Spalthoff R., Nenadić I. (2017). Associations between urban upbringing and cortical thickness and gyrification. *Journal of Psychiatric Research*, 95:114–120.

Bettencourt L.M.A. (2013). The origins of scaling in cities. *Science*, 340(6139):1438–1441.

Bettencourt L.M.A., Lobo J., Helbing D., Kühnert C., West G.B. (2007). Growth, innovation, scaling, and the pace of life in cities. *Proceedings of the National Academy of Sciences of the United States of America*, 104(17):7301–7306.

Beyer K.M.M., Kaltenbach A., Szabo A., Bogar S., Nieto F.J., Malecki K.M. (2014). Exposure to neighborhood green space and mental health: Evidence from the survey of the health of Wisconsin. *International Journal of Environmental Research and Public Health*, 11(3):3453–3472.

Biagi B., Meleddu M. (2024). Exploring urban–rural paradox: Does going rural mean higher life satisfaction? *Italian Economic Journal*, 10:795–823.

Biljanovska N., Dell'Ariccia G. (2023). *Flattening the curve and the flight of the rich: Pandemic-induced shifts in US and European housing markets*. IMF Working Paper 2023/266, International Monetary Fund, Washington, DC.

Biljanovska N., Dell'Ariccia G. (2024). *Reshaping the housing market: The enduring effects of the pandemic*. VoxEU (CEPR Column), CEPR, London.

Bird A. (2007). Perceptions of epigenetics. *Nature*, 447:396–398.

Bloom D.E. et al. (2011). *The global economic burden of noncommunicable diseases*. World Economic Forum, Geneva.

Bloom H. (2001). Instant evolution. The influence of the city on human genes: A speculative case. *New Ideas in Psychology*, 19(3):203–220.

Blouin A.M. et al. (2013). Human hyprocretin and melanin-concentrating hormone levels are linked to emotion and social interaction. *Nature Communications*, 4:1547.

Boden D., Molotch H.L. (1994). The compulsion of proximity. In: Friedland R., Boden D. (Eds.), *NoWhere: Space, time and modernity* (pp. 257–286). University of California Press, Berkeley, CA.

Boesch C. (2012). The ecology and evolution of social behavior and cognition in primates. In: Vonk J., Shackelford T.K. (Eds.), *The Oxford handbook of comparative evolutionary psychology*. Oxford University Press, Oxford.

Bollati V., Baccarelli A. (2010). Environmental epigenetics. *Heredity*, 105:105–112.

Bolund E., Hayward A., Pettay J.E., Lummaa V. (2015). Effects of the demographic transition on the genetic variances and covariances of human life-history traits. *Evolution*, 69:747–755.

Boneva B.S., Frieze I.H., Ferligoj A., Jarošová E., Pauknerová D., Orgocka A. (1998). Achievement, power, and affiliation motives as clues to (e) migration desires: A four-countries comparison. *European Psychologist*, 3:247–254.

Booi H., Boterman W.R. (2020). Changing patterns in residential preferences for urban or suburban living of city dwellers. *Journal of Housing and the Built Environonment*, 35:93–123.

Booij L. et al. (2016). Dopamine cross-sensitization between psychostimulant drugs and stress in healthy male volunteers. *Translational Psychiatry*, 6:e740.

Booth R. (2021). Rural house prices in England and Wales rise twice as fast as in cities. *The Guardian – Housing*. www.theguardian.com/society/2021/jun/20/rural-house-prices-in-england-and-wales-rise-twice-as-fast-as-in-cities.

Bor J., Cohen G.H., Galea S. (2017). Population health in an era of rising income inequality: USA, 1980–2015. *Lancet*, 389:1475–1490.

Borenstein E., Kendal J.R., Feldman M.W. (2006). Cultural niche construction in a metapopulation. *Theoretical Population Biology*, 70:92–104.

Borries C., Larney L., Lu A., Ossi K., Koenig A. (2008). Costs of group size: Lower developmental and reproductive rates in larger groups of leaf monkeys. *Behavioral Ecology*, 19:1186–1191.

Borsellino R., Bernard A., Charles-Edwards E., Corcoran J. (2022). A regional renaissance? The shifting geography of internal migration under COVID-19. *Australian Geographer*, *53*(4):405–423.

Bosworth G. (2026). Rural work, rural workers or working in the rural? In: Avdikos V., Schmidt S., Mariotti I., Capdevila I., Lang T., Fabinyi V. (Eds.), *Collaborative workspaces beyond the urban*. New Geographies of Europe. Palgrave Macmillan, Singapore.

Bosworth G., Bat Finke H. (2020). Commercial counterurbanisation: A driving force in rural economic development. *Environment and Planning A*, 52(3):654–674.

Bouchard T.J. (2014). Genetic influence on human psychological traits: A survey. *Current Directions in Psychological Science*, 13(4):148–151.

Bowler D.E., Buyung-Ali L.M., Knight T.M., Pullin A.S. (2010). A systematic review of evidence for the added benefits to health of exposure to natural environments. *BMC Public Health*, 10:456.

Bratman G.N., Hamilton J.P., Daily G.C. (2012). The impacts of nature experience on human cognitive function and mental health. *Annals of the New York Academy of Sciences*, 1249:118–136.

Brickman P., Campbell D.T. (1971). Hedonic relativism and planning the good science. In: Appley M.H. (Ed.), *Adaptation level theory: A symposium* (pp. 287–302). Academic Press, New York.

Brockmeyer S., D'Angiulli A. (2016). How air pollution alters brain development: The role of neuroinflammation. *Translational Neuroscience*, 7(1):24–30.

Broome J. (1991). Utility. *Economics and Philosophy*, 7:1–12.

Brown C.R., Brown M.B. (2000). Heritable basis for choice of group size in a colonial bird. *Proceedings of the National Academy of Sciences of the United States of America*, 97:14825–14830.

Buecker S., Eber T., Götz F.M., Entringer T.M., Luhmann M. (2021). In a lonely place: Investigating regional differences in loneliness. *Social Psychological and Personality Science*, 12(2):147–155.

Burger M.J., Morrison P.S., Hendriks M., Hoogerbrugge M.M. (2020). Urban-rural happiness differentials across the world. In: Helliwell J.F., Layard R., Sachs J.D., De Neve J.-E. (Eds.), *World happiness report 2020* (pp. 67–94). Sustainable Development Solutions Network, New York.

Burger O., DeLong J.P. (2016). What if fertility decline is not permanent? The need for an evolutionarily informed approach to understanding low fertility. *Philosophical Transactions of the Royal Society B*, 371:20150157.

Burholt V., Scharf T. (2014). Poor health and loneliness in later life: The role of depressive symptoms, social resources, and rural environments. *The Journals of Gerontology. Series B, Psychological Sciences and Social Sciences*, 69(2):311–324.

Buss D.M. (2019). *Evolutionary psychology: The new science of the mind* (6th ed.). Routledge.

Buttimer A., Cosgrove D. (1980). *The human experience of space and place*. Croom Helm, London.

Byars S.G., Ewbank D., Govindaraju D.R., Stearns S.C., Ellison P.T. (2010). Natural selection in a contemporary human population. *Proceedings of the National Academy of Sciences of the United States of America*, 107:1787–1792.

Byars S.G. et al. (2017). Genetic loci associated with coronary artery disease harbor evidence of selection and antagonistic pleiotropy. *PLoS Genetics*, 13:e1006328.

Cackowski J.M., Nasar J.L. (2003). The restorative effects of roadside vegetation: Implications for automobile driver anger and frustration. *Environment and Behavior*, 35:736–751.

Calabrese F., Dahlem D., Gerber A., DeDe P., Chen X., Rowland J., Rath C., Park F., Ratti C., (2011). "The Connected States of America: Quantifying Social Radii of Influence." *IEEE Third International Conference on Privacy, Security, Risk and Trust and 2011* IEEE Third International Conference on Social Computing, Boston, MA, USA, pp. 223–230.

Cain S. (2012). *Quiet: The power of introverts in a world that can't stop talking*. Crown Publishers, New York.

Calderón-Garcidueñas L. et al. (2013). Brain immune interactions and air pollution: Macrophage inhibitory factor (MIF), prion cellular protein (PrPC), Interleukin-6 (IL-6), interleukin 1 receptor antagonist (IL-1Ra), and interleukin-2 (IL-2) in cerebrospinal fluid and MIF in serum differentiate urban children exposed to severe vs. Low air pollution. *Frontiers in Neuroscience*, 7:183.

Calderón-Garcidueñas L., Torres-Jardon R., Kulesza R.J., Park S.B., D'Angiulli A. (2014). Air pollution and detrimental effects on children's brain. The need for a multidisciplinary approach to the issue complexity and challenges. *Frontiers in Human Neuroscience*, 8:613.

Calhoun J.B. (1950). The social behaviour of dogs and wolves: An illustration of sociobiological systematics. *New York Academy of Sciences*, 51:1113–1122.

Calhoun J.B. (1973). From mice to men. *Transactions & Studies of the College of Physicians of Philadelphia*, 41(2):92–118.

Camperio Ciani A.C., Capiluppi C. (2011). Gene flow by selective emigration as a possible cause for personality differences between small Islands and mainland populations. *European Journal of Personality*, 25:53–64.

Cardoso R., Meijers E., van Ham M., Burger M., de Vos D. (2018). Why bright city lights dazzle and illuminate: A cognitive science approach to urban promises. *Urban Studies*, 56(2):452–470.

Caspi A. et al. (2003). Influence of life stress on depression: Moderation by a polymorphism in the 5-HTT gene. *Science*, 301:386–389.

Cassarino M., Setti A. (2015). Environment as 'brain training': A review of geographical and physical environmental influences on cognitive ageing. *Ageing Research Reviews*, 23:167–182.

Castelli C., d'Hombres B., de Dominicis L., Dijkstra L., Montalto V., Pontarollo N. (2022). *What makes people in Europe satisfied with the city where they live*. Working paper WP 05/2022, European Commission.

Castillejos M.C., Martín-Pérez C., Moreno-Küstner B. (2018). A systematic review and meta-analysis of the incidence of psychotic disorders: The distribution of rates and the influence of gender, urbanicity, immigration and socio-economic level. *Psychological Medicine*, 48(13):2101–2115.

Champagne F.A. (2010). Epigenetic influence of social experiences across the lifespan. *Developmental Psychobiology*, 52(4):299–311.

Champagne F.A. (2013). Early environments, glucocorticoid receptors, and behavioural epigenetics. *Behavioral Neuroscience*, 127:628–636.

Chang H. et al (2018). The protocadherin 17 gene affects cognition, personality, amygdala structure and function, synapse development and risk of major mood disorders. *Molecular Psychiatry*, 23(2):400–412.

Chapman C.A., Chapman L.J. (2000). Constraints on group size in red colobus and red-tailed guenons: Examining the generality of the ecological constraints model. *International Journal of Primatology*, 21:565–585.

Chapman C.A., Teichroeb J.A. (2012). What influences the size of groups in which primates choose to live? *Nature Education Knowledge*, 3(10):9.

Chattarji S., Tomar A., Suvrathan A., Ghosh S., Rahman M.M. (2015). Neighborhood matters: Divergent patterns of stress-induced plasticity across the brain. *Nature Neuroscience*, 18:1364–1375.

Chen J., Davis D.S., Wu K., Dai H. (2015). Life satisfaction in urbanizing China: The effect of city size and pathways to urban residency. *Cities*, 49:88–97.

Chen W., Zaid S.M., Nazarali N. (2016). Environmental psychology: The urban built environment impact on human mental health. *Planning Malaysia*, 14(5):23–38.

Choldin H.M. (1978). Urban density and pathology. *Annual Review of Sociology*, 4:91–113.

Christakis N.A. (2019). *Blueprint: The evolutionary origins of a good society*. Little, Brown Spark, New York.

Christmas J.J. (1973). Psychological stresses of urban living: New direction for mental health services in the inner city. *Journal of the National Medical Association*, 65:483–486.

Chung H., van der Lippe T. (2020). Flexible working, work–life balance, and gender equality: Introduction. *Social Indicators Research*, 151(2):365–381.

Cieri R.L., Churchill S.E., Franciscus R.G., Tan J., Hare B. (2014). Craniofacial feminization, social tolerance, and the origins of behavioral modernity. *Current Anthropology*, 55(4):419–443.

Clark G.L. (2018). Behavior, cognition and context. In: Clark G.L., Feldman M., Gertler M.S., Wójcik D. (Eds.), *The new Oxford handbook of economic geography*. Oxford University Press, Oxford.

Clarke K. (2025). The impact of remote work on mobilities in the UK. *Regional Studies, Regional Science*, 12(1):472–487.

Cody M.L. (1971). Finch flocks in the Mojave desert. *Theoretical Population Biology*, 2:141–158.

Cohen P.A. (1982). *Calculating people: The spread of numeracy in early America*. University of Chicago Press, Chicago, IL.

Cohen S., Lezak A. (1977). Noise and inattentiveness to social cues. *Environment and Behavior*, 9(4):559–572.

Collins P.Y. et al. (2024). Making cities mental health friendly for adolescents and young adults. *Nature*, 627:137–148.

Constant A., Ramstead M.J.D., Veissière S.P.L., Campbell J.O., Friston K.J. (2018). Variational approach to niche construction. *Journal of the Royal Society Interface*, 15(141):20170685.

Cooper J.D., Ozcan S., Gardner R.M., Rustogi, N., Wicks, S., van Rees G.F., Leweke F.M., Dalman C., Karlsson H., Bahn S. (2017). Schizophrenia-risk and urban birth are associated with proteomic changes in neonatal dried blood spots. *Translational Psychiatry*, 7(12):1290.

Cornelius A.R. et al. (2013). GWAS of 126,559 individuals identifies genetic variants associated with educational attainment. *Science*, 340:1467–1471.

Cosgrove D. (1985). Prospect, perspective and the evolution of the landscape idea. *Transactions of the Institute of British Geographers*, 10:45–62.

Costa E., Silva J.A., Steffen R.E. (2019). Urban environment and psychiatric disorders: A review of the neuroscience and biology. *Metabolism*, 100S:153940.

Counted V., Cowden R.G., Lomas T. (2024). Global diversity in spatial (rural-urban) well-being in over 100 countries. *Cities*, 149:104987.

Cowlishaw G. (1994). Vulnerability to predation in baboon populations. *Behaviour*, 131:293–304.

Craig J.M., Logan A.C., Prescott S.L. (2016). Natural environments, nature relatedness and the ecological theater: Connecting satellites and sequencing to shinrin-yoku. *Journal of Physiological Anthropology*, 35:1.

Craik K.H. (1973). Environmental psychology. *Annual Review of Psychology*, 24(1):403–422.

Crespi B.J. (2000). The evolution of maladaptation. *Heredity*, 84:623–629.

D'Acci L.S. (2013). Hedonic inertia and underground happiness. *Social Indicators Research*, 113(3):1237–1259.

D'Acci L.S. (2015). Mathematize *urbes* by humanizing them. Cities as isobenefit landscapes: Psycho-economical distances and personal isobenefit lines. *Landscape and Urban Planning*, 139:63–81.

D'Acci L.S. (2019). Aesthetical cognitive perceptions of urban street form. Pedestrian preferences toward straight or curvy route shapes. *Journal of Urban Design*, 24(6):896–912.

D'Acci L. (2019a). New type of cities for liveable futures. Isobenefit urbanism morphogenesis. *Journal of Environmental Management*, 246:128–140.

D'Acci L.S. (2020). Urbanicity mental costs valuation. A review and urban-societal planning consideration. *Mind & Society*, 19:223–223.

D'Acci L.S. (2021). Preferring or needing cities? (Evolutionary?) psychology, utility and life satisfaction of urban life. *City, Culture and Society*, 24:100375.

D'Acci L.S., Voto M. (2023). Morphogenesis of Isobenefit urbanism: Isobenefit-cities simulator. *SoftwareX*, 23:101408.

D'Acci L.S., Banister D., White R.W. (2024). Liveable urban forms: Planning, self-organisation, and a third way (Isobenefit urbanism). *Humanities and Social Sciences Communications*, 11:578.

D'Acci L. (2025). Empirical overview of urban scaling. In: D'Acci L.S. (Ed.), *Urban scaling: Allometry in urban studies and spatial science* (pp. 18–27). Routledge, Advances in Regional Economics. London.

D'Acci L.S. (2025a). Planning new cities and Isobenefit urbanism. In: Kälin C.H. (ed.), *Free global city*. Bloomsbury Hart, London.

Damasio A.R., Grabowski T.J., Bechara A., Damasio H., Ponto L.L., Parvizi J., Hichwa R.D. (2000). Subcortical and cortical brain activity during the feeling of self-generated emotions. *Nature Neuroscience*, 3:1049–1056.

Daniels S., Cosgrove D. (1988). *The iconography of landscape: Essays on the symbolic representation, design and use of past environments*. Cambridge University Press, Cambridge.

Davidson R.J., Irwin W. (1999). The functional neuroanatomy of emotion and affective style. *Trends in cognitive sciences*, 3:11–21.

Dawkins R. (1976). *The selfish gene*. Oxford University Press, Oxford.

Dawkins R. (1982). *The extended phenotype*. Oxford University Press, Oxford.

Dawkins R. (2004). Extended phenotype—but not *too* extended. A reply to Laland, Turner and Jablonka. *Biology & Philosophy*, 19:377–396.

Dawkins R., Wong Y. (2017). *The ancestor's tale*. W&N, London.

Deb S., Okulicz-Kozaryn A. (2023). Exploring the association of urbanisation and subjective well-being in India. *Cities*, 132:104068.

Defra (Department for Environment, Food & Rural Affairs) (2021). *Rural economic bulletin for England: December 2021*. GOV.UK, London. www.gov.uk/government/statistics/quarterly-rural-economic-bulletin.

DeFries J.C., Gervais M.C., Thomas E.A. (1978). Response to 30 generations of selection for open-field activity in laboratory mice. *Behavioral Genetics*, 8(1):3–13.

Dhami S. (2016). *The foundations of behavioral economic analysis*. Oxford University Press, Oxford.

Diener E., Suh E.M., Lucas R.E., Smith H.E. (1999). Subjective well-being: Three decades of progress. *Psychological Bulletin*, 125(2):276–302.

Dilley L., Gkartzios M., Odagiri T. (2022). Developing counterurbanisation: Making sense of rural mobility and governance in Japan. *Habitat International*, 125:102595.

Dingemanse N.J., Araya-Ajoy Y.G. (2015). Interacting personalities: Behavioural ecology meets quantitative genetics. *Trends in Ecology and Evolution*, 30(2):88–97.

Dingemanse N.J., Kazem A.J.N., Réale D., Wright J. (2010). Behavioural reaction norms: Animal personality meets individual plasticity. *Trends in Ecology and Evolution*, 25(2):81–89.

Dockery A.M. (2003). *Happiness, life satisfaction and the role of work: Evidence from two Australian surveys*. Working Paper No. 03.10, School of Economics and Finance, Curtin Business School, Curtin University of Technology.

Doherty T.S., Roth T.L. (2020). Epigenetics in behavior and mental health. In: Paul R.H., Salminen L.E., Heaps J., Cohen L.M. (Eds.), *The wiley encyclopedia of health psychology*. Wiley-Blackwell, Hoboken, NJ.

Dolton P., Howorth C., Abouaziza M. (2016). The optimal length of the working day: Evidence from Hawthorne experiments. Paper presented at Royal Economic Society Conference, University of Sussex, Brighton, 21–23 March, 2016.

Donaldson Z.R., Young L.J. (2008). Oxytocin, vasopressin, and the neurogenetics of sociality. *Science*, 322(5903):900–904.

Donohue K., Dorn L., Griffith C., Kim E., Aguilera A., Polisetty C.R., Schmitt J. (2005a). Niche construction through germination cueing: Life-history responses to timing of germination in *Arabidopsis thaliana*. *Evolution*, 59:771–785.

Donohue K., Polisetty C.R., Wender N.J. (2005b). Genetic basis and consequences of niche construction: Plasticity- induced genetic constraints on the evolution of seed dispersal in *Arabidopsis thaliana*. *American Naturalist*, 165:537–550.

Dougherty D.D, Shina N.L., Alpert N.M., Pitmana R.K., Orr S.P., Lasko M., Macklin M.L., Fischman A.J., Rauch S.L. (1999). Anger in healthy men: A PET study using script-driven imagery. *Biological Psychiatry*, 46(4):466–472.

Downey G. (2016). Being human in cities. *Current Anthropology*, 57(13):52–64.

Duca J.V., Hoesli M., Montezuma J. (2021). The resilience and realignment of house prices in the era of covid-19. *Journal of European Real Estate Research*, 14(3):421–431.

Ducarme F., Couvet D. (2020). What does 'nature' mean? *Palgrave Communications*, 6:14.

Dulac C. (2010). Brain function and chromatin plasticity. *Nature*, 465:728–735.

Dunbar R.I.M. (1988). Habitat quality, population dynamics and group composition in colobus monkeys (Colobus guereza). *International Journal of Primatology*, 9:299–329.

Dunbar R.I.M. (2018). Social structure as a strategy to mitigate the costs of group-living: A comparison of gelada and guereza monkeys. *Animal Behaviour*, 136:53–64.

Dunbar R.I.M., Korstjens A.H., Lehmann J. (2009). Time as an ecological constraint. *Biological Reviews*, 84:413–429.

Dunbar R.I.M., MacCarron P., Robertson C. (2018). Trade-off between fertility and predation risk drives a geometric sequence in the pattern of group sizes in baboons. *Biology Letters*, 14:20170700.

Duque-Wilckens N. et al. (2020). Extra-hypothalamic oxytocin neurons drive stress-induced social vigilance and avoidance. *Proceedings of the National Academy of Sciences of the United States of America*, 117(42):26406–26413.

Durkheim E. (1893). *De la Division du Travail Social*. Alcan, Paris.

Dutton D. (2003). Aesthetics and evolutionary psychology. In: Levinson J. (Ed.), *The Oxford handbook for aesthetics* (pp. 693–705). Oxford University Press, New York.

Dye C. (2008). Health and urban living. *Science*, 319:766–769.

Easterlin R. (2003). Exploring happiness. *PNAS*, 100(19):11176–11183.

Easterlin R.A., Angelescu L., Zweig J.S. (2011). The impact of modern economic growth on urban-rural differences in subjective well-being. *World Development*, 39(12):2187–2198.

Eaton W.W. (1974). Residence, social class, and schizophrenia. *Journal of Health and Social Behavior*, 15:289–299.

Eaton W.W., Mortensen P.B., Frydenberg M. (2000). Obstetric factors, urbanization and psychosis. *Schizophrenia Research*, 43:117–123.

Eimermann M. (2015). Lifestyle migration to the north: Dutch families and the decision to move to rural Sweden. *Population, Space and Place*, 21(1):68–85.

Evans B.E., Buil J.M., Burk W.J., Cillessen A.H.N., van Lier P.A.C. (2018). Urbanicity is associated with behavioral and emotional problems in elementary school-aged children. *Journal of Child and Family Studies*, 27(7):2193–2205.

Ewing R, Handy S. (2009). Measuring the unmeasurable: Urban design qualities related to walkability. *Journal of Urban Design*, 14(1):65–84.

Falk J.H., Balling J.D. (2010). Evolutionary influence on human landscape preference. *Environment and Behavior*, 42(4):479–493.

Faris R.E.L., Dunham H.W. (1939). *Mental disorders in urban areas*. Chicago University Press, Chicago, IL.

Fassio O., Rollero C., De Piccoli N. (2013). Health, quality of life and population density: A preliminary study on "contextualized" quality of life. *Social Indicators Research*, 110:479–488.

Fawcett N.R., Gullone E. (2001). Cute and cuddly and a whole lot more? A call for empirical investigation into the therapeutic benefits of human–animal interaction for children. *Behaviour Change*, 18:124–133.

Feld S., Basso K.H. (Eds.) (1996). *Senses of place*. Santa Fe. School of American Research Press, Santa Fe, NM.

Feldman M.W., Cavalli-Sforza L.L. (1976). Cultural and biological evolutionary processes, selection for a trait under complex transmission. *Theoretical Population Biology*, 9:238–259.

Fernàndez-Castillo N., Cormand B. (2016). Aggressive behavior in humans: Genes and pathways identified through association studies. *Neuropsychiatric Genetic*, 171:676–696.

Fernàndez-Castillo N. et al. (2020). RBFOX1, encoding a splicing regulator, is a candidate gene for aggressive behavior. *European Neuropsychopharmacology*, 30:56–65.

Festinger L.A. (1957). *A theory of cognitive dissonance*. Stanford University Press, Stanford, CA.

Fett A.J., Lemmers-Jansen I.L.J., Krabbendam L. (2019). Psychosis and urbanicity: A review of the recent literature from epidemiology to neurourbanism. *Current Opinion in Psychiatry*, 32(3):232–241.

Fielding T., Ishikawa Y. (2021). COVID-19 and migration: A research note on the effects of COVID-19 on internal migration rates and patterns in Japan. *Population, Space and Place*, 27(6):e2499.

Finnemann A. et al. (2025). Urban-rural differences in anxiety and depression in the UK, New Zealand, and Norway. *Journal of Affective Disorders*, 388:119601.

Finnemann A., Freichel R., van der Maas H., Borsboom D., Wiers R. (2026). Accumulation of psychological problems in UK cities; A quantile regression approach. *Cities*, 170:106630.

Fischer C.S. (1973). Urban malaise. *Social Forces*, 52:221–235.

Fischer C.S. (1977). *Networks and places: Social relations in the urban setting*. Free Press, New York.

Fischer C.S. (1982). *To dwell among friends*. University Chicago Press, Chicago, IL.

Fisher C.S. (1972). Urbanism as a way of life. *Sociological Methods and Research*, 1(2):187–242.

Fisher C.S. (1975). Toward a subcultural theory of urbanism. *American Journal of Sociology*, 80(6):1319–1341.

Fisher C.S. (1976). *The urban experience*. Harcourt Brace Jovanovich, New York.

Fisher C.S. (1978). Sociological comments on psychological approaches to urban life. In: Baum A., Singer J.E., Valins S. (Eds.), *Advances in environmental psychology*. Lawrence Erlbaum, New York.

Fitzgerald D., Rose N., Singh I. (2016). Living well in the neuropolis. *Sociological Review Monograph*, 64(1):221–237.

Florida R. (2004). *Cities and the creative class*. Routledge, New York.

Florida R., Rodríguez-Pose A., Storper M. (2023). Cities in a post-COVID world. *Urban Studies*, 60(8):1509–1531.

Flynn E.G., Laland K.N., Kendal R.L., Kendal J.R. (2013). Target article with commentaries: Developmental niche construction. *Developmental Science*, 16:296–313.

Fonken L.K., Xu X., Weil Z.M., Chen G., Sun Q., Rajagopalan S., Nelson R.J. (2011). Air pollution impairs cognition, provokes depressive-like behaviors and alters hippocampal cytokine expression and morphology. *Molecular Psychiatry*, 16:987–995.

Foucault M. (1984). Space, knowledge, and power. In: Rabinow P. (Ed.), *The foucault reader*. Pantheon Books, New York.

Franck K.A. (1980). Friends and strangers: The social experience of living in urban and non-urban settings. *Journal of Social Issues*, 36:52–71.

Franke B., Reif A. (2020). Special issue on the neurobiology of aggressive behaviour in the context of ADHD and related disorders. *European Neuropsychopharmacology*, 30:1–4.

Freeman D., Emsley R., Dunn G., Fowler D., Bebbington P., Kuipers E., Jolley S., Waller H., Hardy A., Garety P. (2015). The stress of the street for patients with persecutory delusions: A test of the symptomatic and psychological effects of going outside into a busy urban area. *Schizophrenia Bullettin*, 41:971–979.

Freund J., Brandmaier A.M., Lewejohann L., Kirste I., Kritzler M., Krüger A., Sachser N., Lindenberger U., Kempermann G. (2013). Emergence of individuality in genetically identical mice. *Science*, 340:756–759.

Frey B.S. (2020). What are the opportunities for future happiness research? *International Economic Review*, 67:5–12.

Frey D. (1982). Different levels of cognitive dissonance, information seeking and information avoidance. *Journal of Personality and Social Psychology*, 43(6):1175–1183.

Frumkin H. (2001). Beyond toxicity: Human health and the natural environment. *American Journal of Preventive Medicine*, 20:234–240.

Fuentes A. (2017). Human niche, human behaviour, human nature. *Interface Focus*, 7(5):20160136.

Fuguitt G.V., Brown D.L. (1990). Residential preferences and population redistribution: 72-1988. *Demography*, 27:589–600.

Fuguitt G.V., Zuiches J.J. (1975). Residential preferences and population distribution. *Demography*, 12:491–504.

Fujita M. (2009). *Urban economic theory. Land use and city size*. Cambridge University Press.

Fuller R.A., Irvine K.N., Devine-Wright P., Warren P.H., Gaston K.J. (2007). Psychological benefits of greenspace increase with biodiversity. *Biology Letters*, 3:390–394.

Fumagalli M., Sironi M., Pozzoli U., Ferrer-Admettla A., Pattini L., Nielsen R. (2011). Signatures of environmental genetic adaptation pinpoint pathogens as the main selective pressure through human evolution. *PLoS Genetics*, 7(11):e1002355.

Galea S., Uddin M., Koenen K. (2011). The urban environment and mental disorders: Epigenetic links. *Epigenetics*, 6:400–404.

Gans H.J. (2002). The sociology of space: A use–centered view. *City & Community*, 1:329–339.

Garcia J.R., MacKillop J., Aller E.L., Merriwether A.M., Wilson D.S., Lum J.K. (2010). Associations between dopamine D4 receptor gene variation with both infidelity and sexual promiscuity. *PLoS ONE*, 5(11):e14162.

Gardner E.B., Boitano J.J., Mancino N.S., D'Amico D.P. (1975). Environmental enrichment and deprivation: Effects on learning, memory and exploration. *Physiology & Behavior*, 14:321–327.

Gaspar J., Glaeser E.L. (1998). Information technology and the future of cities. *Journal of Urban Economics*, 43(1):136–156.

Geertz C. (1973). *The interpretation of cultures*. Basic Books, New York.

George M.S., Ketter T.A., Parekh P.I., Herscovitch P., Post R.M. (1996). Gender differences in regional cerebral blood flow during transient self-induced sadness or happiness. *Biological Psychiatry*, 40:859–871.

Gerdtham U., Johannesson M. (2001). The relationship between happiness, health, and socio-economic factors: Results based on Swedish microdata. *The Journal of Socio-Economics*, 30(6):553–557.

Ghalambor C.K., Hoke K.L., Ruell E.W., Fischer E.K., Reznick D.N., Hughes K.A. (2015). Non-adaptive plasticity potentiates rapid adaptive evolution of gene expression in nature. *Nature*, 525(7569):372–375.

Gharib M.A., Golembiewski J.A., Moustafa A.A. (2020). Mental health and urban design – zoning in on PTSD. *Current Psychology*, 39(1):167–173.

Gibson M.A., Lawson D.W. (2015). Applying evolutionary anthropology. *Evolutionary Anthropology*, 24(1):3–14.

Gieryn T.F. (2000). A space for place in sociology. *Annual Review of Sociology*, 26:463–496.

Gilad B., Kaish S., Loeb P.B. (1987). Cognitive dissonance and utility maximization. *Journal of Economic Behavior and Organization*, 8(1):61–73.

Gilbert A., Colley K., Roberts D. (2016). Are rural residents happier? A quantitative analysis of subjective wellbeing in Scotland. *Journal of Rural Studies*, 44:37–45.

Gilbert D.T., Pinel E.C., Wilso T.D., Blumberg S.J., Wheatley T. (1998). Immune neglect: A source of durability bias in affective forecasting. *Journal of Personality and Social Psychology*, 75(3):617–638.

Gillespie J.H., Turelli M. (1989). Genotype-environment interactions and the maintenance of polygenic variation. *Genetics*, 121:129–138.

Ginn S., Horder J. (2012). "One in four" with a mental health problem: The anatomy of a statistic. *BMJ*, 344:e1302.

Gintis H. (2011). Gene-culture coevolution and the nature of human sociality. *Philosophical Transactions of the Royal Society of London. Series B, Biological Sciences*, 366(1566):878–888.

Glaese E., Gyourko J. (2008). *Arbitrage in housing markets*. HKS Faculty Research Working Paper Series RWP08-017.

Glaeser E. (2008). *Cities, agglomeration, and spatial equilibrium*. Oxford University Press, New York.

Glaeser E. (2011). *Triumph of the city*. Penguin Books, New York.

Glaeser E., Gottlieb J., Ziv O. (2014). *Unhappy cities*. National Bureao of Economic Research Working Paper 20291.

Glass D.C., Singer J.E. (1972). *Urban stress: Experiments on noise and social stressors*. Academic Press, Waltham, MA.

Glenn N.D., Hill L. (1977). Rural-urban differences in attitudes and behavior in the United States. *The Annals of the American Academy of Political and Social Science*, 429:36–50.

Goldberg A.D., Allis C.D., Bernstein E. (2007). Epigenetics: A landscape takes shape. *Cell*, 128(4):635–638.

González-Leonardo M., López-Gay A., Newsham N., Recaño J., Rowe F. (2022). Understanding patterns of internal migration during the COVID-19 pandemic in Spain. *Population, Space and Place*, 28:e2578.

Gould S.J. (2000). The spice of life. *Leader to Leader*, 15:14–19.

Graetz G., Michaels G. (2018). Robots at work. *Review of Economics and Statistics*, 100(5):753–768.

Graziano M.S., Cooke D.F. (2006). Parieto-frontal interactions, personal space, and defensive behavior. *Neuropsychologia*, 44:2621–2635.

Green A.E. (1997). A question of compromise? Case study evidence on the location and mobility strategies of dual career households. *Regional Studies*, 31(7):641–657.

Green J. (2013). *Moral tribes: Emotion, reason, and the gap between us and them*. Atlantic Books, London.

Gries T., Grundmann R. (2018). Fertility and modernization: The role of urbanization in developing countries. *Journal of International Development*, 30:493–506.

Griffiths P., Linquist S. (Fall 2024). The distinction between innate and acquired characteristics. In: Zalta E.N., Nodelman U. (Eds.), *The Stanford encyclopedia of philosophy*. https://plato.stanford.edu/cgi-bin/encyclopedia/archinfo.cgi?entry=innate-acquired&archive=fall2024.

Grinde B., Husselman T.A. (2023). An attempt to explain visual aesthetic appreciation. *Integrative Psychological and Behavioral Science*, 57(3):840–855.

Grinde B., Patil G.G. (2009). Biophilia: Does visual contact with nature impact on health and well-being? *International Journal of Environmental Research and Public Health*, 6(9):2332–2343.

Groffman P.M. et al. (2014). Ecological homogenization of urban USA. *Frontiers in Ecology and the Environment*, 12:74–81.

Gross R. (2019). *Being human: Psychological perspectives on human nature* (2nd ed.). Routledge, London.

Gruebner O., Rapp M.A., Adli M., Kluge U., Galea S., Heinz A. (2017). Cities and mental health. *Deutsches Ärzteblatt International*, 114(8):121–127.

Grueter C.C., Matsuda I., Zhang P., Zinner D. (2012). Multilevel societies in primates and other mammals: Introduction to the special issue. *International Journal of Primatology*, 33(5):993–1001.

Grueter C.C., Qi X., Li B., Li M. (2017). Multilevel societies. *Current Biology*, 27:R979–R1001.

Gupta A., Mittal V., Peeters J., Van Nieuwerburgh S. (2021). *Flattening the curve: Pandemic-induced revaluation of urban real estate*. NBER Working Paper 28675, National Bureau of Economic Research, Cambridge, MA.

Gwang-Won K., Gwang-Woo J., Tae-Hoon K., Han-Su B., Seok-Kyun O., Heoung-Keun K., Sam-Gyu L., Yoon Soo K., Jin-Kyu S. (2010). Functional neuroanatomy associated with natural and urban scenic views in the human brain: 3.0T functional MR imaging. *Korean Journal of Radiology*, 11(5):507–513.

Haddad L., Schäfer A., Streit F., Lederbogen F., Grimm O., Wüst S., Deuschle M., Kirsch P., Tost H., Meyer-Lindenberg A. (2015). Brain structure

correlates of urban upbringing: An environmental risk factor for schizophrenia. *Schizophrenia Bulletin*, 41(1):115–122.
Hagerhall C.M., Purcell T., Taylor R. (2004). Fractal dimension of landscape silhouette outlines as a predictor of landscape preference. *Journal of Environmental Psychology*, 24(2):247–255.
Hägerstrand T. (1970). What about people in regional science? *Papers – Regional Science Association*, 24:6–21.
Hall E.T. (1966). *The hidden dimension*. Doubleday, New York.
Halpern D. (1995). *Mental health and the built environment*. Taylor & Francis, London.
Haluza D., Schonbauer R., Cervinka R. (2014). Green perspectives for public health: A narrative review on the physiological effects of experiencing outdoor nature. *International Journal of Environmental Research and Public Health*, 11:5445–5461.
Hanell T. (2022). Unmet aspirations and urban malaise. *Social Indicator Research*, 164:83–103.
Hannerz U. (1992). *Cultural complexity: Studies in the social organization of meaning*. Columbia University Press, New York.
Hansen H.K., Aner L.G. (2017). On the location dynamics of highly educated people migrating to peripheral regions of Denmark. *Population, Space and Place*, 23(8):e2076.
Harari Y.N. (2015). *Sapiens: A brief history of humankind*. Harvill Secker, London.
Hare B., Tomasello M. (2005). Human-like social skills in dogs? *Trends in Cognitive Sciences*, 9:439–444.
Hare B., Wobber V., Wrangham R. (2012). The self-domestication hypothesis: Evolution of bonobo psychology is due to selection against aggression. *Animal Behaviour*, 83(3):573–585.
Harlow H.F., Dodsworth R.O., Harlow M.K. (1965). Total social isolation in monkeys. *Proceedings of the National Academy of Sciences of the United States of America*, 54:90–97.
Harris E.E., Meyer D. (2006). The molecular signature of selection underlying human adaptations. *American Journal of Physical Anthropology*, 131:89–130.
Harrison G.L., Fouskakis D., Rasmussen F., Tynelius P., Sipos A., Gunnell D. (2003). Association between psychotic disorder and urban place of birth is not mediated by obstetric complications or childhood socioeconomic position: A cohort study. *Psychological Medicine*, 33:723–731.
Harro J., Laas K., Eensoo D., Kurrikoff T., Sakala K., Vaht M., Parik J., Mäestu J., Veidebaum T. (2019). Orexin/hypocretin receptor gene (HCRTR1) variation is associated with aggressive behaviour. *Neuropharmacology*, 156:107527.

Hartig T., Evans G.W., Jamner L.D., Davis D.S., Gärling T. (2003). Tracking restoration in natural and urban field settings. *Journal of Environmental Psychology*, 23:109–123.

Hartig T., Mitchell R., de Vries S., Frumkin H. (2014). Nature and health. *Annual Review of Public Health*, 35:207–28.

Hartmann P., Apaolaza-Ibáñez V. (2010). Beyond Savanna: An evolutionary and environmental psychology approach to behavioral effects of nature scenery in green advertising. *Journal of Environmental Psychology*, 30:119–128.

Hartmann P., Apaolaza-Ibáñez V. (2013). Desert or rain: Standardisation of green advertising versus adaptation to the target audience's natural environment. *European Journal of Marketing*, 47:917–933.

Harvey D. (1993). From space to place and back again: Reflections on the condition of postmodernity. In: Bird J., Curtis B., Putnam T., Tickner L. (Eds.), *Mapping the future* (pp. 2–29). Routledge, London.

Haukka J., Suvisaari J., Lonnqvist J. (2001). Regional variation in the incidence of schizophrenia in Finland: A study of birth cohorts born from 1950 to 1969. *Psychological Medicine*, 31:1045–1053.

Havens B., Hall M., Sylvestre G., Jivan T. (2004). Social isolation and loneliness: Differences between older rural and urban manitobans. *Canadian Journal on Aging*, 23(2):129–140.

Hawks J., Wang E.T., Cochran G.M., Harpending H.C., Moyzis R.K. (2007). Recent acceleration of human adaptive evolution. *Proceedings of the National Academy of Sciences of the United States of America*, 104:20753–20758.

Hayden B. (1981). Subsistence and ecological adaptations of modern hunter/gatherers. In: Harding S.O., Teleki G. (Eds.), *Omnivorous primates; Gathering and hunting in human evolution*. Columbia University Press, New York.

Hayo B. (2004). *Happiness in eastern Europe*. Marburger Volkswirtschaftliche Beiträge, No. 2004,12, Philipps-Universität Marburg, Fachbereich Wirtschaftswissenschaften, Marburg.

Hebb D.O. (1995). The mammal and his environment. *American Journal of Psychiatry*, 111:826–831.

Heinrich B. (2013). The biological roots of aesthetics and art. *Evolutionary Psychology*, 11(3):743–761.

Heinrich Mora E., Heine C., Jackson J.J., West G.B., Yang V.C., Kempes C.P. (2021). Scaling of urban income inequality in the USA. *Journal of the Royal Society Interface*, 18(181):20210223.

Heins S. (2004). Rural living in city and countryside: Demand and supply in the Netherlands. *Journal of Housing and the Built Environment*, 19:391–408.

Heinz A., Deserno L., Reininghaus U. (2013). Urbanicity, social adversity and psychosis. *World Psychiatry*, 12:187–197.

Heinz A.J., Beck A., Meyer-Lindenberg A., Sterzer P., Heinz A. (2011). Cognitive and neurobiological mechanisms of alcohol-related aggression. *Nature Reviews Neuroscience*, 12:400–413.

Helliwell J.F., Shiplett H., Barrington-Leigh C.P. (2018). *How happy are your neighbours? Variation in life satisfaction among 1200 Canadian neighbourhoods and communities*. National Bureau of Economic Research NBER Working Paper No. 24592.

Helson H. (1964). *Adaptation-level theory: An experimental and systematic approach to behavior*. Harper and Row, New York.

Henderson N.D. (1970). Brain weight increases resulting from environmental enrichment: A directional dominance in mice. *Science*, 169:776–778.

Henning-Smith C., Moscovice I., Kozhimannil K. (2019). Differences in social isolation and its relationship to health by rurality. *Journal of Rural Health*, 35(4):540–549.

Henrich J. (2015). *The secret of our success: How culture is driving human evolution, domesticating our species, and making us smarter*. Princeton University Press, New York.

Henricks T.S. (2022). *Anatomies of modern discontent: Visions from the human sciences*. Routledge, London.

Herman J.P., Cullinan W.E. (1997). Neurocircuitry of stress: Central control of the hypothalamo-pituitary-adrenocortical axis. *Trends in Neuroscience*, 20:78–84.

Herrel A., Joly D., Danchin E. (2020). Epigenetics in ecology and evolution. *Functional Ecology*, 34:381–384.

Herzog T., Miller E. (1998). The role of mystery in perceived danger and environmental preference. *Environmental and Behavior*, 30:429–449.

Hill K., Barton M., Hurtado A.M. (2009). The emergence of human uniqueness: Characters underlying behavioral modernity. *Evolutionary Anthropology*, 18:187–200.

Hill R.A., Lycett J., Dunbar R.I.M. (2000). Ecological determinants of birth intervals in baboons. *Behavioral Ecology*, 11:560–564.

Hirsch E. (1995). Landscape: Between place and space. In: O'Hanlon M. (Eds.), *Anthropological studies of landscape: Perspectives on space and place* (pp. 1–30). Clarendon Press, Oxford.

Hirsh E., O'Hanlon M. (Eds.) (1995). *Anthropological studies of landscape: Perspectives on space and place*. Clarendon Press, Oxford.

Hoare E., Jacka F., Berk M. (2019). The impact of urbanization on mood disorders: An update of recent evidence. *Current Opinion in Psychiatry*, 32(3):198–203.

Holt-Lunstad J., Smith T.B., Baker M., Harris T., Stephenson D. (2015). Loneliness and social isolation as risk factors for mortality: A meta-analytic review. *Perspectives on Psychological Science*, 10(2):227–237.

Hoogerbrugge M., Burger M. (2022). Selective migration and urban–rural differences in subjective well-being: Evidence from the United Kingdom. *Urban Studies*, 59(10):2092–2109.

Houghton S., Hattie J., Carroll A., Wood L., Baffour B. (2016). It hurts to be lonely! Loneliness and positive mental wellbeing in Australian rural and urban adolescents. *Journal of Psychologists and Counsellors in Schools*, 26(1):52–67.

Houghton S., Hattie J., Wood L., Carroll A., Martin K., Tan C. (2014). Conceptualising loneliness in adolescents: Development and validation of a self-report instrument. *Child Psychiatry & Human Development*, 45:604–616.

Hu Y., Shmygelska A., Tran D. Eriksson N., Tung J.Y., Hinds D.A. (2016). GWAS of 89,283 individuals identifies genetic variants associated with self-reporting of being a morning person. *Nature Communications*, 7:10448.

Huggins R., Thompson P. (2019). The behavioural foundations of urban and regional development: Culture, psychology and agency. *Journal of Economic Geography*, 19(1):121–146.

Hunt E.K., Lautzenheiser M. (2015). *History of economic thought. A critical perspective*. Routledge, New York.

Ihara Y., Feldman M.W. (2004). Cultural niche construction and the evolution of small family size. *Theoretical Population Biology*, 65:105–111.

Inglehart R.F. (2018). *Cultural evolution*. University Cambridge Press, Cambridge.

Irwin F.W. (1944). The realism of expectations. *Psychological Review*, 51(2):120–126.

Isbell L.A. (2024). *Primate socioecology: Shifting perspectives*. Johns Hopkins University Press.

Jacobs Z., Roberts R.G. (2009). Human history written in stone and blood. *American Scientist*, 97:2–9.

Jaenike J., Holt R.D. (1991). Genetic variation for habitat preference: Evidence and explanations. *American Naturalist*, 137:S67–S90.

Jain K., Stephan W. (2017). Modes of rapid polygenic adaptation. *Molecular Biology and Evolution*, 34:3169–3175.

Jansen S.J.T. (2020). Urban, suburban or rural? Understanding preferences for the residential environment. *Journal of Urbanism: International Research on Placemaking and Urban Sustainability*, 13(2):213–235.

Janson C.H. (1988). Food competition in brown capuchin monkeys (*Cebus apella*): Quantitative effects of group size and tree productivity. *Behaviour*, 105(1–2):53–76.

Janson C.H., Goldsmith M.L. (1995). Predicting group size in primates: Foraging costs and predation risks. *Behavioral Ecology*, 6:326–336.

Jevons W.S. (1871). *The theory of political economy*. Macmillan, London.

Joens-Matre R.R., Welk G.J., Calabro M.A., Russell D.W., Nicklay E., Hensley L.D. (2008). Rural-urban differences in physical activity, physical fitness, and overweight prevalence of children. *Journal of Rural Health*, 24:49–54.

Johnson A.W., Earle T.K. (2001). *The evolution of human societies: From foraging group to agrarian state* (2nd ed.). Stanford University Press, Stanford, CA.

Johnson M.T.J., Munshi-South J. (2017). Evolution of life in urban environments. *Science*, 358(6363):eaam8327.

Jokela M. (2009). Personality predicts migration within and between U.S. states. *Journal of Research in Personality*, 43:79–83.

Jokela M. (2014). Flow of cognitive capital across urban and rural United States. *Intelligence*, 46:47–53.

Jokela M., Elovainio M., Kivimäki M., Keltikangas-Järvinen L. (2008). Temperament and migration patterns in Finland. *Psychological Science*, 19:831–837.

Jones L.J., Norton W.H. (2015). Using zebrafish to uncover the genetic and neural basis of aggression, a frequent comorbid symptom of psychiatric disorders. *Behavioural Brain Research*, 276:171–180.

Jurčišinová V., Želinský T. & Hudec O. (2026). The urban paradox and rural appeal: Subjective well-being across diverse European living environments. *Applied Research Quality Life*, 21:71–99.

Kahneman D. (2000). Experienced utility and objective happiness: A moment-based approach. In: Kahneman D., Tversky A. (Eds.), *Choices, values and frames* (pp. 673–692). Cambridge University Press and the Russell Sage Foundation, New York.

Kahneman D. (2003). Maps of bounded rationality: Psychology for behavioral economics. *The American Economic Review*, 93:1449–1475.

Kahneman D., Schkade D. (1999). *Predicting the well-being effect of new circumstances: Changes are proxies for states*. Working Paper, Princeton University.

Kalyuzhnova Y, Kambhampati U. (2008). The determinants of individual happiness in Kazakhstan. *Economic Systems*, 32:285–299.

Kaplan H.S. (1996). A theory of fertility and parental investment in traditional and modern human societies. *Yearbook of Physical Anthropology*, 39:91–135.

Kaplan J.T., Freedman J., Iacoboni M. (2007). US versus them: Political attitudes and party affiliation influence neural response to faces of presidential candidates. *Neuropsychologia*, 45:55–64.

Kaplan R., Kaplan S. (1989). *The experience of nature: A psychological perspective*. Cambridge University Press, New York.

Kaplan S. (1987). Aesthetics, affect, and cognition: Environmental preference from an evolutionary perspective. *Environment and Behavior*, 19(1):3–32.

Kaplan S. (1988). Where cognition and affect meet: A theoretical analysis of preference. In Nasar J.L. (Ed.), *Environmental aesthetics: Theory, research and applications* (pp. 56–63). Cambridge University Press, Cambridge.

Kaplan S., Berman M.G. (2010). Directed attention as a common resource for executive functioning and self-regulation. *Perspectives on Psychological Science*, 5:43–57.

Karsten L. (2020). Counterurbanisation: Why settled families move out of the city again. *Journal of Housing and the Built Environment*, 35(2):429–442.

Kasarda J.D., Janowitz M. (1974). Community attachment in mass society. *American Sociological Review*, 39:328–339.

Katz P.S. (2011). Neural mechanisms underlying the evolvability of behaviour. *Philosophical Transactions of the Royal Society B: Biological Sciences*, 366(1574):2086–2099.

Kaufman J., Yang B., Douglas-Palumberi H., Houshyar S., Lipschitz D., Krystal J., Gelernter J. (2004). *Proceedings of the National Academy of Sciences of the United States of America*, 101(49):17316–17321.

Kayser M., Brauer S., Stoneking M. (2003). A genome scan to detect candidate regions influenced by local natural selection in human populations. *Molecular Biology and Evolution*, 20:893–900.

Kelly B.D. et al. (2010). Schizophrenia and the city: A review of literature and prospective study of psychosis and urbanicity in Ireland. *Schizophrenia Research*, 116:75–89.

Kempermann G., Kuhn H.G., Gage F.H. (1997). More hippocampal neurons in adult mice living in an enriched environment. *Nature*, 386:493–495.

Kendal J., Tehrani J.J., Odling-Smee J. (2011). Human niche construction in interdisciplinary focus. *Philosophical Transactions of the Royal Society B*, 366(1566):785–792.

Kennedy D.P., Adolphs R. (2011). Stress and the city. *Nature*, 474:452–453.

Kennedy D.P., Glascher J., Tyszk J.M., Adolphs R. (2009). Personal space regulation by the human amygdala. *Nature Neuroscience*, 12:1226–1227.

Kent R. (1989). The role of mystery in preferences for shopping malls. *Landscape Journal: Design, Planning and Management*, 8(1):28.

Key W.H. (1968). Rural-urban social participation. In: Fava S.F. (Ed.), *Urbanism in world perspective*. Crowell, New York.

Kiive E., Laas K., Vaht M., Veidebaum T., Harro J. (2017). Stressful life events increase aggression and alcohol use in young carriers of the GABRA2 rs279826/rs279858 A-allele. *European Neuropsychopharmacology*, 27:816–827.

Kimball M., Willis R. (2006). *Utility and happiness*. University of Michigan.

Kinnison M.T., Hendry A.P. (2001). The pace of modern life II: From rates of contemporary microevolution to pattern and process. *Genetica*, 112–113:145–164.

Kirkbride J.B. et al. (2006). Heterogeneity in incidence rates of schizophrenia and other psychotic disorders: Findings from the 3-center ÆSOP Study. *Archives of General Psychiatry*, 63(3):250–258.

Kirkbride J.B., Keyes K.M., Susser E. (2018). City living and psychotic disorders-implications of global heterogeneity for theory development. *JAMA Psychiatry*, 75(12):1211–1212.

Klasios J. (2016). Evolutionizing human nature. *New Ideas in Psychology*, 51:27–33.

Klepeis N.E., Nelson W.C., Ott W.R., Robinson J.P., Tsang A.M., Switzer P., Behar J.V., Hern S.C., Engelmann W.H. (2001). The national human activity pattern survey (NHAPS): A resource for assessing exposure to environmental pollutants. *Journal of Exposure Analysis and Environmental Epidemiology*, 11(3):231–252.

Knight J., Gunatilaka R. (2010). The rural–urban divide in China: Income but not happiness? *The Journal of Development Studies*, 46(3):506–534.

Knoke K. (1996). *Bold new world: The essential road map to the twenty-first century*. Kodansha, New York.

Knox P., Pinch S. (2006). *Urban social geography: An introduction*. Pearson, Kuala Lumpur, Malaysia.

Kong A. et al. (2017). Selection against variants in the genome associated with educational attainment. *Proceedings of the National Academy of Sciences of the United States of America*, 114:E727–E732.

Kovess-Masfety V., Lecoutour X., Delavelle S., (2005). Mood disorders and urban/rural settings. *Social Psychiatry and Psychiatric Epidemiology*, 40:613.

Krabbendam L., Hooker C.I., Aleman A. (2014). Neural effects of the social environment. *Schizophrenia Bulletin*, 40(2):248–251.

Krabbendam L., van Os J. (2005). Schizophrenia and urbanicity: A major environmental influence–conditional on genetic risk. *Schizophrenia Bulletin*, 31:795–799.

Krabbendam L. et al. (2021). Understanding urbanicity: How interdisciplinary methods help to unravel the effects of the city on mental health. *Psychological Medicine*, 51(7):1099–1110.

Krebs J.R., Davies N.B. (1991). *An introduction to behavioural ecology* (3rd ed.). Blackwell Scientific Publications, Oxford.

Krech D., Rosenzweig M.R., Bennett E.L. (1962). Relations between chemistry and problem-solving among rats raised in enriched and impoverished environments. *Journal of Comparative and Physiological Psychology*, 55(5):801–807.

Krzywicka P., Byrka K. (2017). Restorative qualities of and preference for natural and urban soundscapes. *Frontiers in Psychology*, 8:1705.

Kubinyi E., Vas J., Hejjas K., Ronai Z., Brúder I., Turcsán B., Sasvari-Szekely M., Miklósi Á. (2012). Polymorphism in the tyrosine hydroxylase (TH) gene is associated with activity-impulsivity in German shepherd dogs. *PLoS ONE*, 7(1):e30271.

Kühn S. et al. (2017). In search of features that constitute an "enriched environment" in humans: Associations between geographical properties and brain structure. *Scientific Report*, 7:11920.

Kuźmar S., Woźniak-Jęchorek B., Bole D. (2026). Will remote work drive a new wave of suburbanisation in Poland? Analysing the relocation preferences of Polish office employees. *Applied Geography*, 186:103848.

Kweon B.S., Ulrich R.S., Walker V.D., Tassinary L.G. (2008). Anger and stress: The role of landscape posters in an office setting. *Environment and Behavior*, 40:355–381.

Kwiatkowski D.P. (2005). How malaria has affected the human genome and what human genetics can teach us about malaria. *American Journal of Human Genetics*, 77(2):171–192.

Kylafis G., Loreau M. (2008). Ecological and evolutionary consequences of niche construction for its agent. *Ecology Letters*, 11:1072–1081.

Laas K., Reif A., Kiive E., Domschke K., Lesch K.P., Veidebaum T., Harro J. (2014). A functional NPSR1 gene variant and environment shape personality and impulsive action: A longitudinal study. *Journal of Psychopharmacology*, 28:227–236.

Lachance J., Tishkoff S.A. (2013). Population genomics of human adaptation. *Annual Review of Ecology, Evolution, and Systematics*, 44:123–143.

Lai K.Y., Sarkar C., Kumari S., Ni M.Y., Gallacher J., Webster C. (2021). Calculating a national anomie density ratio: Measuring the patterns of loneliness and social isolation across the UK's residential density gradient using results from the UK Biobank study. *Landscape and Urban Planning*, 215:104194.

Laland K.N., Odling-Smee F.J., Feldman M.W. (1996). The evolutionary consequences of niche construction. *Journal of Evolutionary Biology*, 9:293–316.

Laland K.N., Odling-Smee F.J., Feldman M.W. (1999). Evolutionary consequences of niche construction and their implications for ecology. *Proceedings of the National Academy of Sciences of the United States of America*, 96(10):242–210.

Laland K.N., Odling-Smee F.J., Feldman M.W. (2000). Niche construction, biological evolution, and cultural change. *Behavioral and Brain Sciences*, 23:131–175.

Laland K.N., Odling-Smee F.J., Feldman M.W. (2001). Cultural niche construction and human evolution. *Journal of Evolutionary Biology*, 14:22–33.

Laland K.N., Odling-Smee F.J., Feldman M.W., Kendal J.R. (2009). Conceptual barriers to progress within evolutionary biology. *Foundations of Science*, 4:195–216.

Laland K.N., Odling-Smee J., Myles S. (2010). How culture shaped the human genome: Bringing genetics and the human sciences together. *Nature Reviews Genetics*, 11:137–148.

Lambert K.G., Nelson R.J., Jovanovic T., Cerdá M. (2015). Brains in the city: Neurobiological effects of urbanization. *Neuroscience and Biobehavioral Reviews*, 58:107–122.

Landwehr J.R., Labroo A.A., Herrmann A. (2011). Gut liking for the ordinary: Incorporating design fuency improves automobile sales forecasts. *Marketing Science*, 30(3):416–429.

Lane R.D., Chua P.M., Dolan R.J. (1999). Common effects of emotional valence, arousal and attention on neural activation during visual processing of pictures. *Neuropsychologia*, 37:989–997.

Lane R.D., Reiman E.M., Ahern G.L., Schwartz G.E., Davidson R.J. (1997b). Neuroanatomical correlates of happiness, sadness, and disgust. *The American Journal of Psychiatry*, 154:926–933.

Lane R.D., Reiman E.M., Bradley M.M., Lang P.J., Ahern G.L., Davidson R.J., Schwartz G.E. (1997a). Neuroanatomical correlates of pleasant and unpleasant emotion. *Neuropsychologia*, 35:1437–1444.

Larson N., Ward D.S., Neelon S.B., Story M. (2011). What role can child-care settings play in obesity prevention? A review of the evidence and call for research efforts. *Journal of the American Dietetic*, 111:1343–1362.

Lawless N.M., Lucas R.E. (2010). Predictors of regional well-being: A county level analysis. *Social Indicators Research*, 101(3):341–357.

Lecic-Tosevski D. (2019). Is urban living good for mental health? *Current Opinion in Psychiatry*, 32(3):204–209.

Lederbogen F. et al. (2011). City living and urban upbringing affect neural social stress processing in humans. *Nature*, 474:498–501.

Lee K.O., Kaufman P. (2020). The effect of urban density on mental health: A systematic review. *University of Toronto Medical Journal*, 97(2):21–29.

Lehmann J., Dunbar R.I.M. (2009). Implications of body mass and predation for ape social system and biogeographical distribution. *Oikos*, 118:379–390.

Lenski G. (2005). *Ecology-evolution theory: Principles and applications*. Routledge, London; New York.

Lenzi C., Perucca G. (2021). Not too close, not too far: Urbanisation and life satisfaction along the urban hierarchy. *Urban Studies*, 58(13):2742–2757.

Lenzi C., Perucca G. (2022). No place for poor men: On the asymmetric effect of urbanization on life satisfaction. *Social Indicator Resesrch*, 164:165–187.

Lesch K.P, Merschdorf U. (2000). Impulsivity, aggression, and serotonin: A molecular psychobiological perspective. *Behavioral Sciences & the Law*, 18:581–604.

Levesque S., Surace M.J., McDonald J., Block M.L. (2011). Air pollution and the brain: Subchronic diesel exhaust exposure causes neuroinflammation and elevates early markers of neurodegenerative disease. *Journal of Neuroinflammation*, 8:105.

Lewin R. (2005). *Human evolution*. Blackwell, Oxford.

Lewis G., David A., Andreasson S., Allebeck P. (1992). Schizophrenia and city life. *Lancet*, 340:137–40.

Lewontin R.C. (1983). Gene, organism, and environment. In: Bendall D.S. (Ed.), *Evolution from molecules to men* (pp. 273–286). Cambridge University Press, Cambridge.

Lipowski Z.J. (1971). Surfeit of attractive information inputs: A hallmark of our environment. *Behavioral Science*, 16(5):467–471.

Liu J., Green R.J. (2026). Examining the biophilia hypothesis through assessing children's preferences for outdoor environments and perception of nature in Beijing, China. *Cities*, 168:106428.

Lo M.T. et al. (2017). Genome-wide analyses for personality traits identify six genomic loci and show correlations with psychiatric disorders. *Nature Genetics*, 49:152–156.

Loewenstei G., Schkade D. (1999). Wouldn't it be nice: Predicting future feelings. In: Kahneman D., Diener E., Schwarz N. (Eds.), *Wellbeing: The foundation of hedonic psychology* (pp. 85–108). Russell Sage Foundation, New York.

Lofland L.H. (1973). *A world of strangers: Order and action in urban public space*. Basic Books, New York.

Long E., Thomson M., Milicev J., Goodfellow C., Letina S., Bradley S., McCann M. (2025). Loneliness, social support, and social networks: Urban–rural variation and links to wellbeing in Scotland. *Journal of Public Health*, 33(12):2651–2661.

Longman D.P., Shaw C.N. (2026). *Homo sapiens*, industrialisation and the environmental mismatch hypothesis. *Biological Reviews*.

Lopreato J. (1984). *Human nature and biocultural evolution*. Routledge, London.

Lorenz K. (1963). *Das sogenannte Böse zur Naturgeschichte der Aggression*. Verlag, Vienna. English translation (1966). *On aggression*. Methuen Publishing, London.

Lothian A. (1999). Landscape and the philosophy of aesthetics: Is landscape quality inherent in the landscape or in the eye of the beholder? *Landscape and Urban Planning*, 44(4):177–198.

Low S.M., Lawrence-Zuñiga D. (2003). *The anthropology of space and place: Locating culture*. Blackwell, Oxford.

Lowe J. (2019). Urban mental health. In: Vojnovic I., Pearson A.L., Asiki G., DeVerteuil G., Allen A. (Eds.), *Handbook of global urban health* (pp. 217–231). Routledge, London.

Lowry I.S. (1967). Comments on britton Harris. *Papers – Regional Science Association*, 19:197–198.

Lu Y., Qin L. (2014). Healthy migrant and Salmon Bias hypotheses: A study of health and internal migration in China. *Social Science & Medicine*, 102:41–48.

Luttmer Erzo F.P. (2005). Neighbors as negatives: Relative earnings and well-being. *Quarterly Journal of Economics*, 120(3):963–1002.

Lykken D., Tellegen A. (1996). Happiness is a stochastic phenomenon. *Psychological Science*, 7:186–189.

Lynch K. (1960). *The image of the city*. The MIT Press, Boston, MA.

Lynch K. (1984). *Good city form*. The MIT Press, Cambridge, MA; London.

Maas J., Verheij R.A., Groenewegen P.P., de Vries S., Spreeuwenberg P. (2006). Green space, urbanity, and health: How strong is the relation? *Journal of Epidemiology and Community Health*, 60:587–592.

Mace G.M. (2008). Reproducing in cities. *Science*, 319:764–766.
Maller C., Townsend M., Pryor A., Brown P., St Leger L. (2005). Healthy nature healthy people: 'Contact with nature' as an upstream health promotion intervention for populations. *Health Promotion International*, 21:45–54.
Malzberg B. (1930). Mental disease and "the melting pot". *The Journal of Nervous and Mental Disease*, 72(4):379–395.
Manning N. (2019). Sociology, biology and mechanisms in urban mental health. *Social Theory and Health*, 17(1).
Marcelis M., Navarro-Mateu F., Murray R.M., Selten J.P., Van Os J. (1998). Urbanization and psychosis: A study of 1942–1978 birth cohorts in the Netherlands. *Psychological Medicine*, 28(4):871–879.
Marcelis M., Takei N., van Os J. (1999). Urbanization and risk for schizophrenia: Does the effect operate before or around the time of illness onset? *Psychological Medicine*, 29(5):1197–1203.
March D., Hatch S.L., Morgan C., Kirkbride J.B., Bresnahan M., Fearon P., Susser E. (2008). Psychosis and place. *Epidemiology Review*, 30(1):84–100.
Marlowe F.W. (2005). Hunter-gatherers and human evolution. *Evolutionary Anthropology*, 14(2):54–67.
Marquez J., Goodfellow C., Hardoon D., Inchley J., Leyland A.H., Qualter P., Simpson S.A., Long E. (2023). Loneliness in young people: A multilevel exploration of social ecological influences and geographic variation. *Journal of Public Health*, 45(1):109–117.
Martinotti G. (1996). Four populations: Human settlements and social morphology in the contemporary metropolis. *European Review*, 4(1):3–23.
Mascayano F., Lee J., Yang X., Li Z., Casanueva R., Hernández V., Burgos J., Florence A.C., Yang L.H., Susser E. (2025). Defining urbanicity in the context of psychosis research: A qualitative systematic literature review. *Schizophrenia Bulletin*, 51(5):1312–1327.
Mascherek A., Murphy L., Lisanik M., Kühn S. (2025). Comparing aesthetic preferences and agreement ratings in depictions of natural and urban environments. *Journal of Environmental Psychology*, 106:102709.
Massey D. (2002). A brief history of human society: The origin and role of emotion in social life: 2001 presidential address. *American Sociological Review*, 67(1):1–29.
Mathieson I. et al. (2015). Genome-wide patterns of selection in 230 ancient Eurasians. *Nature*, 528(7583):499–503.
Matsumoto N., Koyanagi E., Seta S. (1997). "Physical and Mental Factors of Anticipation in the Streetscape." *Conference Proceedings of the International Conference on Environment-Behavior Studies for the 21st Century*, November 4–6, Tokyo, Japan, pp. 283–286.
McClung C.A. (2007). Circadian genes, rhythms and the biology of mood disorders. *Pharmacology & Therapeutics*, 114(2):222–232.

McClung C.A. (2011). Circadian rhythms and mood regulation: Insights from pre-clinical models. *European Neuropsychopharmacology*, 21(Suppl 4):S683–S693.

McCord M., Lo D., McCord J., Davis P., Haran M., Turley P. (2022). The impact of COVID-19 on house prices in Northern Ireland: Price persistence, yet divergent? *Journal of Property Research*, 39(3), 237–267.

McCrae R.R., Terracciano A., 79 Members of the Personality Profiles of Cultures Project (2005). Personality profiles of cultures: Aggregate personality traits. *Journal of Personality and Social Psychology*, 89(3):407–425.

McDonnell M.J. (2011). The history of urban ecology: An ecologist's perspective. In: Niemelä J. (Ed.), *Urban ecology: Patterns, processes and applications* (pp. 5–13). Oxford University Press, Oxford.

McEwen B.S. (2013). The brain on stress: Toward an integrative approach to brain, body, and behavior. *Perspective in Psychological Science*, 8(6):673–675.

McGowan P., Sasaki A., D'Alessio A. Dymov S., Labonté B., Szyf M., Turecki G., Meaney M.J. (2009). Epigenetic regulation of the glucocorticoid receptor in human brain associates with childhood abuse. *Nature Neuroscience*, 12(3):342–348.

McGrath J., Saha S., Welham J., El Saadi O., MacCauley C., Chant D. (2004). A systematic review of the incidence of schizophrenia: The distribution of rates and the influence of sex, urbanicity, migrant status and methodology. *BMC Medicine*, 2:13.

Mealey L., Theis P. (1995). The relationship between mood and preferences among natural landscapes: An evolutionary perspective. *Ethology and Sociobiology*, 16(3):247–256.

Menec V.H., Newall N.E., Mackenzie C.S., Shooshtari S., Nowicki S. (2019). Examining individual and geographic factors associated with social isolation and loneliness using Canadian Longitudinal Study on Aging (CLSA) data. *PLoS ONE*, 14(2):e0211143.

Meyer-Lindenberg A. (2010). From maps to mechanisms through neuroimaging of schizophrenia. *Nature*, 468(7321):194–202.

Milgram S. (1970). The experience of living in cities. *Science*, 167(3924):1461–1468.

Mill J.S. (1863). *Utilitarianism*. (Thrift ed., 2007), Dover, New York.

Mill J.S. (1874). *Dissertations and discussions*. Henry Holt, New York.

Miller G. (2016). Roots of the urban mind. *Science*, 352(6288):908–911.

Milot E., Stearns S.C. (2020). Selection on humans in cities. In: Szulkin M., Munshi-South J., Charmantier A. (Eds.), *Urban evolutionary biology*. Oxford University Press, Oxford.

Milton K. (1984). Habitat, diet, and activity patterns of free-ranging woolly spider monkeys (*Brachyteles arachnoides* E. Geoffroy 1806). *International Journal of Primatology*, 5(5):491–514.

Mitchell C.J.A. (2004). Making sense of counterurbanization. *Journal of Rural Studies*, 20(1), 15–34.

Mitchell R., Popham F. (2008). Effect of exposure to natural environment on health inequalities: An observational population study. *The Lancet*, 372(9650):1655–1660.

Mizrahi R. (2010). Social stress and psychosis risk: Common neurochemical substrates? *Neuropsychopharmacology*, 41:666–674.

Morris D. (1967). *The naked ape*. Random house, New York.

Morris D. (2006). *The nature of happiness*. Little Books, London.

Morrison P.S. (2010). Local expressions of subjective well-being: The New Zealand experience. *Regional Studies*, 45(8):1039–1058.

Morrison P.S. (2020). Wellbeing and the region. In: Fischer M., Nijkamp P. (Eds.), *Handbook of regional science* (pp. 779–798). Springer, Berlin; Heidelberg.

Morrison P.S., Weckroth M. (2017). Human values, subjective well-being and the metropolitan region. *Regional Studies*, 52(3):325–337.

Mortensen P.B., Pedersen C.B., Westergaard T., Wohlfahrt J., Ewald H., Mors O., Andersen P.K., Melbye M. (1999). Effects of family history and place and season of birth on the risk of schizophrenia. *New England Journal of Medicine*, 340(8):603–608.

Mortensen P.B., Pedersen M.G., Pedersen C.B. (2010). Psychiatric family history and schizophrenia risk in Denmark: Which mental disorders are relevant? *Psychological Medicine*, 40(2):201–210.

Morton T. (2000). *The descent of man*. Episode 2: Stone age minds in modern skulls. Australian Broadcasting Corporation, Sydney, NSW.

Mostafavi H. et al. (2017). Identifying genetic variants that affect viability in large cohorts. *PLoS Biology*, 15:e2002458.

Moura J.M.B., Júnior W.S.F., Silva T.C., Albuquerque U.P. (2018). The influence of the evolutionary past on the mind: An analysis of the preference for landscapes in the human species. *Frontiers in Psychology*, 9:2485.

Murdoch G.P. (1981). *Atlas of world cultures*. University of Pittsburgh Press, Pittsburgh, PA.

Murray G., Judd F., Jackson H., Fraser C., Komiti A., Hodgins G., Pattison P., Humphreys J., Robins G. (2005). The five factor model and accessibility/remoteness: Novel evidence for person–environment interaction. *Personality and Individual Differences*, 39(4):715–725.

Muzet A. (2007). Environmental noise, sleep and health. *Sleep Medicine Reviews*, 11(2):135–142.

Myers D.G., Diener E. (1995). Who is happy? *Psychological Science*, 6:10–19.

Naisbitt R. (1995). *The global paradox*. Avon Books, New York.

Negroponte N. (1995). *Being digital*. Vintage Books, New York.

Nettle D., Gibson M.A., Lawson D.W., Sear R. (2013). Human behavioral ecology: Current research and future prospects. *Behavioral Ecology*, 24(5):1031–1041.

Newbury J., Arseneault L., Caspi A., Moffitt T.E., Odgers C.L., Fisher H.L. (2016). Why are children in urban neighborhoods at increased risk for psychotic symptoms? Findings from a UK longitudinal cohort study. *Schizophrenia Bulletin*, 42(6):1372–1383.

Niepoth N., Bendesky A. (2020). How natural genetic variation shapes behavior. *Annual Review of Genomics and Human Genetics*, 21:437–463.

Nunn C.L., Samson D.R., Krystal A.D. (2016). Shining evolutionary light on human sleep and sleep disorders. *Evolution, Medicine, and Public Health*, 2016:227–243.

Nzabona A., Ntozi J., Ruraremwa G. (2016). Loneliness among older persons in Uganda: Examining social, economic and demographic risk factors. *Ageing and Society*, 36(4):860–888.

Obschonka M., Schmitt-Rodermund E., Silbereisen R.K., Gosling S.D., Potter J. (2013). The regional distribution and correlates of an entrepreneurship-prone personality profile in the United States, Germany, and the United Kingdom: A socioecological perspective. *Journal of Personality and Social Psychology*, 105:104–122.

Odling-Smee F.J. (1988). Niche constructing phenotypes. In: Plotkin H.C. (Ed.), *The role of behavior in evolution* (pp. 73–132). MIT Press, Cambridge, MA.

Odling-Smee F.J. (1995). Niche construction, genetic evolution and cultural change. *Behavioural Processes*, 35(1–3):195–205.

Odling-Smee J., Erwin D.H., Palkovacs E.P., Feldman M.W., Laland K.N. (2013). Niche construction theory: A practical guide for ecologists. *Quarterly Review of Biology*, 88(1):3–28.

Odling-Smee J.F., Laland K.N., Feldman M. (2003). *Niche construction: The neglected process in evolution*. Princeton University Press, New York.

Odling-Smee J.F., Laland K.N., Feldman M.W. (1996). Niche construction. *The American Naturalist*, 147(4):641–648.

Office for National Statistics (ONS) (2016). *Social capital across the UK: 2011 to 2012. Release date: 19 May 2016*. Office for National Statistics.

Oishi S. (2010). The psychology of residential mobility: Implications for the self, social relationships, and well-being. *Perspectives on Psychological Science*, 5:5–21.

Okkels N., Kristiansen C.B., Munk-Jørgensen P., Sartorius N. (2018). Urban mental health: Challenges and perspectives. *Current Opinion in Psychiatry*, 31(3):258–264.

Okulicz-Kozaryn A. (2017). Unhappy metropolis (when American city is too big). *Cities*, 61:144–155.

Okulicz-Kozaryn A. (2023). A. Unhappy metros: Panel evidence. *Applied Research Quality Life*, 18:753–763.
Okulicz-Kozaryn A., Mazelis J.M. (2018). Urbanism and happiness: A test of Wirth's theory of urban life. *Urban Studies*, 55(2):349–364.
Okulicz-Kozaryn A., Valente R.R. (2021). Urban unhappiness is common. *Cities*, 118:103368.
O'Leary A., Laas K., Vaht M., Kiive E., Veidebaum T., Reif A., Harro J. (2019). Nitric oxide synthase genotype interacts with stressful life events to increase aggression in male subjects in a population-representative sample. *European Neuropsychopharmacology*, 30:56–65.
Olivier C.-A., Martin J.S., Pilisi C., Agnania P., Kauffmanna C., Hayes L., Jaeggi A.V., Schradin C. (2024). Primate social organization evolved from a flexible pair-living ancestor. *Proceedings of the National Academy of Sciences of the United States of America*, 121(1):e2215401120.
Open Science Collaboration (2015). Estimating the reproducibility of psychological science. *Science*, 349(6251):4716.
Orians G.H., Heerwagen J.H. (1992). Evolved responses to landscapes. In: Barkow J.H., Cosmides L., Tooby J. (Eds.), *The adapted mind: Evolutionary psychology and the generation of culture* (pp. 555–579). Oxford University Press, New York.
Pani L., Porcella A., Gessa G.L. (2000). The role of stress in the pathophysiology of the dopaminergic system. *Molecular Psychiatry*, 5:14–21.
Papadimitriou F. (2020). Spatial complexity, visual complexity and aesthetics. In: Papadimitriou F. (Ed.), *Spatial complexity: Theory, mathematical methods and applications* (pp. 243–261). Springer, Cham.
Paradiso S., Johnson D.L., Andreasen N.C., O'Leary D.S., Watkins G.L., Ponto L.L., Hichwa R.D. (1999). Cerebral blood flow changes associated with attribution of emotional valence to pleasant, unpleasant, and neutral visual stimuli in a PET study of normal subjects. *The American Journal of Psychiatry*, 156:1618–1629.
Park B.J., Tsunetsugu Y., Kasetani T., Kagawa T., Miyazaki Y. (2010). The physiological effects of Shinrin-yoku (taking in the forest atmosphere or forest bathing): Evidence from field experiments in 24 forests across Japan. *Environmental Health and Preventive Medicine*, 15:18–26.
Park R.E. (1915). The city: Suggestion for the investigation of human behaviour in the city environment. *The American Journal of Sociology*, 20:577–612.
Park R.E., Burgess E.W. (1967) [1925]. *The city*. University of Chicago Press, Chicago, IL.
Parker K., Horowitz J., Brown A., Fry R., Cohn D., Igielnik R. (2018). *What unites and divides urban, suburban and rural communities*. Pew Research Center, Washington, DC.
Parsons R., Tassinary L.G., Ulrich R.S., Hebl M.R., Grossman-Alexander M. (1998). The view from the road: Implications for stress recovery and immunization. *Journal of Environmental Psychology*, 18:113–1404.

Peachey K. (2021). How Covid has changed where we want to live. *BBC News*. London. www.bbc.co.uk/news/business-56359865.

Pearce E., Wlodarski R., Machin A., Dunbar R.I.M. (2017). Variation in the β-endorphin, oxytocin, and dopamine receptor genes is associated with different dimensions of human sociality. *Proceedings of the National Academy of Sciences of the United States of America* , 114(20): 5300–5305.

Pedersen C.B., Mortensen P.B. (2001a). Evidence of a dose-response relationship between urbanicity during upbringing and schizophrenia risk. *Archives of General Psychiatry*, 58:1039–1046.

Pedersen C.B., Mortensen P.B. (2001b). Family history, place and season of birth as risk factors for schizophrenia in Denmark: A replication and reanalysis. *British Journal of Psychiatry*, 179:46–52.

Pedersen C.B., Mortensen P.B. (2006a). Are the cause(s) responsible for urban-rural differences in schizophrenia risk rooted in families or in individuals? *American Journal of Epidemiology*, 163:971–978.

Pedersen C.B., Mortensen P.B. (2006b). Urbanization and traffic related exposures as risk factors for schizophrenia. *BMC Psychiatry*, 6:1–7.

Peen J., Dekker J., Schoevers R.A., ten Have M., de Graaf R., Beekman A.T. (2007). Is the prevalence of psychiatric disorders associated with urbanization? *Social Psychiatry and Psychiatric Epidemiology*, 42:984–989.

Peen J., Schoevers R.A., Beekman A.T., Dekker J. (2010). The current status of urban-rural differences in psychiatric disorders. *Acta Psychiatrica Scandinavica*, 121:84–93.

Peiró A. (2006). Happiness, satisfaction and socio-economic conditions: Some international evidence. *Journal of Socio-Economics*, 35:348–365.

Pelletier F., Pigeon G., Bergeron P., Mayer F.M., Boisvert M., Réale D., Milot E. (2017). Eco evolutionary dynamics in a contemporary human population. *Nature Communications*, 8:15947.

Penke L., Jokela M. (2016). The evolutionary genetics of personality revisited. *Current Opinion in Psychology*, 7:104–109.

Pepper G.V., Nettle D. (2014). Socioeconomic dis parities in health behaviour: An evolutionary perspective. In: Gibson M.A., Lawson D.W. (Eds.), *Applied evolutionary anthropology* (pp. 225–243). Springer, New York.

Persson B. (2020). Genotype−environment correlation and its relation to personality — A twin and family study. *Twin Research and Human Genetics*, 23(4):228–234.

Peterson B.S. et al. (2015). Effects of prenatal exposure to air pollutants (polycyclic aromatic hydrocarbons) on the development of brain white matter, cognition, and behavior in later childhood. *JAMA Psychiatry*, 72(6):531–540.

Pickrell J.K. et al. (2009). Signals of recent positive selection in a worldwide sample of human populations. *Genome Research*, 19(5):826–837.

Pinker S. (2002). *The blank slate*. (2019 ed.). Penguin, London, p. x.

Plomin R., DeFries J.C., Knopik V.S., Neiderhiser J.M. (2016). Top 10 replicated findings from behavioral genetics. *Perspectives on Psychological Science*, 11(1):3–23.

Polderman T.J.C., Benyamin B., De Leeuw C.A., Sullivan P.F., Van Bochoven A., Visscher P.M., Posthuma D. (2015). Meta-analysis of the heritability of human traits based on fifty years of twin studies. *Nature Genetics*, 47(7):702–709.

Prati G. (2024). The relationship between rural-urban place of residence and subjective well-being is nonlinear and its substantive significance is questionable. *International Journal of Applied Positive Psychology*, 9:27–43.

Prattley J., Buffel T., Marshall A., Nazroo J. (2020). Area effects on the level and development of social exclusion in later life. *Social Science & Medicine*, 246:112722.

Pred A. (1967). *Behavior and location. Foundations for a geographic and dynamic location theory*. C.W.K Gleerup, Lund.

Pritchard J.K., Di Rienzo A. (2010). Adaptation—Not by sweeps alone. *Nature Reviews Genetics*, 11:665–667.

Probst J.C., Laditka S.B., Moore C.G., Harun N., Powell M.P., Baxley E.G. (2006). Rural-urban differences in depression prevalence: Implications for family medicine. *Family Medicine*, 38(9):653–660.

Pulver A., Kiive E., Kanarik M., Harro J. (2020). Association of orexin/hypocretin receptor gene (HCRTR1) with reward sensitivity, and interaction with gender. *Brain Research*, 1746:147013.

Pykett J., Osborne T., Resch B. (2020). From urban stress to neurourbanism: How should we research city well-being? *Annals of the American Association of Geographers*, 110(6):1936–1951.

Ramsden E. (2012). Rats, stress and the built environment. *History of the Human Sciences*, 25(5):123–147.

Réale D., Reader S.M., Sol D., McDougall P.T., Dingemanse N.J. (2007). Integrating animal temperament within ecology and evolution. *Biological Reviews*, 82:291–318.

Reed J.L. et al. (2018). Interaction of childhood urbanicity and variation in dopamine genes alters adult prefrontal function as measured by functional magnetic resonance imaging (fMRI). *PLoS ONE*, 13(4):e0195189.

Reichert M., Braun U., Lautenbach S., Zipf A., Ebner-Priemer U., Tost H., Meyer-Lindenberg A. (2020). Studying the impact of built environments on human mental health in everyday life: Methodological developments, state-of-the-art and technological frontiers. *Current Opinion in Psychology*, 32:158–164.

Reiss A.J. (1959). Rural-urban and status differences in interpersonal contacts. *American Journal of Sociology*, 65:182–195.

Rentfrow P.J. (Ed.) (2013). *Geographical psychology: Exploring the interaction of environment and behavior*. American Psychological Association, Washington, DC.

Rentfrow P.J., Gosling S.D., Jokela M., Stillwell D.J., Kosinski M., Potter J. (2013). Divided we stand: Three psychological regions of the United States and their political, economic, social, and health correlates. *Journal of Personality and Social Psychology*, 105:996–1012.

Rentfrow P.J., Gosling S.D., Potter J. (2008). A theory of the emergence, persistence, and expression of regional variation in basic traits. *Perspectives on Psychological Science*, 3:339–369.

Rentfrow P.J., Jokela M., Lamb M.E. (2015). Regional personality differences in Great Britain. *PLoS ONE*, 10(3):e0122245.

Rentfrow P.J., Mellander C., Florida R. (2009). Happy states of America: A state-level analysis of psychological, economic, and social well-being. *Journal of Research in Personality*, 43:1073–1082.

Reznick D.N., Bryga H., Endler J.A. (1990). Experimentally induced life-history evolution in anatural population. *Nature*, 346:357–359.

Reznick D.N., Endler J. (1982). The impact of predation on life history evolution in Trinidadianguppies (*Poecilia reticulata*). *Evolution*, 36:160–177.

Reznick D.N., Shaw F.H., Rodd F.H., Shaw R.G. (1997). Evaluation of the rate of evolution innatural populations of guppies (*Poecilia reticulata*). *Science*, 275:1934–1937.

Rice D., Barone S., Jr. (2000). Critical periods of vulnerability for the developing nervous system: Evidence from humans and animal models. *Environ Health Perspect*, 108(Suppl 3):511–533.

Richerson P.J., Boyd R. (2004). *Not by genes alone*. University of Chicago Press, Chicago, IL.

Richerson P.J., Boyd R., Bettinger R.L. (2009). Cultural innovations and demographic change. *Human Biology*, 81(2–3):211–235.

Richerson P.J., Boyd R., Henrich J. (2010). Gene–culture coevolution in the age of genomics. *Proceedings of the National Academy of Sciences of the United States of America*, 107:8985–8992.

Rivkin L.R. et al. (2019). A roadmap for urban evolutionary ecology. *Evolutionary Applications*, 12(3):384–398.

Roberts P., Boivin N., Lee-Thorp J., Petraglia M., Stock J. (2016). Tropical forests and the genus Homo. *Evolutionary Anthropology*, 25:306–317.

Robertson D.S. (1991). Feedback theory and Darwinian evolution. *Journal of Theoretical Biology*, 152:469–484.

Robinson G.E., Fernald R.D., Clayton D.F. (2008). Genes and social behavior. *Science*, 322(5903):896–900.

Roe J.J., Thompson C.W., Aspinall P.A., Brewer M.J., Duff E.I., Miller D., Mitchell R., Clow A. (2013). Green space and stress: Evidence from cortisol measures in deprived urban communities. *International Journal of Environmental Research and Public Health*, 10(9):4086–4103.

Royet J., Zald D., Versace R., Costes N., Lavenne F., Koenig O., Gervais R. (2000). Emotional responses to pleasant and unpleasant olfactory, visual, and auditory stimuli: A positron emission tomography study. *Journal of Neuroscience*, 20(20):7752–7759.

Rowe F., Calafiore A., Arribas-Bel D., Samardzhiev K., Fleischmann M. (2023). Urban exodus? Understanding human mobility in Britain during the COVID-19 pandemic using Meta-Facebook data. *Population, Space and Place*, 29:e2637.

Røysamb E., Nes R.B., Czajkowski N.O., Vassend O. (2018). Genetics, personality and wellbeing. A twin study of traits, facets and life satisfaction. *Scientific Reports*, 8:12298.

Rubin K.H., Bukowski W., Parker J.G. (2006). Peer interactions, relationships, and groups. In: Eisenberg N. (Ed.), *Handbook of child psychology: Vol. 3. Social, emotional, and personality development* (pp. 571–645). Wiley, New York.

Ryan S.C., Sugg M.M., Runkle J.D., Thapa B. (2024). Advancing understanding on greenspace and mental health in young people. *Geohealth*, 8(3):e2023GH000959.

Rybski D., Arcaute E., Batty M. (2019). Urban scaling laws. *Environment and Planning B: Urban Analytics and City Science*, 46(9):1605–1610.

Sachs J. (2000). Notes on a new sociology of economic development. In: Harrison L.E., Huntington S.P. (Eds.), *Culture matters: How values shape human progress*. Basic Books, New York.

Saltz J.B. (2011). Natural genetic variation in social environment choice: Context-dependent gene-environment correlation in *Drosophila melanogaster*. *Evolution*, 65:2325–2334.

Saltz J.B., Nuzhdin S.V. (2014). Genetic variation in niche construction: Implications for development and evolutionary genetics. *Trends in Ecology and Evolution*, 29(1):8–14.

Sampson L., Ettman C.K., Galea S. (2020). Urbanization, urbanicity, and depression: A review of the recent global literature. *Current Opinion in Psychiatry*, 33(3):233–244.

Sánchez-Moral S., Arellano A., Díez-Pisonero R. (2026). The impact of remote working on residential mobility in the metropolitan region of Madrid. *Cities*, 169:106462.

Sanchez-Roige S., Gray J.C., MacKillop J., Chen C.H., Palmer A.A. (2018). The genetics of human personality. *Genes, Brain, and Behavior*, 17(3): e12439.

Sander W. (2011). Location and happiness in the United States. *Economics Letters*, 112:277–279.

Schelin E., Munk-Jorgensen P., Olesen A., Gerlach J. (2000). Regional differences in schizophrenia incidence in Denmark. *Acta Psychiatrica Scandinavica*, 101:293–299.

Schkade D., Kahneman D. (1998). Does living in California make people happy? A focusing illusion in judgments of life satisfaction. *Psychological Science*, 9:340–346.

Schläpfer M., Bettencourt L.M.A., Grauwin S., Raschke M., Claxton R., Smoreda Z., West G.B., Ratti C. (2014). The scaling of human interactions with city size. *Journal of the Royal Society Interface*, 1120130789.

Schopler J., Stockdale J.E. (1977). An interference analysis of crowding. *Environmental Psychology & Nonverbal Behavior*, 1(2):81–88.

Schroeder C.W. (1942). Mental disorders in cities. *American Journal of Sociology*, 48(91):40–47.

Scitovsky T. (1976). *The joyless economy*. Oxford University Press, Oxford.

Scott M., Kelleher L., Fox-Rogers L., Gkartzios M. (2025). From 'counterurbanisation as practice' to the 'governance of counterurbanisation': Structuring pro-rural relocations through planning regulation of housing. *Journal of Rural Studies*, 120:103868.

Scottish Government (2020). *Scottish household survey 2019: Annual report*. Scottish Government, Edinburgh. www.gov.scot/publications/scottish-household-survey-2019-annual-report/pages/5/.

Seeman M. (1975). Alienation studies. *Annual Review of Sociology*, 1:91–123.

Selye H. (1946). The general adaptation syndrome and the diseases of adaptation. *The Journal of Clinical Endocrinology and Metabolism*, 6:117–230.

Selye H. (1950). Stress and the general adaptation syndrome. *British Medical Journal*, 1(4667):1383–1392.

Selye H. (1951). The general-adaptation-syndrome. *Annual Review of Medicine*, 2:327–342.

Senior W.N. (2002) [1938]. *An outline of the science of political economy*. University Press of the Pacific, New York.

Sennett R. (1990). *The conscience of the eye: The design and social life of cities*. Norton, New York.

Sennett R. (1994). *Flesh and stone: The body and the city in western civilization*. Norton, New York.

Shackelford T.K., Welling L.L.M. (Eds.) (2019). *The Oxford handbook of evolutionary psychology and behavioral endocrinology*. Oxford University Press, Oxford.

Shucksmith M., Cameron S., Merridew T., Pichler F. (2009). Urban-rural differences in quality of life across the European Union. *Regional Studies*, 43(10):1275–1289.

Shukla P., Kang T.K. (2017). Perceived loneliness among rural and urban adolescents: A comparative study. *Indian Journal of Positive Psychology*, 8(3):386–388.

Shultz S., Finlayson L.V. (2010). Large body and small brain and group sizes are associated with predator preferences for mammalian prey. *Behavioral Ecology*, 21:1073–1079.

Shultz S., Noe R., McGraw S., Dunbar R.I.M. (2004). A community-level evaluation of the impact of prey behavioural and ecological characteristics on predator diet composition. *Proceedings of the Royal Society B*, 271B:725–732.

Silva J.A., Steffen R.E. (2019). Urban environment and psychiatric disorders: A review of the neuroscience and biology. *Clinical and Experimental, Metabolism*, 100:153940.

Silver M., Di Paolo E. (2006). Spatial effects favour the evolution of niche construction. *Theoretical Population Biology*, 20:387–400.

Simmel G. (1950) [1903]. The metropolis and mental life. In: Wolff K.H. (Ed.), *The sociology of George Simmel*. Macmillan, New York.

Simon H.A. (1959). Theories of decision-making in economics and behavioral science. *The American Economic Review*, 49(3):253–283.

Sinha R., Lacadie C., Skudlarski P., Wexler B.E. (2004). Neural circuits underlying emotional distress in humans. *Annals of the New York Academy of Sciences*, 1032:254–257.

Škorić M., Kišjuhas A. (2020). Habitat selection and the evolutionary aesthetics of landscape preference. *Documenta Praehistorica*, 47:494–507.

Smith C.U.M. (2005). Evolutionary neurobiology and aesthetics. *Perspectives in Biology and Medicine*, 48(1):17–30.

Sommer R. (2002). Personal space in a digital age. In: Bechtel R.B., Churchman A. (Eds.), *Handbook of environmental psychology* (pp. 647–660). Wiley, New York.

Sørensen J.F.L (2014). Rural–urban differences in life satisfaction: Evidence from the European Union. *Regional Studies*, 48(9):1451–1466.

Srivastava A., Dunbar R.I.M. (1996). The mating system of hanuman langurs: A problem in optimal foraging. *Behavioral Ecology and Sociobiology*, 39:219–226.

Stafford T. (2012). Why are we so curious? *BBC Future*, 19 June.

Stajich J.E., Hahn M.W. (2005). Disentangling the effects of demography and selection in human history. *Molecular Biology and Evolution*, 22:63–73.

Stawarz N., Rosenbaum-Feldbrügge M., Sander N., Sulak H., Knobloch V. (2022). The impact of the COVID-19 pandemic on internal migration in Germany: A descriptive analysis. *Population, Space and Place*, 28(6):e2566.

Steel Z., Marnane C., Iranpour C., Chey T., Jackson J.W., Patel V., Silove D. (2014). The global prevalence of common mental disorders: A systematic review and meta-analysis 1980–2013. *International Journal of Epidemiology*, 43(2):476–493.

Steemers K. (2015). *The 6th VELUX daylight symposium*: (0:38 www.youtube.com/watch?v=NAJYcO-htxg).

Steinheuser V., Ackermann K., Schönfeld P., Schwabe L. (2014). Stress and the city: Impact of urban upbringing on the (re)activity of the hypothalamus-pituitary-adrenal axis. *Psychosomatic Medicine*, 76(9):678–685.

Stevens R.G., Brainard G.C., Blask D.E., Lockley S.W., Motta M.E. (2013). Adverse health effects of nighttime lighting: Comments on American Medical Association policy statement. *American Journal of Preventive Medicine*, 45:343–346.

Stokols D. (1978). Environmental psychology. *Annual Review of Psychology*, 29:253–295.

Storz J.F., Payseur B.A., Nachman M.W. (2004). Genome scans of DNA variability in humans reveal evidence for selective sweeps outside of Africa. *Molecular Biology and Evolution*, 21:1800–1811.

Stotz K. (2017). Why developmental niche construction is not selective niche construction: And why it matters. *Interface Focus*, 7:2016015720160157.

Streit F. et al. (2014). A functional variant in the neuropeptide S receptor 1 gene moderates the influence of urban upbringing on stress processing in the amygdala. *The International Journal on the Biology of Stress*, 17:352–361.

Stringer C., Andrews P. (2014). *The complete world of human evolution*. Thames & Hudson, Naturally History Museum, London.

Ströbele M., Hunziker M. (2017). Are suburbs perceived as rural villages? Landscape-related residential preferences in Switzerland. *Landscape and Urban Planning*, 163:67–79.

Stulp G., Barrett L. (2016). Wealth, fertility and adaptive behaviour in industrial populations. *Philosophical Transactions of the Royal Society B*, 371:20150153.

Stulp G., Barrett L., Tropf F.C., Mills M. (2015). Does natural selection favour taller stature among the tallest people on earth? *Proceedings of the Royal Society B: Biological Sciences*, 282:20150211.

Sudradjat I. (2012). Foucault, the other spaces, and human behaviour. *Procedia – Social and Behavioral Sciences*, 36:28–34.

Sukopp H. (1998). Urban ecology—scientific and practical aspects. In Breuste J., Feldmann H., Uhlmann O. (Eds.), *Urban ecology* (pp. 3–16). Springer, Basel.

Sun Y., Liang C. (2022). Urban-rural comparison of the association between unsupportive relationships, perceived stress, authentic self-presentation, and loneliness among young adults in Taiwan. *International Journal of Environmental Research and Public Health*, 19(14):8808.

Sundquist K., Frank G., Sundquist J. (2004). Urbanisation and incidence of psychosis and depression. *British Journal of Psychiatry*, 84:293–298.

Sutcliffe J.P., Crabbe B.D. (1963). Incidence and degrees of friendships in urban and rural areas. *Social Forces*, 42:60–67.

Tae-Hoon K., Gwang-Woo J., Han-Su B., Gwang-Won K., Thirunavukkarasu S., Heoung-Keun K., Seung-Won L., Hyung-Joong K., Jin-Kyu S., (2010). Human brain activation in response to visual stimulation with rural and urban scenery pictures: A functional magnetic resonance imaging study. *Science of the Total Environment*, 408(12):2600–2607.

Takano T., Nakamura K., Watanabe M. (2002). Urban residential environments and senior citizens' longevity in megacity areas: The importance of walkable green spaces. *Journal of Epidemiology and Community Health*, 56:913–918.

Tandon P.S., Zhou C., Christakis D.A. (2012). Frequency of parent-supervised outdoor play of US preschool-aged children. *Archives of Pediatric and Adolescent Medicine*, 166:707–712.

Tassinari F., Kleine-Rueschkamp L., Veneri P. (2023). *Life satisfaction along the urban-rural continuum: A global assessment*. OECD Regional Development Papers, No. 44, OECD Publishing.

Taylor A.F., Kuo F.E. (2009). Children with attention deficits concentrate better after walk in the park. *Journal of Attention Disorders*, 12(5): 402–409.

Taylor R.P., Spehar B., Donkelaar P.V., Hagerhall C.M. (2011). Perceptual and physiological responses to Jackson Pollock's fractals. *Frontier in Human Neuroscience*, 5:60.

Teng L.B., Sharif R., Ishaki W.S.W., Kozlowski M., Ismail S. (2018). Urban setting: Induce or reduce mental health? *Alam Cipta*, 11(2):19–24.

Tennessen C.M., Cimprich B. (1995). Views to nature: Effects on attention. *Journal of Environmental Psychology*, 15:77–85.

The Economist (2021, December 18). *Why Americans are rethinking where they want to live*. www.economist.com/united-states/why-americans-are-rethinking-where-theywant-to-live/21806771.

The Economist (2021, July 4). *Covid-19 has persuaded Americans to leave city centres*. www.economist.com/graphic-detail/2021/07/04/covid-19-has-persuadedamericans-to-leave-city-centres.

The Economist (2021, October 30). *Remote-first is taking over the rich world*. www.economist.com/finance-and-economics/2021/10/30/remote-first-work-istaking-over-the-rich-world.

The Globe and Mail. (2021, January 22). *Toronto, Montreal see exodus pick up pace, aggravated by COVID-19 pandemic*. www.theglobeandmail.com/business/articletoronto-montreal-see-exodus-pick-up-pace-aggravated-by-covid-19/.

The Guardian (2020, September 26). *Escape to the country: How Covid is driving an exodus from Britain's cities*. www.theguardian.com/world/2020/sep/26/escape-countrycovid-exodus-britain-cities-pandemic-urban-green-space.

The New York Times (2020). *Coronavirus escape: To the suburbs*. www.nytimes.com/2020/05/08/realestate/coronavirus-escape-city-to-suburbs.html.

The Sydney Morning Herald (2021, August 3). Lockdowns spark city exodus as thousands head to the hills. www.smh.com.au/politics/federal/lockdowns-spark-city-exodus-as-thousandshead-to-the-hills-20210803-p58fh3.html.

Thornhill R. (1998). Darwinian aesthetics. In: Crawford C., Krebs D. (Eds.), *Handbook of evolutionary psychology* (pp. 543–572). Erlbaum, Mahwah, NJ; New York.

Thornicroft G., Bisoffi G., De Salvia D., Tansella M. (1993). Urban-rural differences in the associations between social deprivation and psychiatric service utilization in schizophrenia and all diagnoses: A case-register study in Northern Italy. *Psychological Medicine*, 23(2):487–496.

Tielbeek J.J. et al. (2017). Genome-wide association studies of a broad spectrum of antisocial behavior. *JAMA Psychiatry*, 74:1242–1250.

Tiger L., Fox R. (1966). The zoological perspective in social science. *Man*, 1(1):75–81.

Tiger L., Fox R. (1971). *The imperial animal*. Holt, Rinehart & Winston, Oxford.

Tikhodeyev O.N., Shcherbakova O.V. (2019). The problem of non-shared environment in behavioral genetics. *Behavior Genetics*, 49:259–269.

Tinbergen N. (1951). *The study of instinct*. Clarendon Press, Oxford.

Tishkoff S.A. et al. (2007). Convergent adaptation of human lactase persistence in Africa and Europe. *Nature Genetics*, 39(1):31–40.

Tobiasz-Adamczyk B., Zawisza K. (2017). Urban-rural differences in social capital in relation to self-rated health and subjective well-being in older residents of six regions in Poland. *Annals of Agricultural and Environmental Medicine*, 24(2):162–170.

Toffler A. (1980). *The third wave*. Bantam Books, New York.

Tomson K., Vaht M., Laas K., Veidebaum T., Harro J. (2016). Effect of a human serotonin 5-HT2A receptor gene polymorphism on impulsivity: Dependence on cholesterol levels. *Journal of Affective Disorders*, 206:23–30.

Tong Y., Piotrowski M. (2012). Migration and health selectivity in the context of internal migration in China, 1997–2009. *Population Research and Policy Review*, 31(4):497–543.

Tönnies F. (2002) [1887]. *Community and society*. Dover, New York.

Torrey E.F., Mortensen P.B., Pedersen C.B., Wohlfahrt J., Melbye M. (2001). Risk factors and confounders in the geographical clustering of schizophrenia. *Schizophrenia Research*, 49(3):295–299.

Tost H., Champagne F.A., Meyer-Lindenberg A. (2015). Environmental influence in the brain, human welfare and mental health. *Nature Neuroscience*, 18:1421–1431.

Townsend J.B., Barton S. (2018). The impact of ancient tree form on modern landscape preferences. *Urban Forestry & Urban Greening*, 34:205–216.

Tropf F.C. et al. (2015). Human fertility, molecular genetics, and natural selection in modern societies. *PLoS ONE*, 10:e0126821.

Tsunetsugu Y., Miyazaki Y. (2005). Measurement of absolute hemoglobin concentrations of prefrontal region by near-infrared time-resolved spectroscopy: Examples of experiments and prospects. *Journal of Physiological Anthropology and Applied Human Science*, 24(4):469–472.

Tuan Y.F. (1977). *Space and place: The perspective of experience*. Edward Arnold, London.

Tubadji A., Nijkamp P. (2015). Cultural impact on regional development: Application of a PLS-PM model to Greece. *The Annals of Regional Science*, 54:687–720.

Turchin M.C., Chiang C.W.K., Palmer C.D., Sankararaman S., Reich D., Genetic Investigation of ANthropometric Traits (GIANT) Consortium (2012). Evidence of widespread selection on standing variation in Europe at height-associated SNPs. *Nature Genetics*, 44(9):1015–1019.

Turkheimer E., Waldron M. (2000). Nonshared environment: A theoretical, methodological, and quantitative review. *Psychological Bulletin*, 126(1):78–108.

Turner J.H., Machalek R. (2018). *The new evolutionary sociology: Recent and revitalized theoretical and methodological approaches*. Routledge, New York.

Turner K.M., Burne T.H. (2013). Interaction of genotype and environment: Effect of strain and housing conditions on cognitive behavior in rodent models of schizophrenia. *Frontiers in Behavioral Neuroscience*, 7:1–7.

Tyree S.M., Borniger J.C., de Lecea L. (2018). Hypocretin as a hub for arousal and motivation. *Frontiers in Neurology*, 9:413.

Ullman E.L. (1962). The nature of cities reconsidered. *Papers – Regional Science Association*, 9:7–23.

Ulrich R.S., Simons R.F., Losito B.D., Fiorito E., Miles M.A., Zelson M. (1991). Stress recovery during exposure to natural and urban environments. *Journal of Environmental Psychology*, 11:201–230.

Vaessen T., Hernaus D., Myin-Germeys I., van Amelsvoort T. (2015). The dopaminergic response to acute stress in health and psychopathology: A systematic review. *Neuroscience & Biobehavioral Reviews*, 56:241–251.

Valk S.L., Bernhardt B.C., Trautwein F.M., Böckler A., Kanske P., Guizard N., Collins D.L., Singer T. (2017). Structural plasticity of the social brain: Differential change after socio-affective and cognitive mental training. *Science Advances*, 4(10):e17004893.

van den Berg A.E., Custers M.H. (2011). Gardening promotes neuroendocrine and affective restoration from stress. *Journal of Health Psychology*, 16(1):3–11.

van den Berg A.E., Maas J., Verheij R.A., Groenewegen P.P. (2010). Green space as a buffer between stressful life events and health. *Social Science & Medicine*, 70(8):1203–1210.

van den Berg S.M. et al. (2016). Meta-analysis of genome-wide association studies for extraversion: Findings from the genetics of personality consortium. *Behavioral Genetics*, 46(2):170–182.

Van Os J. (2004). Does the urban environment cause psychosis? *The British Journal of Psychiatry*, 184:287–288.

Van Os J., Hanssen M., Bijl R.V., Vollebergh W. (2001). Prevalence of psychotic disorder and community level of psychotic symptoms. *Archives of General Psychiatry*, 58:663–668.

Van Os J., Kenis G., Rutten B.P.F. (2010). The environment and schizophrenia. *Nature*, 648:203–212.

Van Os J., Pedersen C.B., Mortensen P.B. (2004). Confirmation of synergy between urbanicity and familial liability in the causation of psychosis. *American Journal of Psychiatry*, 161:2312–2314.

van Schaik C.P. (1983). Why are diurnal primates living in groups? *Behaviour*, 87:120–144.

van Vugt M., Giphart R. (2018). *Mismatch: How our stone age brain deceives us every day*. Robinson, London.

Vassos E., Agerbo E., Mors O., Pedersen C.B. (2016). Urban–rural differences in incidence rates of psychiatric disorders in Denmark. *The British Journal of Psychiatry*, 208:435–440.

Veenhoven R. (1988). The utility of happiness. *Social Indicator Research*, 20(4):333–354.

Versigghel J., Ermagun A., Hook H., De Vos J., Witlox F. (2026). The new commute: Is teleworking stimulating residential and workplace relocations? *Journal of Transport Geography*, 130:104471.

Vilhelmson B., Thulin E. (2013). Does the internet encourage people to move? Investigating Swedish young adults' internal migration experiences and plans. *Geoforum*, 47:209–216.

Vilhelmson B., Thulin E., Gil Solá A. (2026). The new geography of hybrid work: Do we live more locally when work moves home? *Applied Geography*, 186:103834.

Vogiazides L., Kawalerowicz J. (2022). Urban exodus in Covid times: Who moves out of the inner city of Stockholm and where do they go? *Stockholm Research Reports in Demography*, 2022:4, Stockholm University, Stockholm.

Voight B.F., Kudaravalli S., Wen X., Pritchard J.K. (2006). A map of recent positive selection in the human genome. *PLoS Biology*, 4(3):e72.

Waddington C.H. (1959). Evolutionary systems; animal and human. *Nature*, 183:1634–1638.

Wand G.S. et al. (2007). Association of amphetamine-induced striatal dopamine release and cortisol responses to psychological stress. *Neuropsychopharmacology*, 32:2310–2320.

Wang J.L. (2004). Rural–urban differences in the prevalence of major depression and associated impairment. *Social Psychiatry and Psychiatric Epidemiology*, 39:19.

Ward Thompson C., Roe J., Aspinall P., Mitchell R., Clow A., Miller D. (2012). More green space is linked to less stress in deprived communities: Evidence from salivary cortisol patterns. *Landscape and Urban Planning*, 105:221–229.

Waring T.M., Wood Z.T., Szathmáry E. (2024). Characteristic processes of human evolution caused the Anthropocene and may obstruct its global solutions. *Philosophical Transactions of the Royal Society B: Biological Sciences*, 379(1893):20220259.

Waterman A.S. (1993). Two conceptions of happiness: Contrasts of personal expressiveness (Eudaimonia) and hedonic enjoyment. *Journal of Personality and Social Psychology*, 64(4):678–691.

Weaver I., Cervoni N., Champagne F., D'Alessio A.C., Sharma S., Seckl J.R., Dymov S., Szyf M., Meaney M.J. (2004). Epigenetic programming by maternal behavior. *Nature Neuroscience*, 7(8):847–854.

Weber M., Martindale D., Neuwirth G. (1962) [1921]. *The city*. Collier Books, New York.

Weckroth M. et al. (2022). Urbanity, neighbourhood characteristics and perceived quality of life (QoL): Analysis of individual and contextual determinants for perceived QoL in 3300 postal code areas in Finland. *Social Indicator Research*, 164:139–164.

Weich S., Twigg L., Lewis G. (2006). Rural/non-rural differences in rates of common mental disorders in Britain: Prospective multilevel cohort study. *British Journal of Psychiatry*, 188:51–57.

Weinhold B. (2006). Epigenetics: The science of change. *Environmental Health Perspectives*, 114(3):A160–A167.

Wells N.M., Evans G.W. (2003). Nearby nature: A buffer of life stress among rural children. *Environment and Behavior*, 35:311–330.

Werbner P. (2018). Commentary: Urban friendship: Towards an alternative anthropological genealogy. *Urban Studies*, 55(3):662–674.

West G. (2011). *The surprising math of cities and corporations*. [TED talk].TEDGlobal 2011.

West G. (2017). *Scale*. Penguin Random House, New York.

West M.J., King A.P., Arberg A.A. (1988). The inheritance of niches: The role of ecological legacies in ontogeny. In: Blass E. (Ed.), *Handbook of behavioral neurobiology* (pp. 41–62). Plenum, New York.

Whitaker S.D. (2021). Did the COVID-19 pandemic cause an urban exodus? *Cleveland Fed District Data Briefs* (20210205), Federal Reserve Bank of Cleveland, Cleveland, OH.

White E.A. (1903). The geographical distribution of insanity in the United States. *Journal of Nervous and Mental Disease*, 30:257–279.

White T.D. (2018). The origin of our species. In: *Becoming Human (New Scientist: The Collection, Vol.5 Issue 4, 2nd ed.)*.New Scientist, The Collection, London.

WHO (2014). *Mental health: A state of well-being*. World Health Organization.

Wiers R.W., Urban Mental Health Researchers, El Marroun H., Bockting C., Krugers H. (2025). Debate: Urban versus rural environments – which is better for mental health? The one good thing about a small town…. *Child Adolesc Ment Health*, 30:189–191.

Wilker E.H. et al. (2015). Long-term exposure to fine particulate matter, residential proximity to major roads and measures of brain structure. *Stroke*, 46(5):1161–1166.

Willems E., Hill R.A. (2009). Predator-specific landscapes of fear and resource distribution: Effects on spatial range use. *Ecology*, 90:546–555.

Williams K.J., Lee K.E., Hartig T., Sargent L.D., Williams N.S., Johnson K.A. (2018). Conceptualising creativity benefits of nature experience: Attention restoration and mind wandering as complementary processes. *Journal of Environmental Psychology*, 59:36–45.

Williamson S.H., Hubisz M.J., Clark A.G., Payseur B.A., Bustamante C.D., Nielsen R. (2007). Localizing recent adaptive evolution in the human genome. *PLoS Genetics*, 3(6):0901–0915.

Wilson E.O. (1975). *Sociobiology: The new synthesis*. Harvard University Press, Cambridge, MA.

Wilson E.O. (1984). *Biophilia*. Harvard University Press, Cambridge, MA.

Wilson E.O. (1998). *Consilience: The unity of knowledge*. Alfred A. Knopf, New York.

Wilson E.O. (2000). *Sociobiology. The new synthesis* (25th Anniversary ed.). Belknap Harvard, Cambridge, MA.

Wilson E.O. (2004). *On human nature*. Harvard University Press, Cambridge, MA; London.

Wilson E.O. (2004a). *The future of life*. Random House, New York.

Winters J.V., Li Y. (2017). Urbanisation, natural amenities and subjective well-being: Evidence from US counties. *Urban Studies*, 54(8):1956–1973.

Winston R.M.L. (2002). *Human instinct*. London: Bantam Press.

Wirth L. (1938). Urbanism as a way of life. *American Journal of Sociology*, 44:1–24.

Wolf J.B. (2000). Indirect genetic effects and gene interactions. In: Wolf J.B., Brodie E.D., Wade M.J. (Eds.), *Epistasis and the evolutionary process*. Oxford University Press, New York.

Workman L., Reader W. (2021). *Evolutionary psychology*. Cambridge University Press, Cambridge.

Wrangham R.W. (1980). An ecological model of female-bonded primate groups. *Behaviour*, 75:262–300.

Wrangham R.W. (1987). Evolution of social structure. In: Smuts B.B., Cheney D.L., Seyfarth R.M., Wrangham R.W., Struhsaker T.T. (Eds.), *Primate societies* (pp. 282–296). The University of Chicago Press, Chicago, IL.

Wrangham R.W., Gittleman J.L., Chapman C.A. (1993). Constraints on group size in primates and carnivores: Population density and day-range as assays of exploitation competition. *Behavioral Ecology and Sociobiology*, 32(3):199–209.

Wu J. et al. (2026). Urban-rural differences in depressive symptoms and related factors among employed middle-aged and older adults: a national cross-sectional study in China. *BMC Public Health*, 26:791.

Xenakis I., Arnellos A., Darzentas J. (2012). The functional role of emotions in aesthetic judgment. *New Ideas in Psychology*, 30(2):212–226.

Xu C., Miao L., Turner D., DeRubeis R. (2023). Urbanicity and depression: A global meta-analysis. *Journal of Affective Disorders*, 340:299–311.

Xu H.A., Modirshanechi A., Lehmann M.P., Gerstner W., Herzog M.H. (2021). Novelty is not surprise: Human exploratory and adaptive behavior in sequential decision-making. *PLoS Computational Biology*, 17(6):e1009070.

Yamaguchi M., Deguchi M., Miyazaki Y. (2006). The effects of exercise in forest and urban environments on sympathetic nervous activity of normal young adults. *Journal of International Medical Research*, 34(2):152–159.

Yi X. et al. (2010). Sequencing of 50 human exomes reveals adaptation to high altitude. *Science*, 329(5987):75–78.

Young I.M. (1990). *Justice and the politics of difference*. Princeton University Press, New York.

Zagorsky J.L., Smith P.K. (2017). The association between socioeconomic status and adult fast-food consumption in the U.S. *Economics and Human Biology*, 27:12–25.

Zald D.H., Pardo J.V. (1997). Emotion, olfaction, and the human amygdala: Amygdala activation during aversive olfactory stimulation. *Proceedings of the National Academy of Sciences of the United States of America*, 94:4119–4124.

Zhang Y., Yasin S.M., Sun L. (2025). The implications of urban-to-rural migration on rural development: A systematic literature review. *GeoJournal*, 90:97.

Zeller E., Timmermann A., Yun K.-S., Raia P., Stein K., Ruan J. (2023). Human adaptation to diverse biomes over the past 3 million years. *Science*, 380(6645):604–608.

Zerilli J. (2020). *The adaptable mind*. Oxford University Press, Oxford.

Zhai W., Peng Z. (2021). Where to buy a house in the United States amid COVID-19? *Environment and Planning A*, 53(1):9–11.

Zielinska-Dabkowska K.M., Schernhammer E.S., Hanifin J.P., Brainard G.C. (2023). Reducing nighttime light exposure in the urban environment to benefit human health and society. *Science*, 380(6650):1130–1135.

Ziemann V. et al. (2023). *Urban house price gradients in the post-COVID-19 era*. OECD Economics Department Working Papers, No. 1756, OECD Publishing, Paris.

Zijlema W., Cerin E., Cirach M., Bartoll X., Borrell C., Dadvand P., Nieuwenhuijsen M.J. (2024). Cities and mental health: The role of the built environment, and environmental and lifestyle factors in Barcelona. *Environmental Pollution*, 346:123559.

Zwir I. et al. (2020). Uncovering the complex genetics of human character. *Molecular Psychiatry*, 25:2295–2312.

Index